I0763118

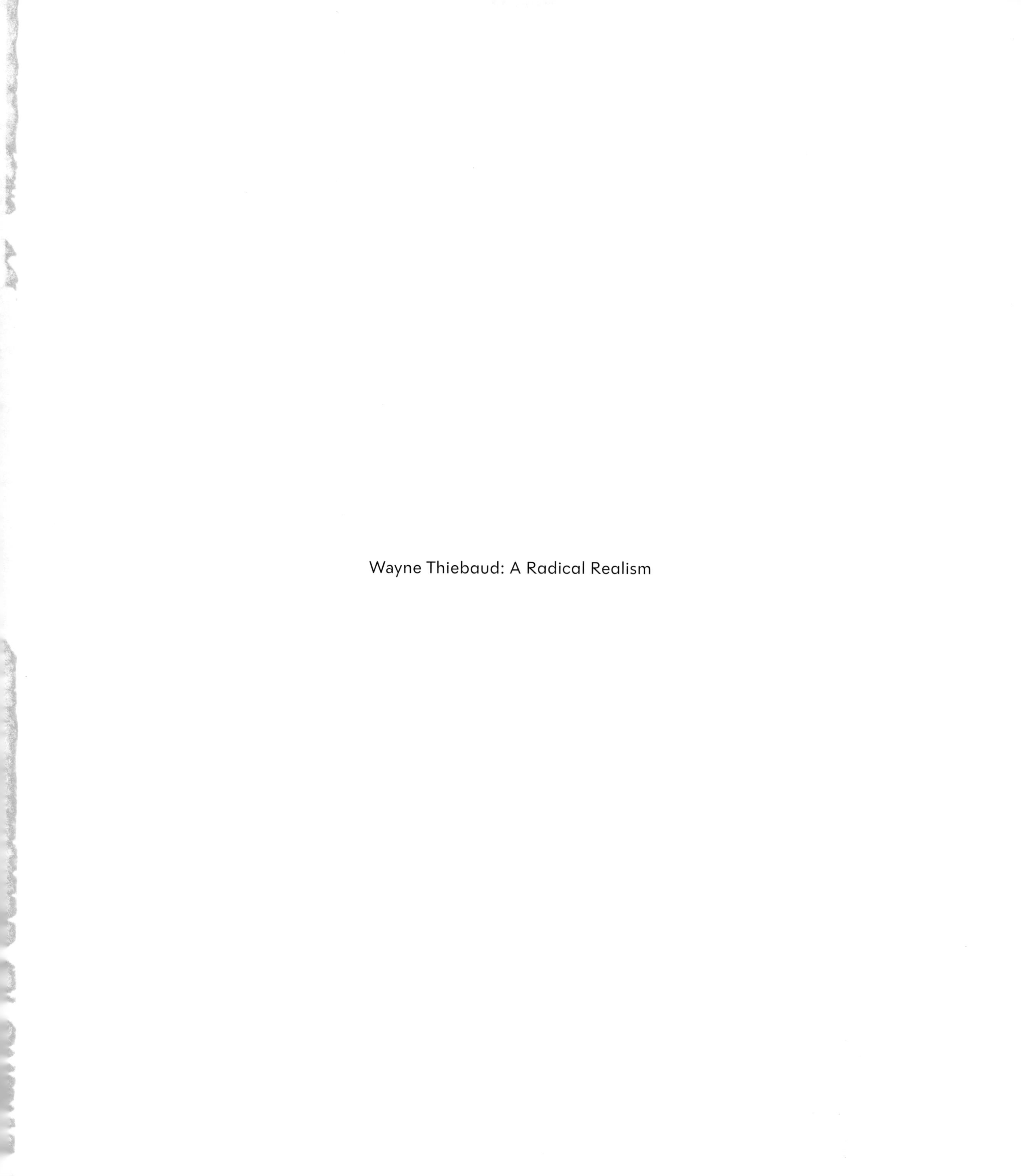

Wayne Thiebaud: A Radical Realism

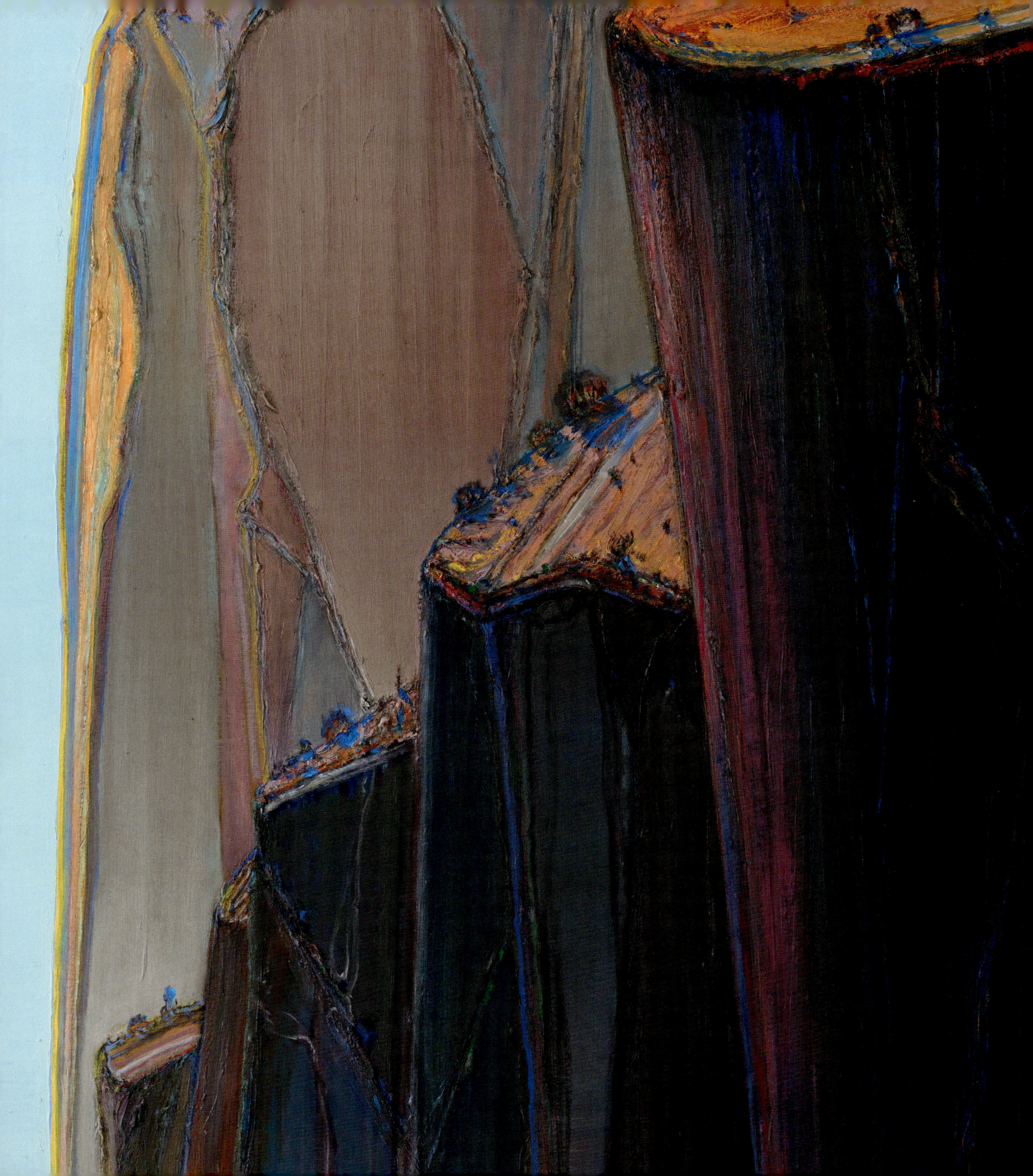

# Wayne Thiebaud
# A Radical Realism

Essays by Derrick R. Cartwright, Gene Cooper,
Peter Frank, Julia Friedman, and Rachel Teagle

Introduction by Peter Frank

Interview with Wayne Thiebaud by Derrick R. Cartwright

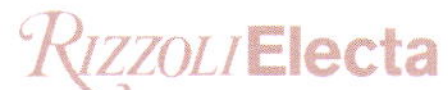

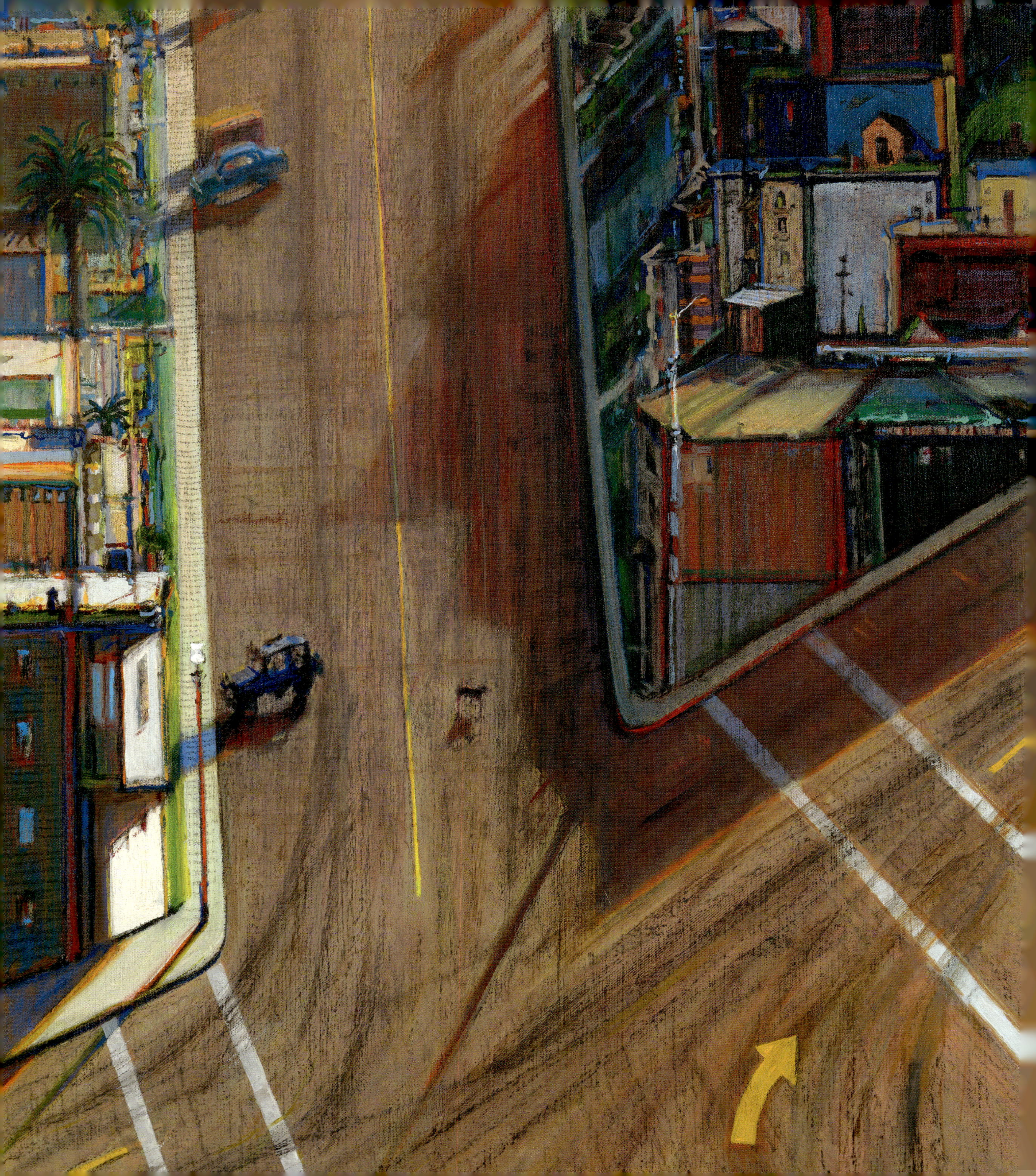

# Contents

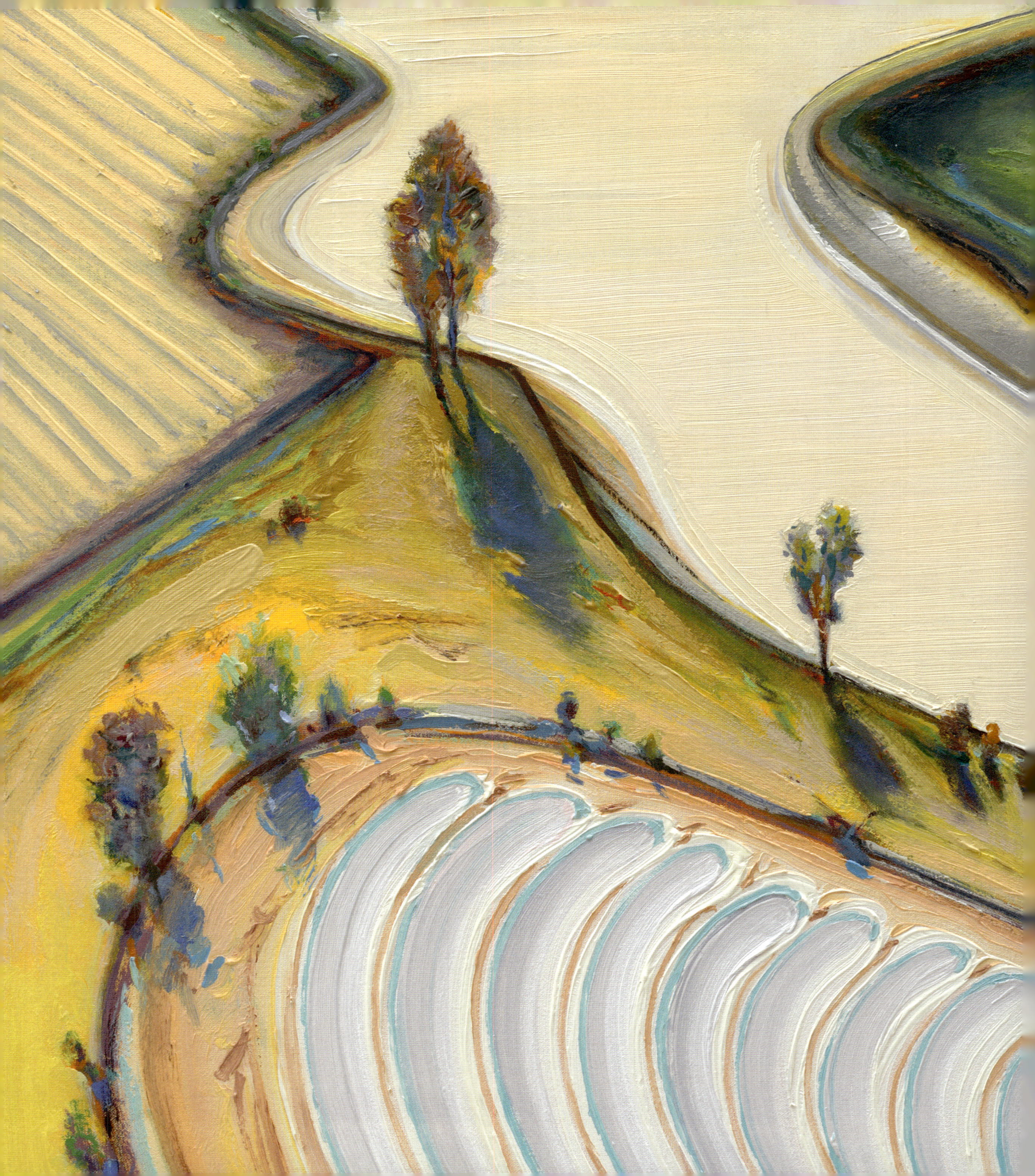

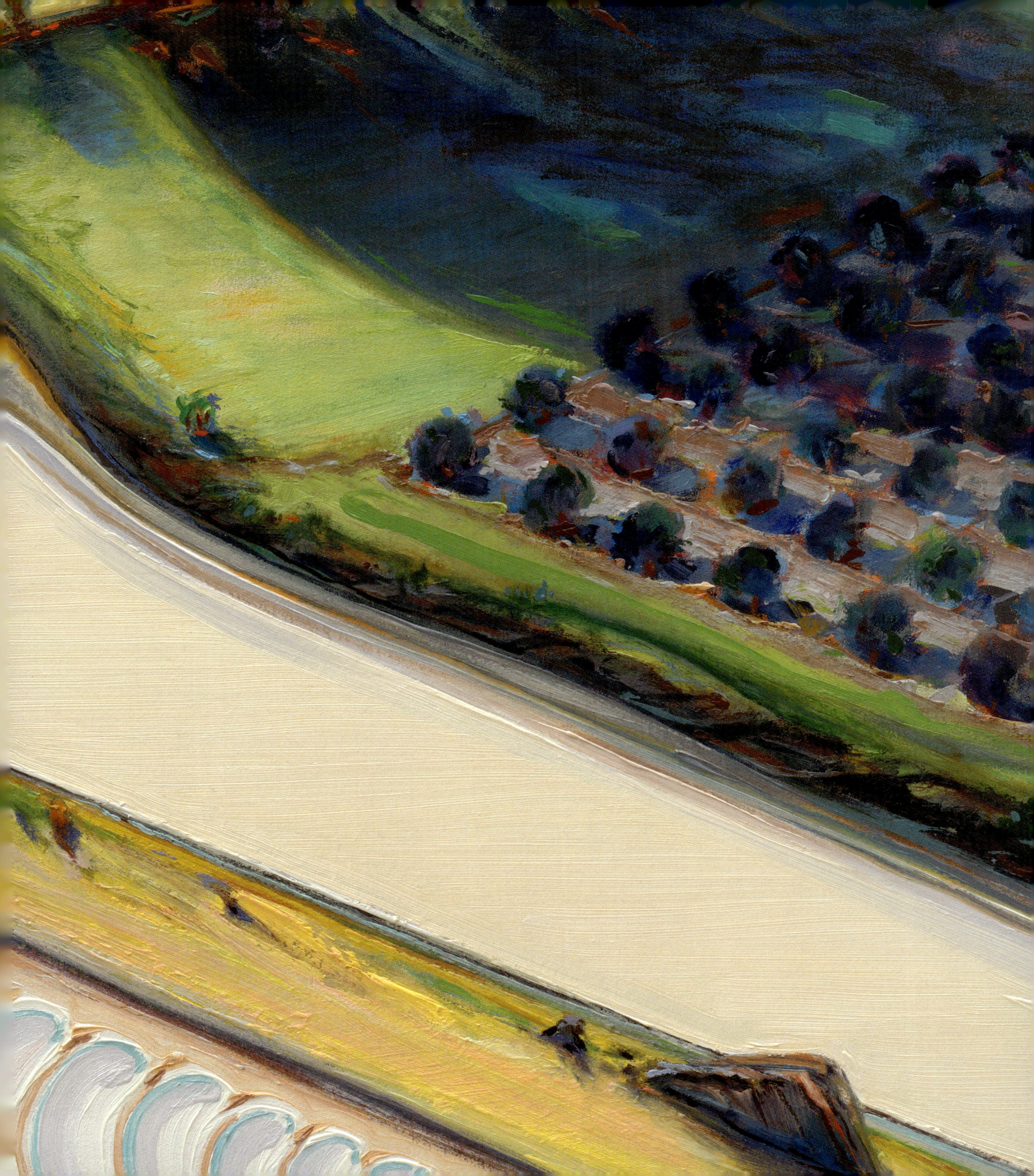

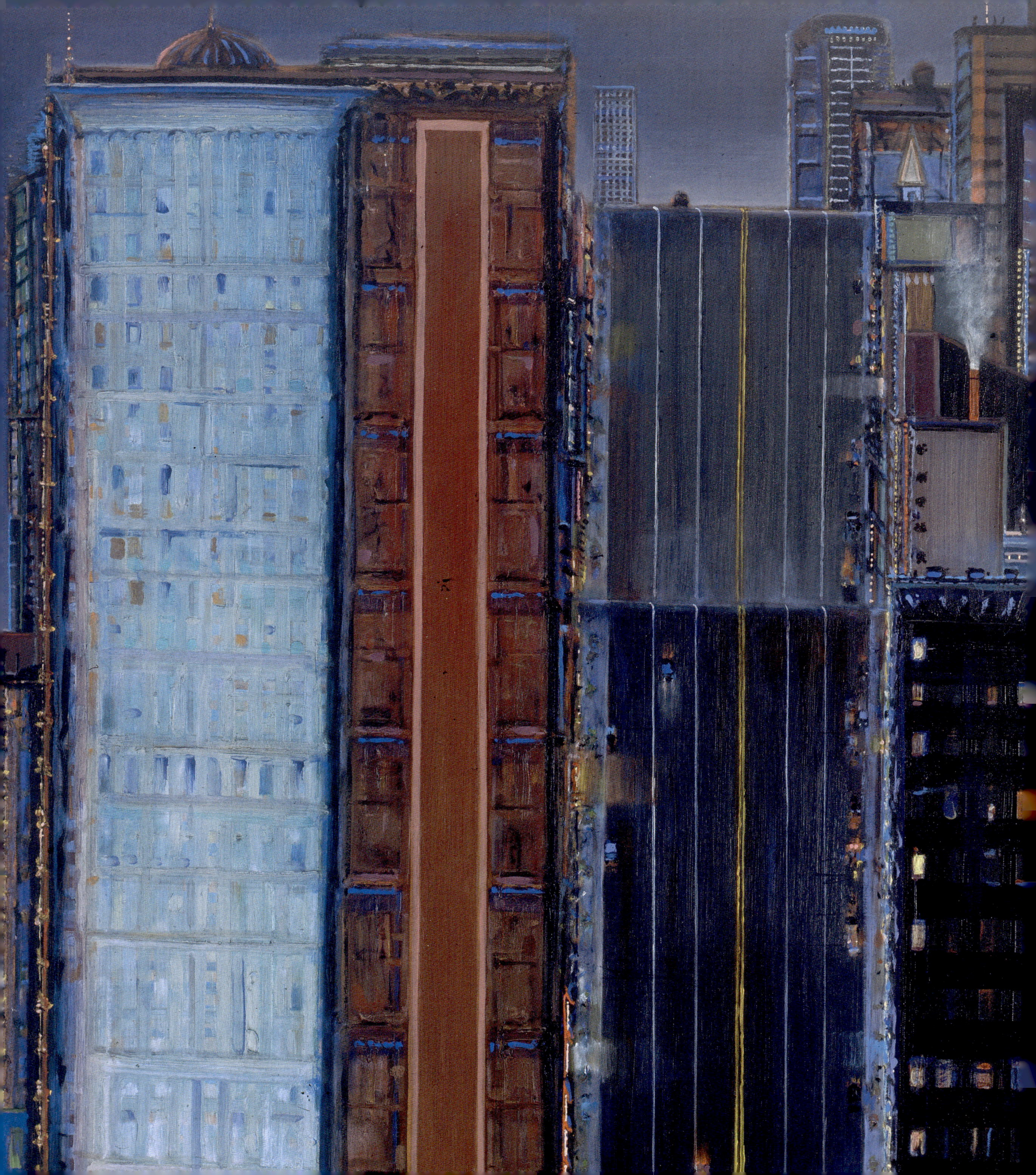

# Introduction

Peter Frank

Past 100 when he died, Wayne Thiebaud painted for large parts of two centuries. As sweeping as his legacy is in this regard, he was a dedicated regionalist for his entire career, taking endless inspiration from the Northern California milieu he inhabited most of his life (and no little inspiration from his Southern California childhood). Thiebaud has always been best known for his expansive meditations on food and often-quizzical depictions of fellow humans. Neither subject would seem to pin the painter as a specifically Northern California artist; rather, they present him as a specifically *American* painter, devoting skill and sensuous rendition to people and objects so mundane they otherwise disappear into the day. Thiebaud was the Edward Hopper of his generation (and locale), infusing the banal with a meditative poetry.

These figures and still lifes, of people in suits and bathing suits and of sandwiches and cake slices in display cases, prompted observers in the early to mid-1960s to brand Thiebaud a Pop artist. This was not an unfair assessment in the context of the time, considering both the subject matter and his treatment of it; but it reduced Thiebaud's achievement to his imagery (and to a certain extent his palette). What he depicted and how he rendered and ordered what he depicted signified the same kind of American consumerist anomie as that conveyed by Rosenquist's and Ruscha's billboard compositions, Lichtenstein's and Ramos's cartoons, and Warhol's and Bengston's emblems. But Thiebaud, clearly, was emotionally closer to his subject matter, as his rich brushstroke and almost pedagogically academic compositions signaled. (He already enjoyed a local reputation as an inspired and devoted teacher—after backing into the profession in the first place.) Thiebaud was indeed making "new painting of common objects," but of a different tenor than his peers on both coasts. They emphasized "common objects"; he emphasized "painting."

Thiebaud made two significant shifts in subject matter during the earlier part of his career. The success of his still life material—or perhaps his discomfort at their being branded "Pop"—led him to take up the figure in the mid-1960s. By the end of that decade he had come to embrace the landscape as well—finding in this latter rubric a way out of objecthood and into thoroughgoing visual conjuration. From then on, all these subject categories were fair game to the artist, lines of inquiry at once personally acute and art-historically aware, and ripe for subtle or exaggerated variation. Thiebaud maintained an open and ongoing dialogue with the image—that is, with the subject freighted with significance but not necessarily "meaning." Such a process of intimation added to the persuasive commitment Thiebaud's art evinced to the perceptual process of recognition. In Thiebaud's practice, cognition was one step, recognition the next.

An artist this accessible yet this intricate, this forthright yet this clever, invites much critical as well as popular attention. Thiebaud's unemotional yet passionate attitude was of his time, but—like Degas's, for instance, or Hopper's—his style wasn't quite in it. This aloof

Wayne Thiebaud, **Dark City** (detail), 1999

relationship to his contemporaries was less a reactionary streak than it was a prior responsiveness to art history, and to the lessons in perception gained by studying Chardin and Morandi, Velázquez and Manet. Art historians thus feel especially comfortable addressing Thiebaud's quirks and apparent inconsistencies, recognizing the source(s) and the meaning(s) of such anomalies. Thiebaud himself readily admitted to, even preached this eccentric—or, perhaps, bespoke—engagement of the Old and Modern Masters.

All the writers represented in this album had contact with Wayne Thiebaud, mostly on an ongoing basis, some incidental, some for decades, some only in the decade or so before the centenarian's passing. Already mesmerized by the man's unique exploration of a lucid yet mysterious metarealism, we were charmed by his observations on art in general—especially as those observations maintained the mystery while dispelling the seeming dissonances.

Thanks go to longtime Thiebaudaires Gene Cooper, Rachel Teagle, and Derrick R. Cartwright for their richly cultivated understanding of a man and an oeuvre they recognize transcended ordinary art by not transcending the ordinary. Julia Friedman and I admired him and his accomplishments over a shorter amount of time but with no lesser awe. This assembly—a kind of memorial Festschrift—honors not only the man and his art, but the spirit in which his art has changed minds and eyes.



OPPOSITE
Wayne Thiebaud in his studio at Rosebud, Hood, California, ca. 1968
Photo: Betty Jean Thiebaud

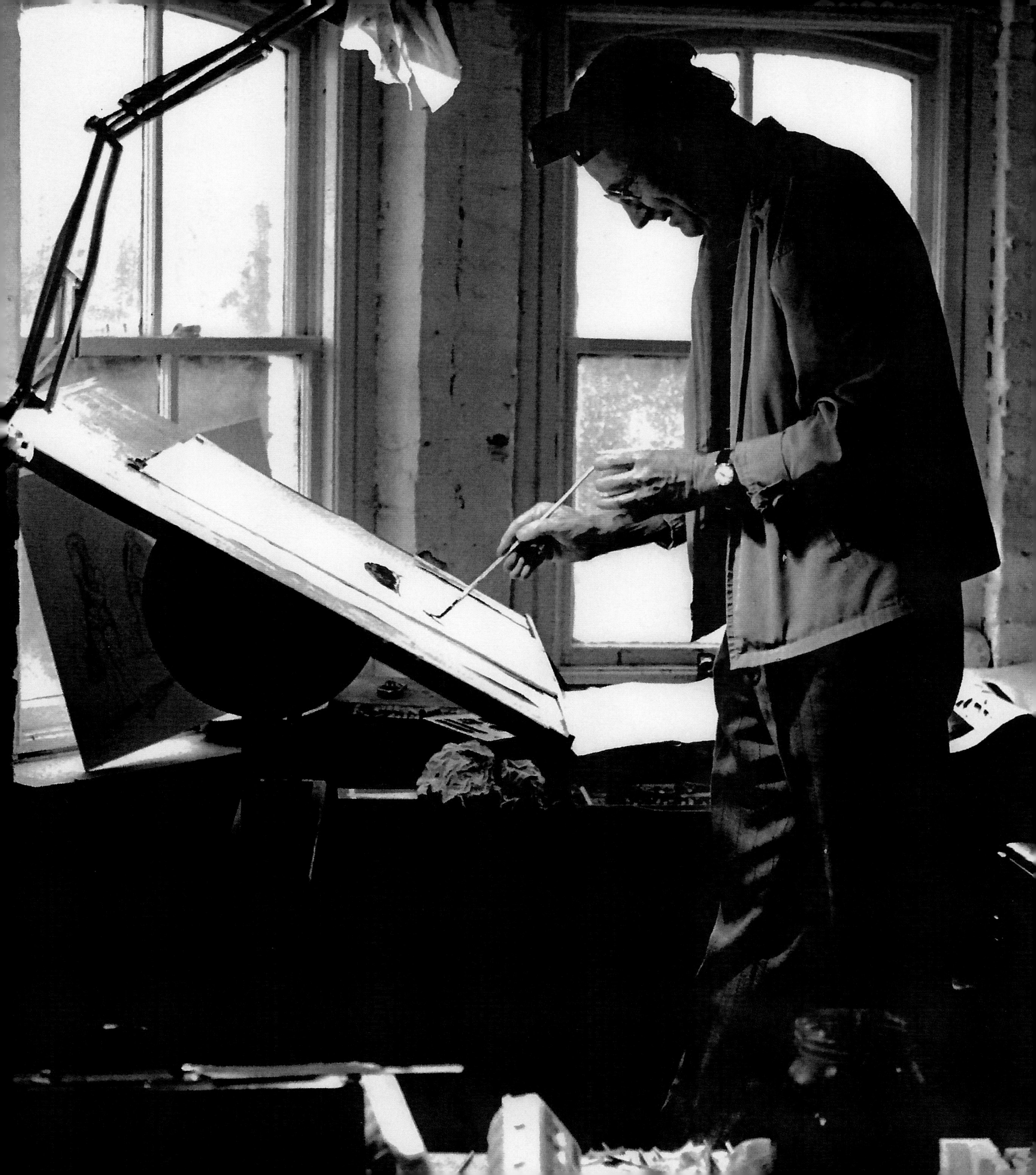

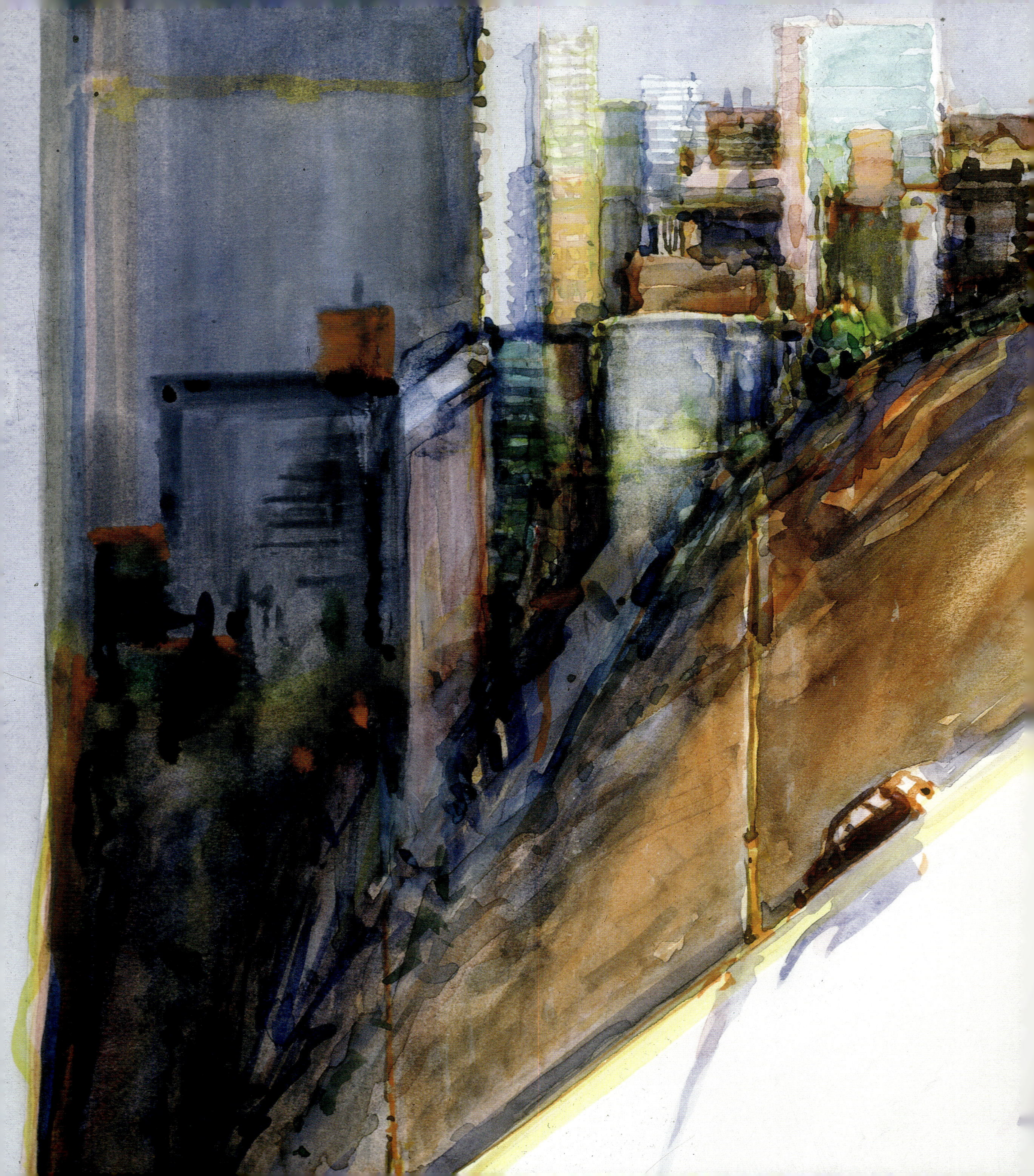

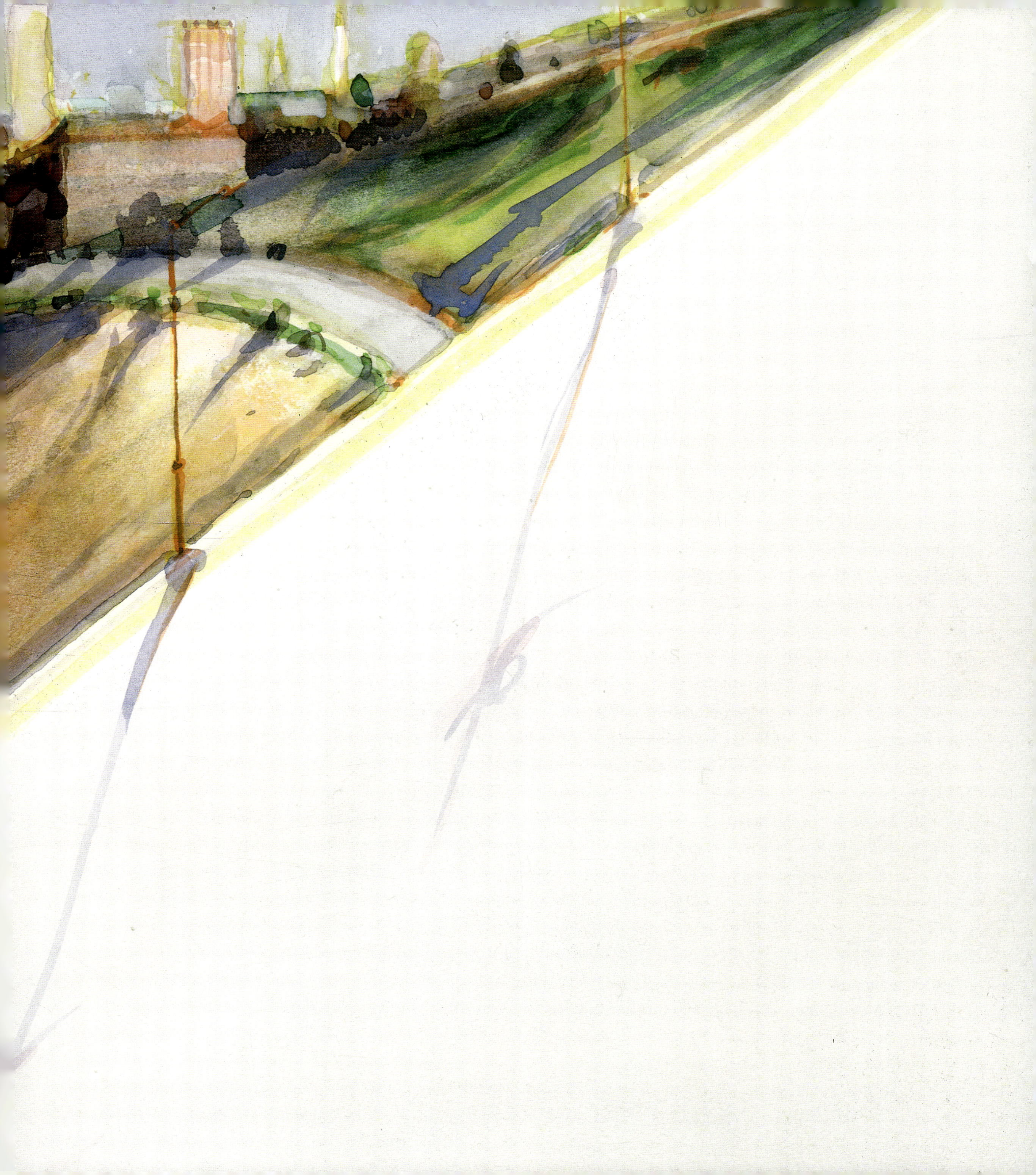

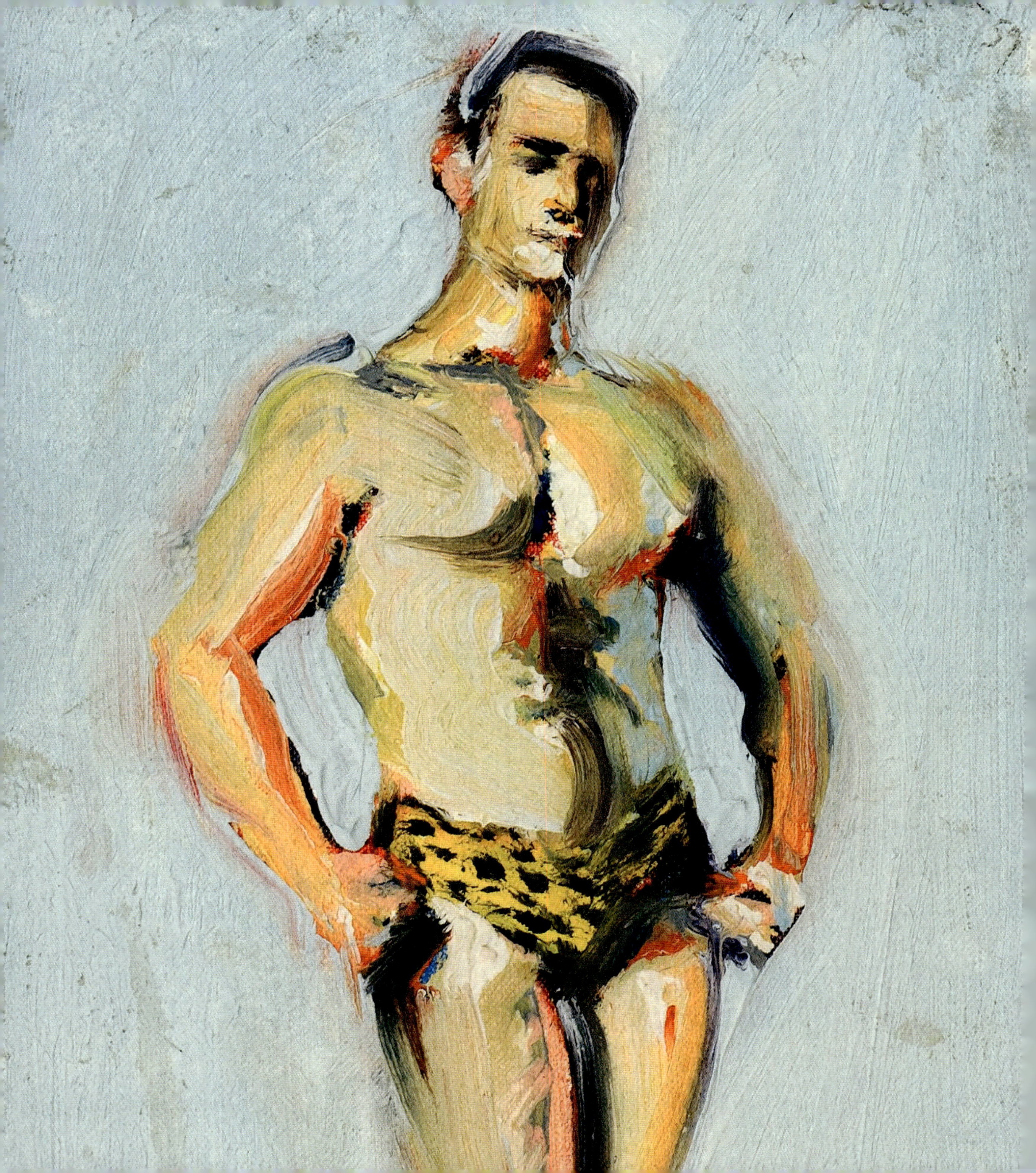

# "Art Comes from Art"

## Gene Cooper

> "The Louvre is the book in which we learn to read."
> —Paul Cézanne

As much as cultural forces impact the history of art, art itself has had the most direct effect on determining its own changing character. Pablo Picasso, for example, spent his whole life probing art history for material on which to develop his own strategies. Without his attraction to Paul Cézanne, in particular, Picasso's work would have had a very different look and art history would have been dramatically changed. Then there was Vincent van Gogh, who started his career influenced by Rembrandt and died shortly after copying Jean Millet. In Wayne Thiebaud's case, he came to art history accidentally, on a high school field trip to the Huntington Museum in Southern California. Here Thiebaud saw his first "real" art. It was Thomas Gainsborough's life-size *The Blue Boy* (ca. 1770), centerpiece of the museum's vast collection of eighteenth-century English portraits that would stick forever in Thiebaud's memory (P. 16). He would always recall being dazzled by the illusion of the young aristocrat's blue satin vest. Thus the teenage Thiebaud had his first memorable taste of art history.

Couple this event with his life at home in nearby Long Beach. Thiebaud was raised in a warm, supportive, Mormon community headed by his father, bishop of the local ward. One especially relevant aspect was the church's regular practice of using Mormon history as a way to teach its scriptures. Historical references defined the church's identity and made difficult issues more accessible. For Thiebaud the discursive, reflective Mormon method could easily be transferred into a teaching tool for, notable among others, artists.

In 1946, Thiebaud met Robert Mallary, a highly sophisticated sculptor who would become his first mentor. Mallary guided Thiebaud through the gallery scenes in Los Angeles and New York. He explained the dynamics of the art world, emphasizing that if he wanted to be a significant artist and leave his mark in art history, he had to be well grounded in the study of art history. At this point, Thiebaud decided to leave the commercial art world he'd been working in for years and become a fine artist.

His first step was to get an art education at San Jose State College and Sacramento State College (1949–52). However, Thiebaud discovered that very little teaching actually took place. There was little support for art history, and studio classes lacked the rigor that he sought. So Thiebaud turned to copying paintings selected at random from art books and magazines. At the same time, he took a teaching position at Sacramento City College (1951–59), where he was assigned to teach the Survey of Western Art History even though he was ill-prepared to do so. But it forced him not only to gain the requisite factual knowledge, but also to recognize the interactive synergisms that define art history. Thiebaud now had an awareness of the territory, and of key individuals that he would add to his educational pool. After reading biographies

Wayne Thiebaud, **Charles Atlas** (detail), 1959

on Rembrandt and Van Gogh in the 1950s, he came to regard genre subjects as respectable and closer to his own middle-class values.

From this point on, Thiebaud would search for historical influences that would both deepen his understanding of art and provide aesthetic pleasure. He expanded his search to include paintings found in a variety of locations. Some were those anonymous ones resting on dusty thrift store shelves, while others hung properly on brightly lit museum walls. In particular, he liked to copy primary works done by painters who represented transitions between Western art historical periods. He gravitated towards artists who carried history forward. For example, he studied the seminal work of Giovanni Bellini (late medieval), Giotto (early Renaissance), Paul Signac (neo-Impressionism), Édouard Manet (sometimes called the "father of modern art"), and Richard Diebenkorn (Thiebaud copied his close friend's early still lifes of tableware).

Eventually his educational journey took Thiebaud into the Islamic world through the stylizations of Persian manuscripts. Since the Muslim storylines were largely alien to the Westerner, the idealized styling became the subject matter. Thiebaud used the miniatures' device of fragmenting a landscape or cityscape into different delineated pieces. By working with the Persian styles, Thiebaud brought another dimension to the then-current popularity of the emotionally charged gesturalism that characterized Abstract Expressionism.

During our sixty-year friendship, Wayne Thiebaud did six portraits of me (PP. 30 AND 127). While he was painting, we would share our knowledge of art history and art theory. It was a "teaching moment" for both of us. We also visited museums together. New York's Metropolitan Museum of Art was our favorite. He often said that he would like to be "buried in the Met."

For Thiebaud, copying selections of art history was the basis of his art education. It was also an important means for him to fulfill his longtime desire to become a "significant" member of that special fraternity that has shaped art history.



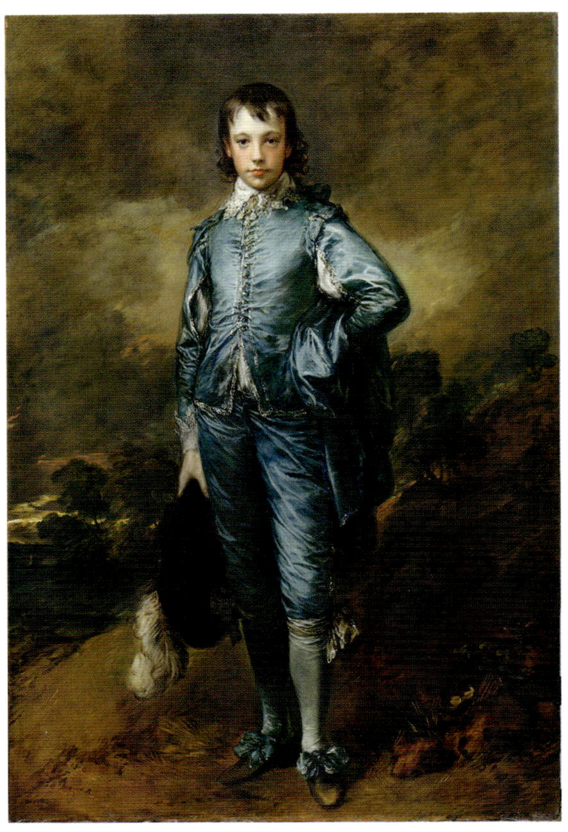

"An artist has to train his responses more than other people do . . . He has to be disciplined as a mathematician. Discipline is not a restriction but an aid to freedom. It prepares an artist to choose his own limitations."
—Wayne Thiebaud

"Art comes from art and nothing else. Copy pictures. Enjoy the hell out of it."
—Wayne Thiebaud

Thomas Gainsborough (British, 1727–1788)
**The Blue Boy**, ca. 1770
Oil on canvas
70 ⅝ × 48 ¾ × 1 in.
The Huntington Library, Art Museum, and Botanical Gardens

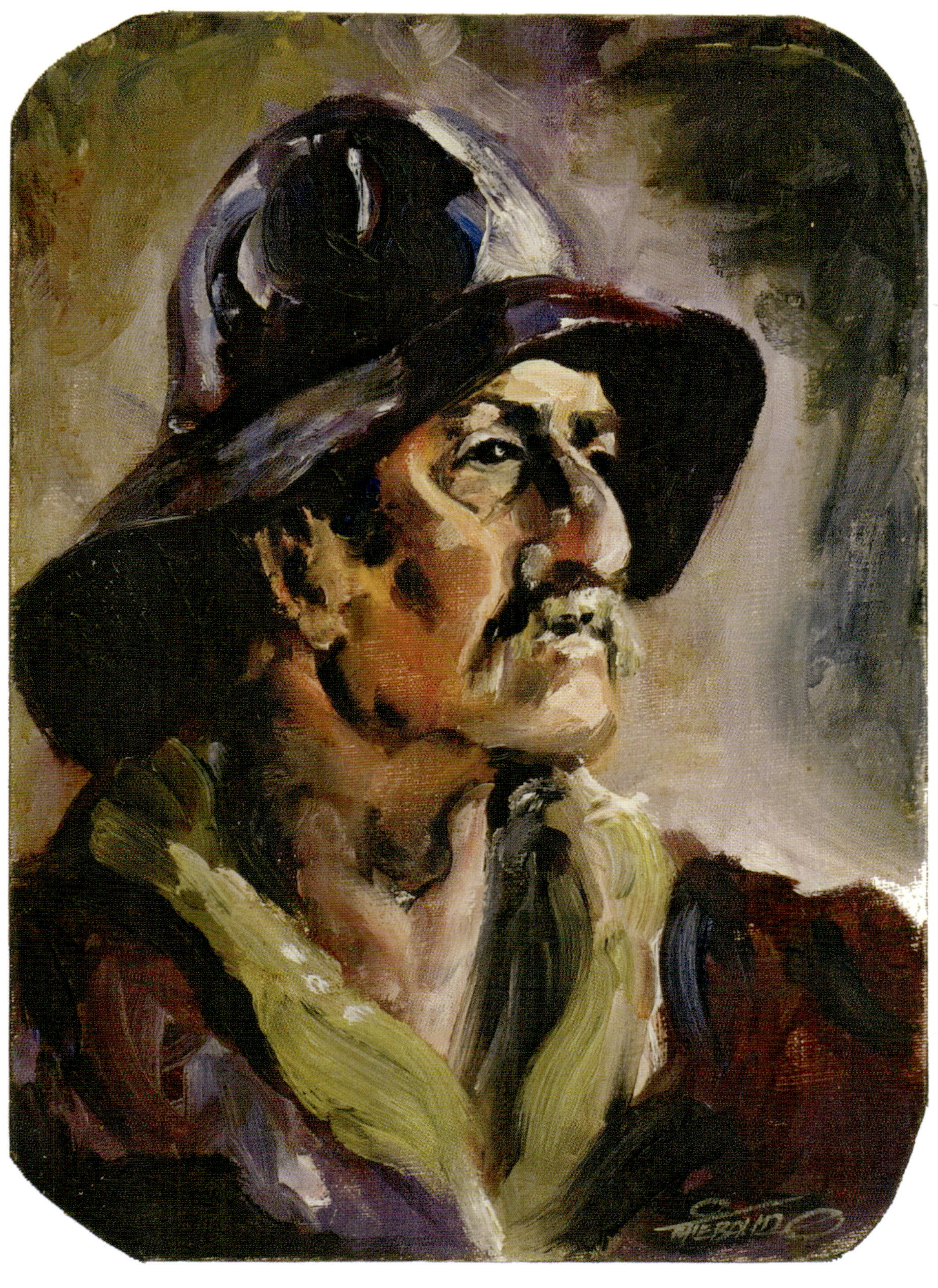

Wayne Thiebaud
**Fisherman**, 1936
Oil on canvas board
15 ¾ × 11 ¾ in.
Collection of Wayne Thiebaud Foundation

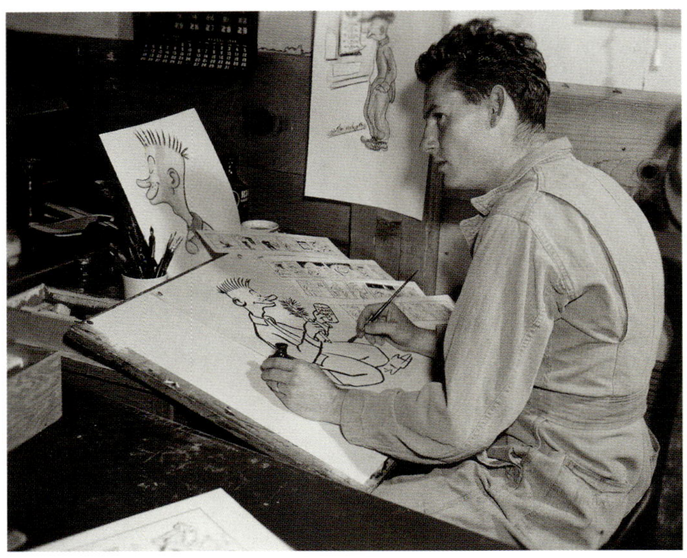

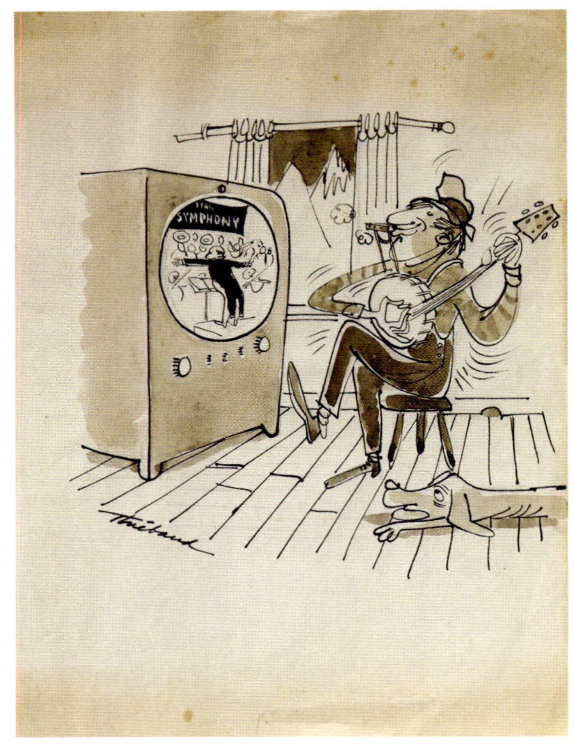




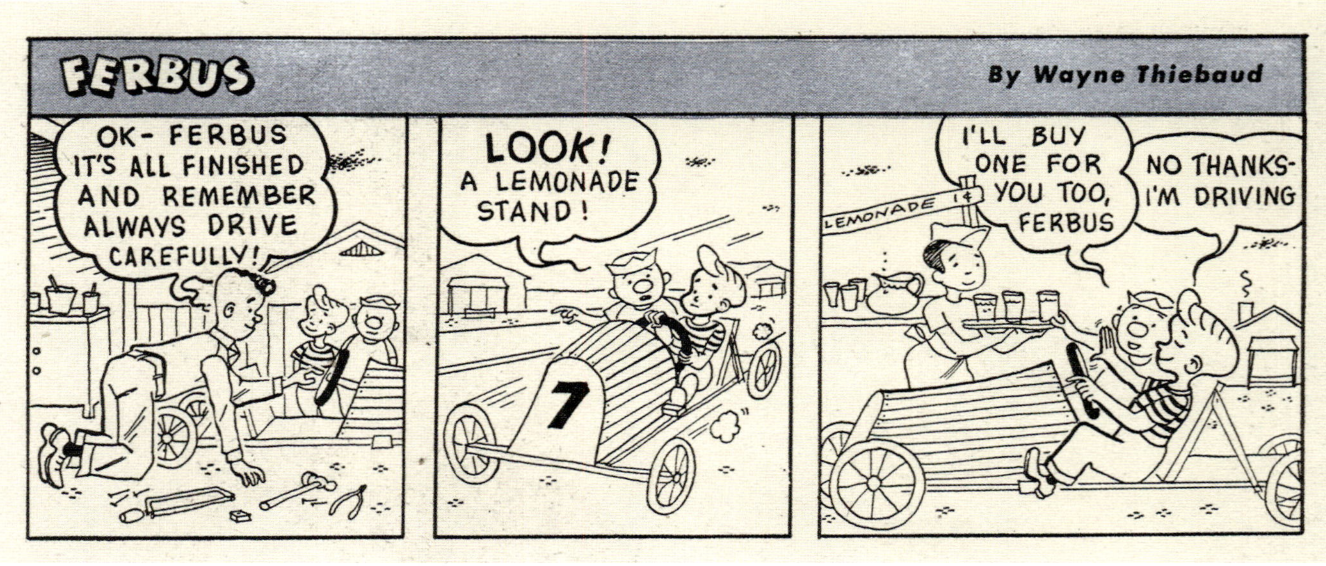


TOP LEFT
Thiebaud working on **Aleck** cartoons
Mather Army Field, California, 1944
Courtesy of Wayne Thiebaud Foundation
and The Morgan Library

TOP RIGHT
Wayne Thiebaud
**Untitled (Man with Banjo)**, ca. 1940s
Pen, ink, and wash on paper
11 × 8 ½ in.
Courtesy of Wayne Thiebaud Foundation
and The Morgan Library

BOTTOM
Wayne Thiebaud
**Ferbus** comic strip published in *Rexall Magazine*
August 1947
Courtesy of Wayne Thiebaud Foundation
and The Morgan Library

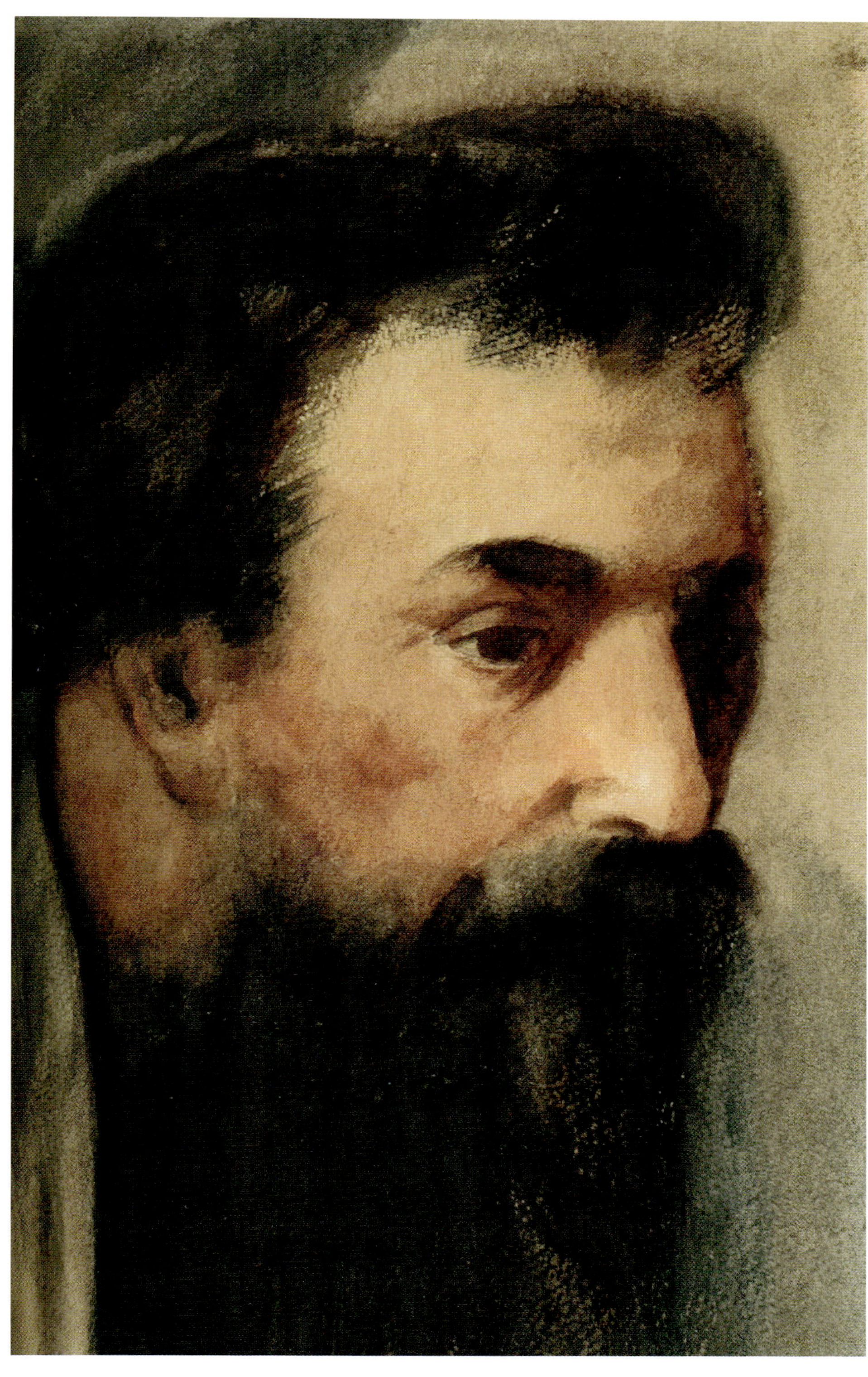



Wayne Thiebaud
**Male Portrait**, ca. 1947
(Rembrandt)
Watercolor on paper
13 ⅝ × 9 ¼ in.
Collection of Wayne Thiebaud Foundation

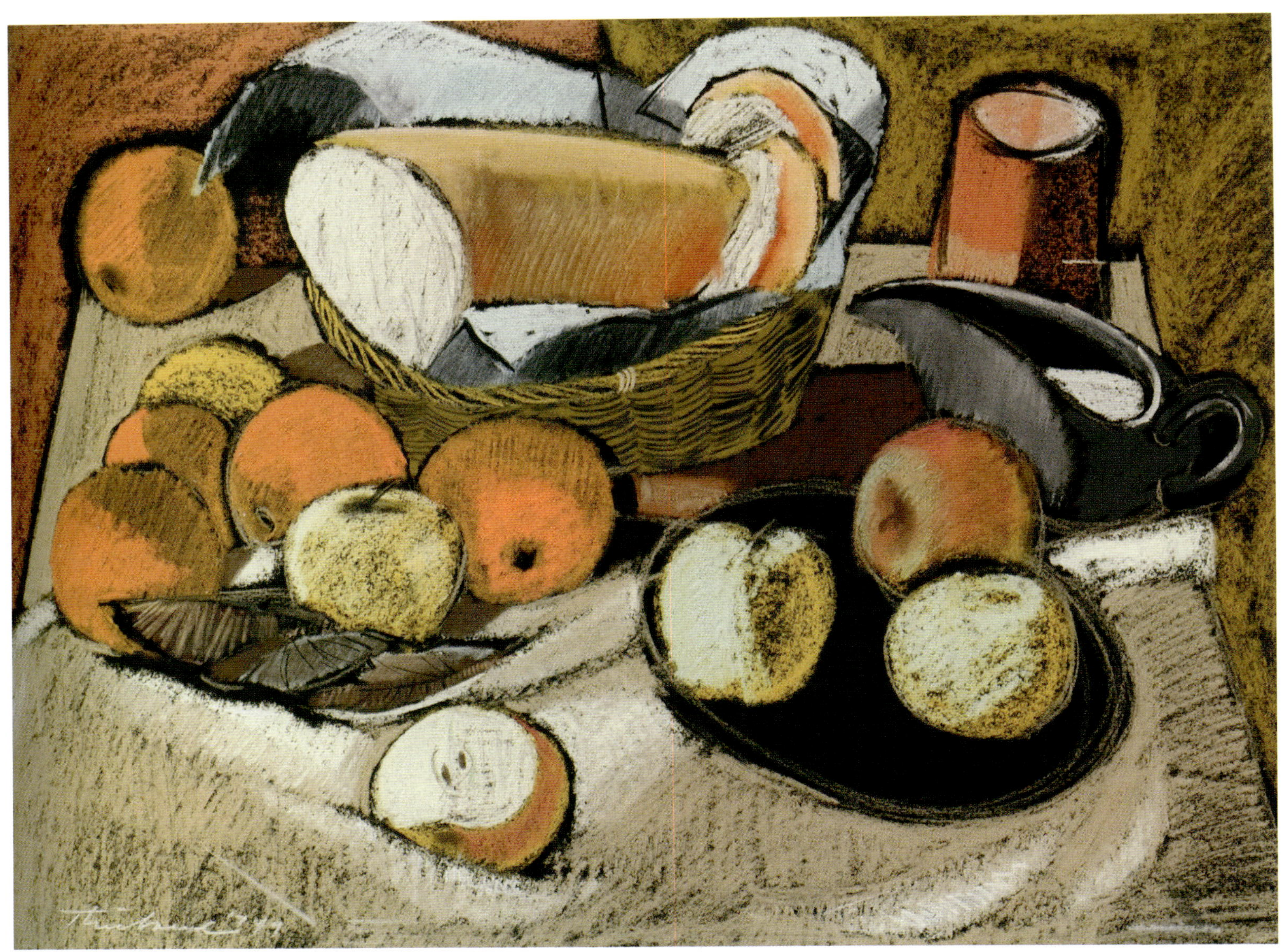

Wayne Thiebaud
**Table Still Life**, 1949
Pastel on black paper
16 ¼ × 22 ¾ in.
Collection of Wayne Thiebaud Foundation

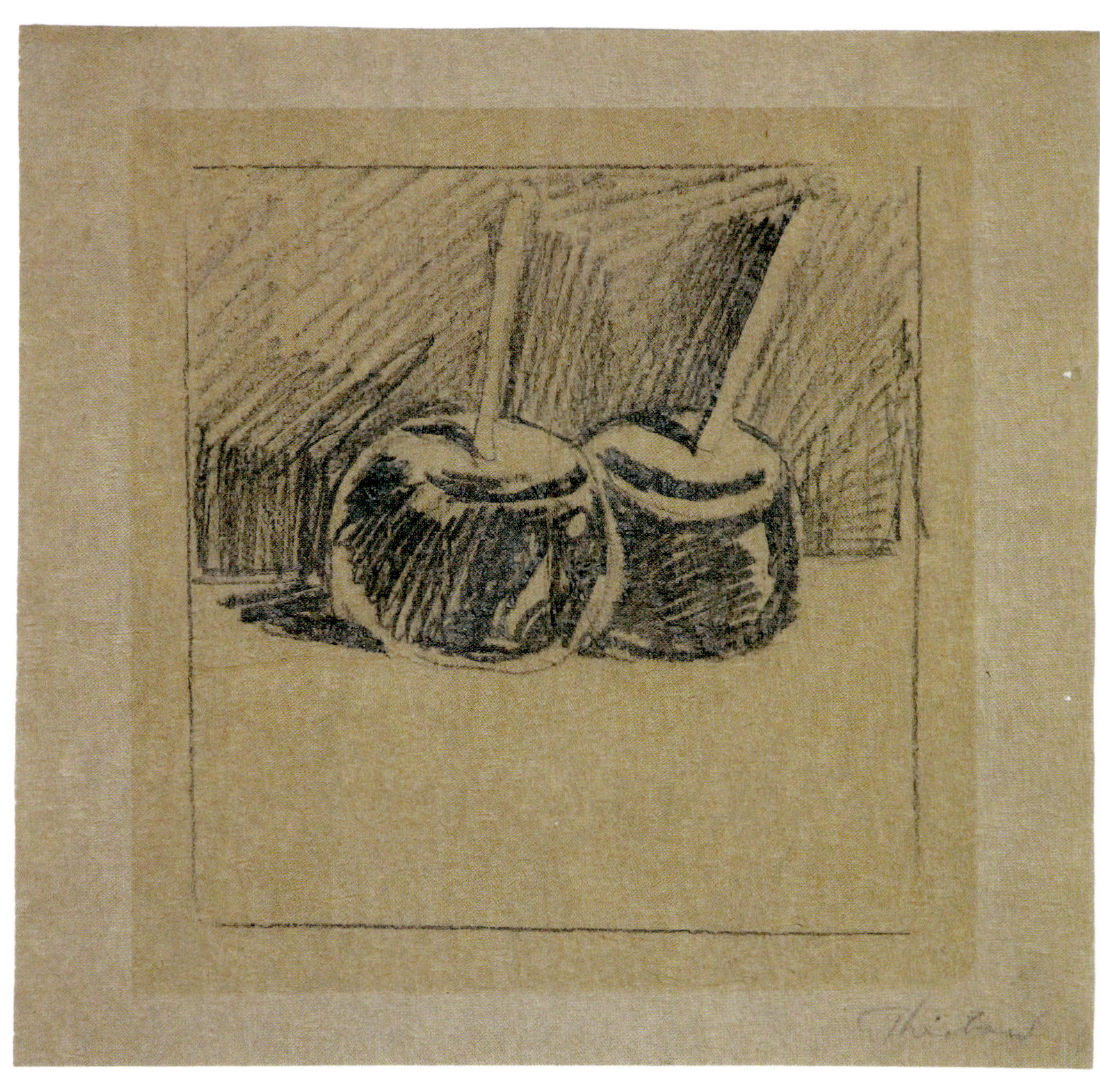



Wayne Thiebaud
**Candy Apples**, 1961
Graphite on paper
10 ⅛ × 10 ⅝ in.
Private Collection

Wayne Thiebaud
**Charles Atlas**, 1959
Oil on board
12 ½ × 7 in.
Collection of Paul LeBaron Thiebaud Trust

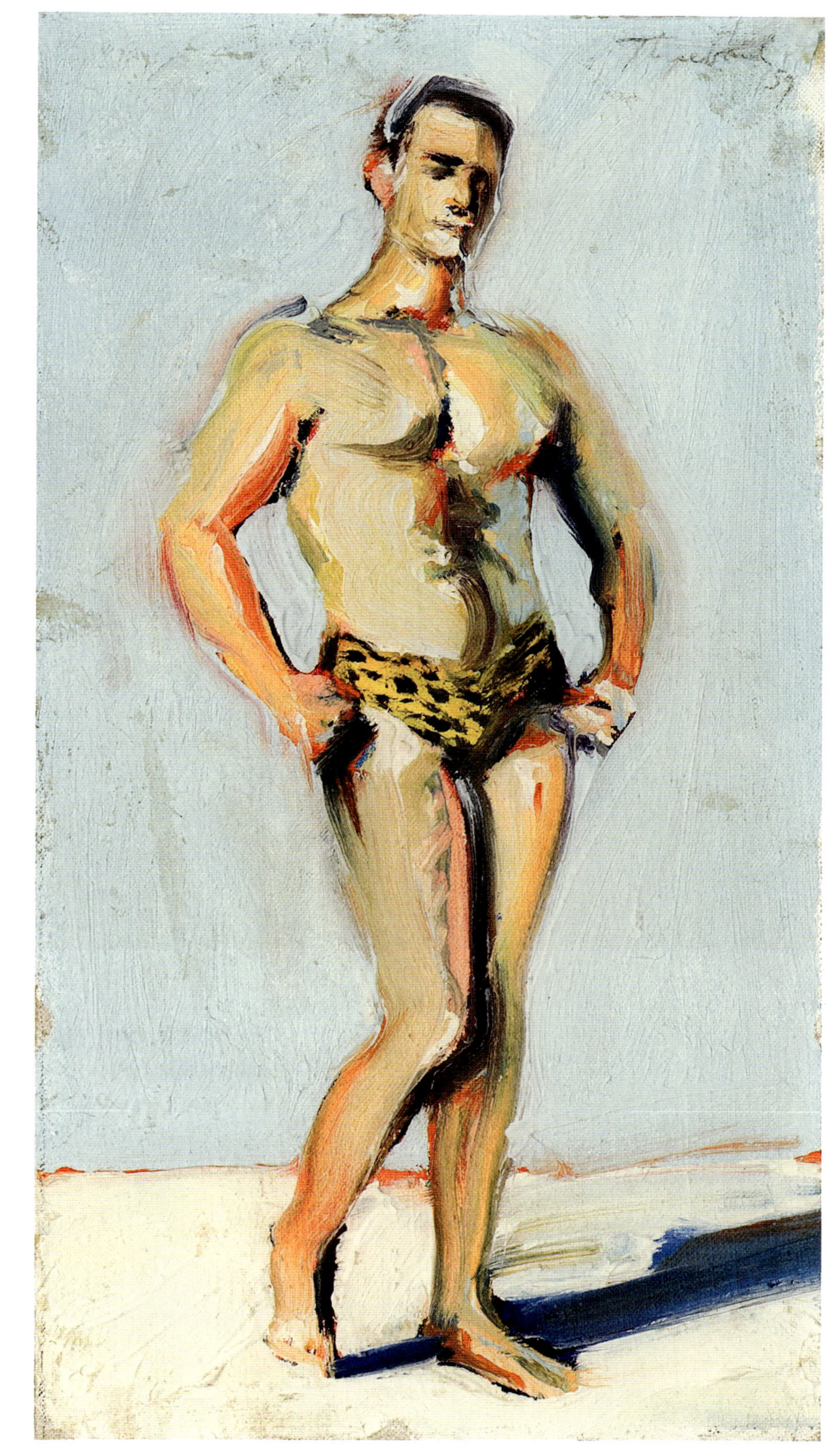

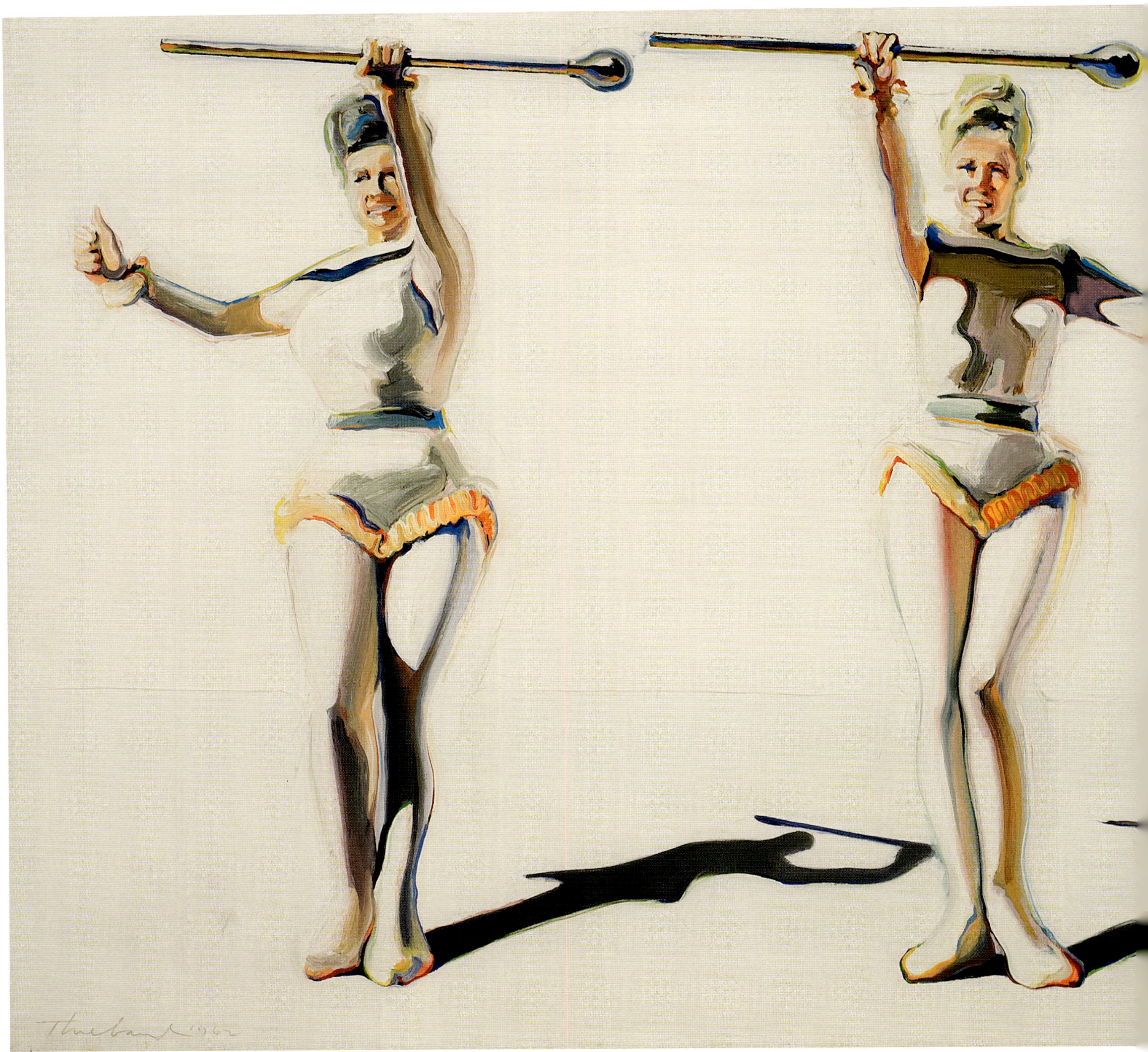

Wayne Thiebaud
**Majorettes**, 1962
Oil on canvas
36 × 48 in.
Collection of Paul LeBaron Thiebaud Trust

Wayne Thiebaud
**35 Cent Masterworks**, 1970–72
Oil on canvas
36 × 27 ¾ in.
Collection of Wayne Thiebaud Foundation

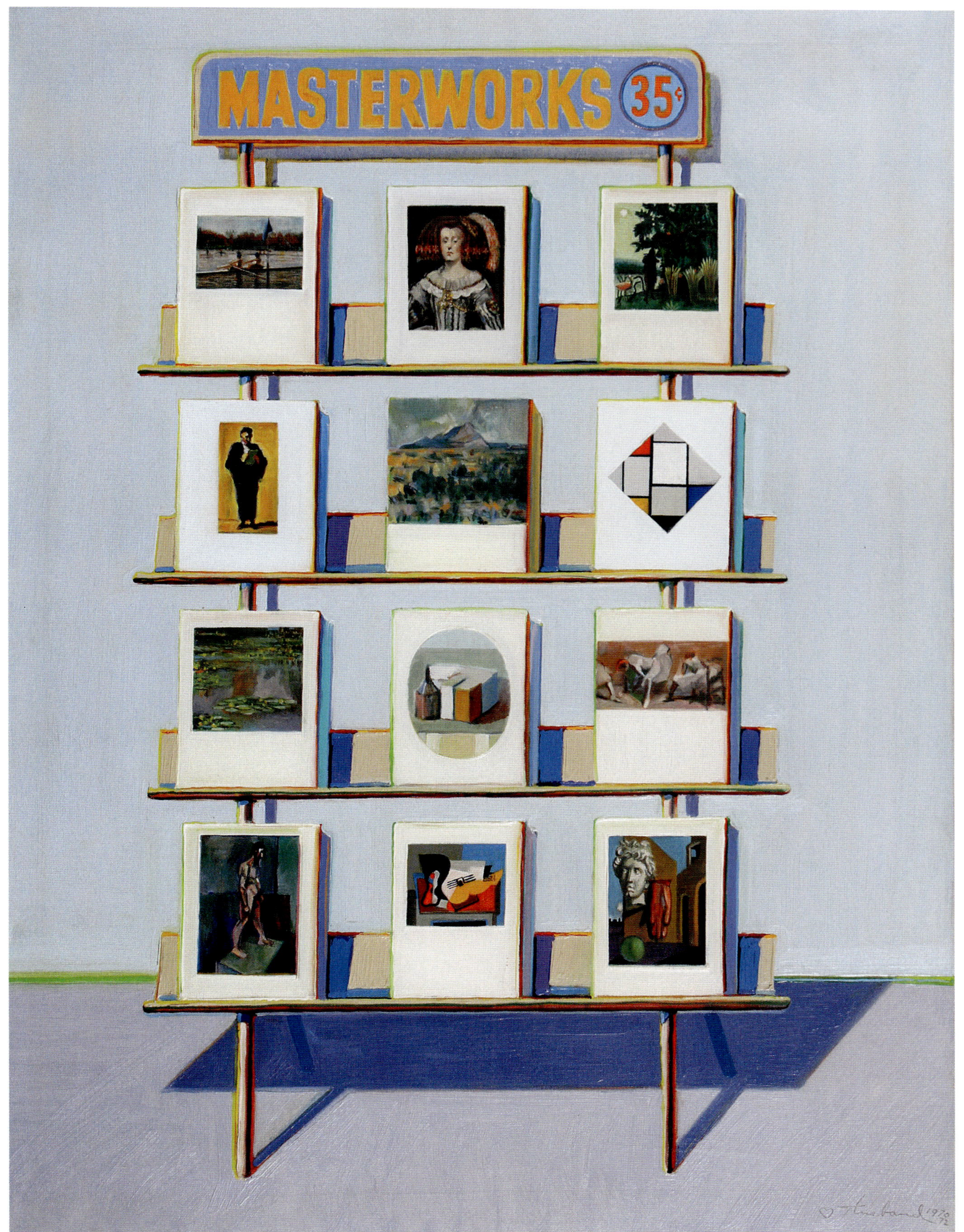
MASTERWORKS
35¢

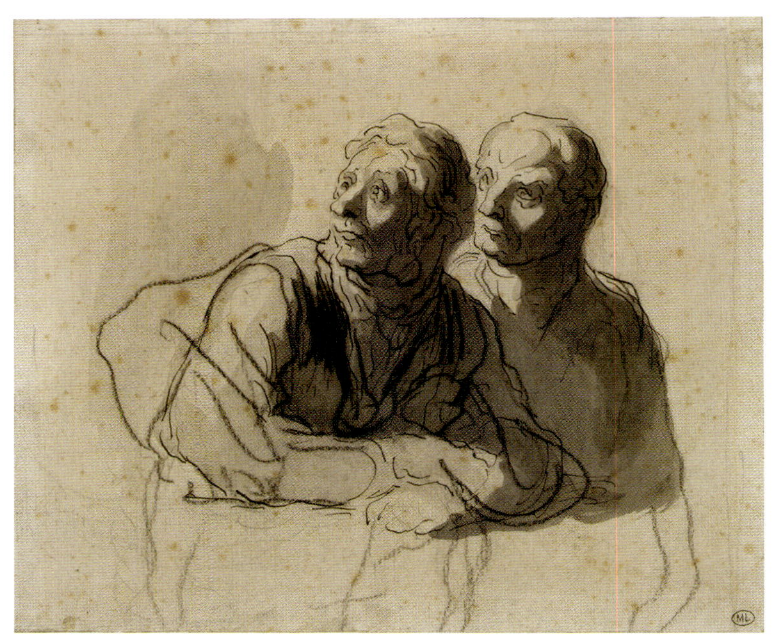

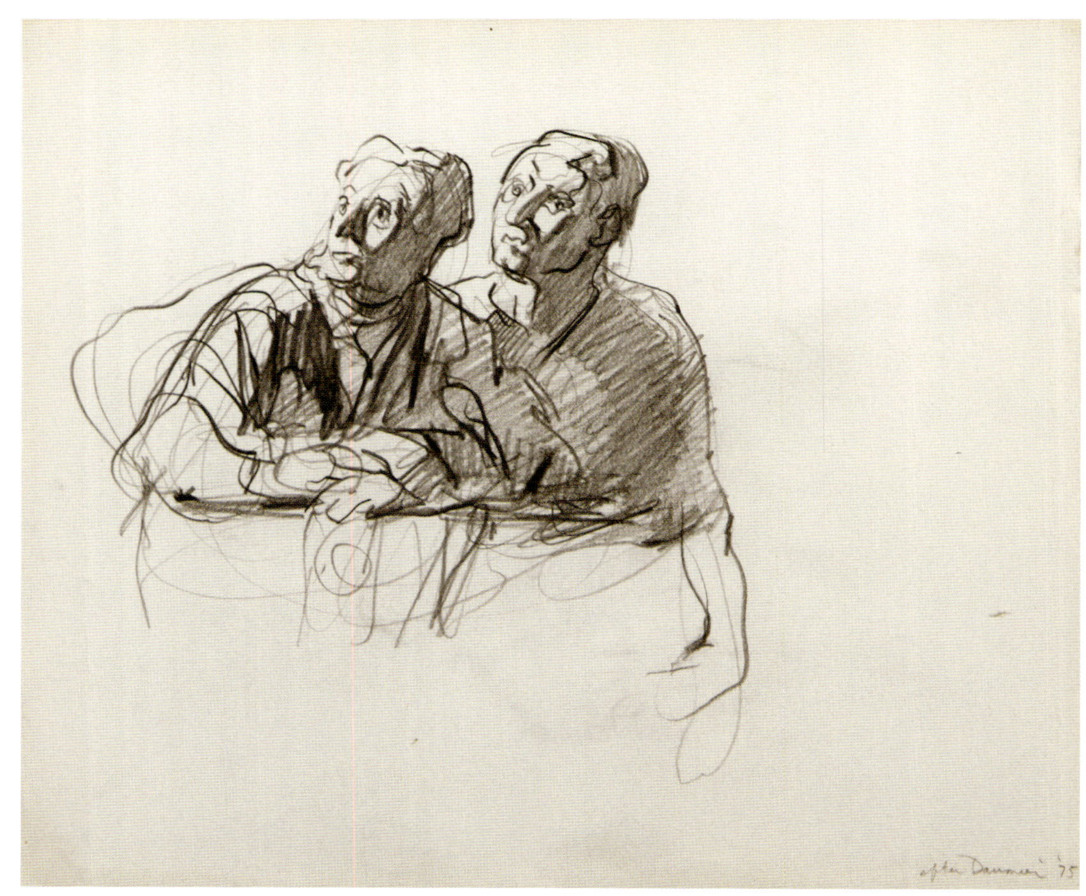

TOP
Honoré Daumier
**Two Men, bust-length, looking towards the left**, ca. 1860s
Pen and gray ink, gray wash, over charcoal on paper
6 × 7 ¼ in.
Musée d'Orsay, Paris

BOTTOM
Wayne Thiebaud
**Untitled (After Daumier)**, 1975
Graphite on paper
9 × 11 in.
Courtesy of Wayne Thiebaud Foundation and The Morgan Library

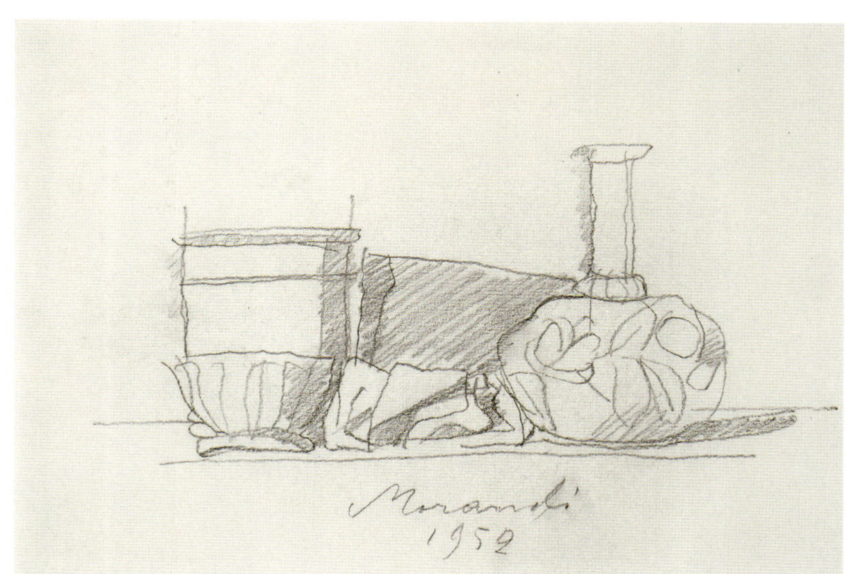


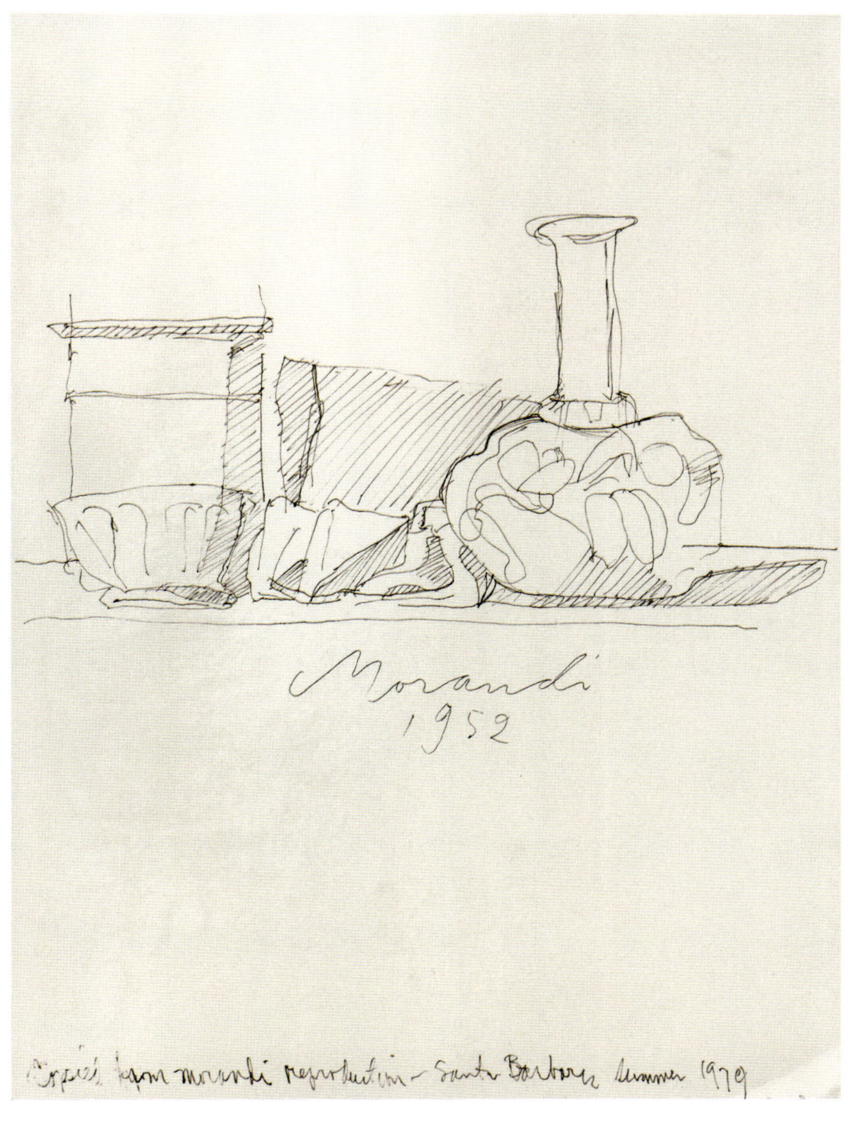

TOP
Giorgio Morandi
**Still Life**, 1952
Graphite on paper
9 ¼ x 12 ¾ in.
Courtesy of Museo Morandi/Settore Musei Civici Bologna

BOTTOM
Wayne Thiebaud
**Untitled (After Morandi)**, 1979
Graphite on paper
11 × 8 ½ in.
Courtesy of Wayne Thiebaud Foundation and The Morgan Library

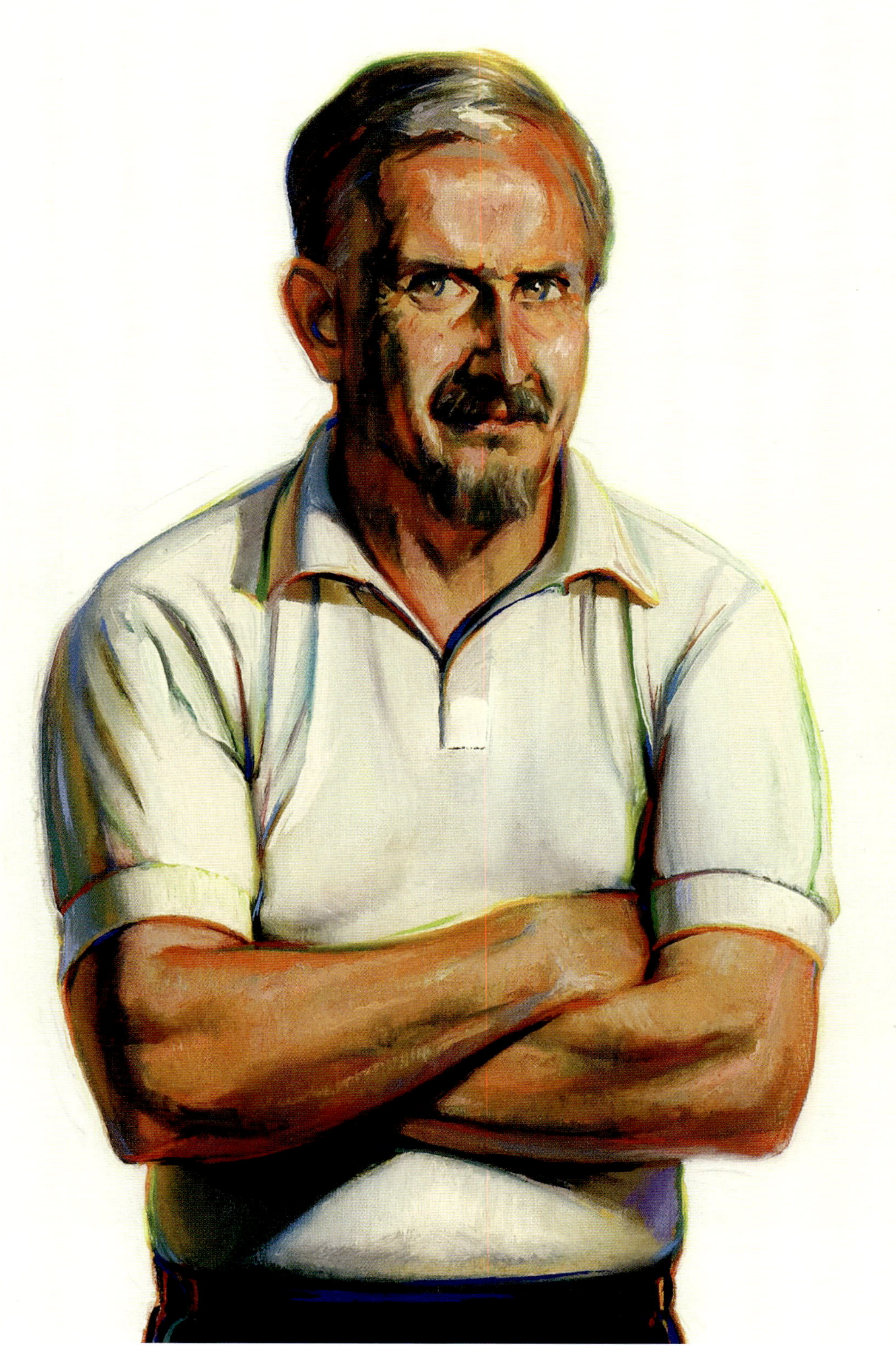

Wayne Thiebaud
**Player**, 1982
Oil on canvas
60 × 36 in.
Collection of Wayne Thiebaud Foundation

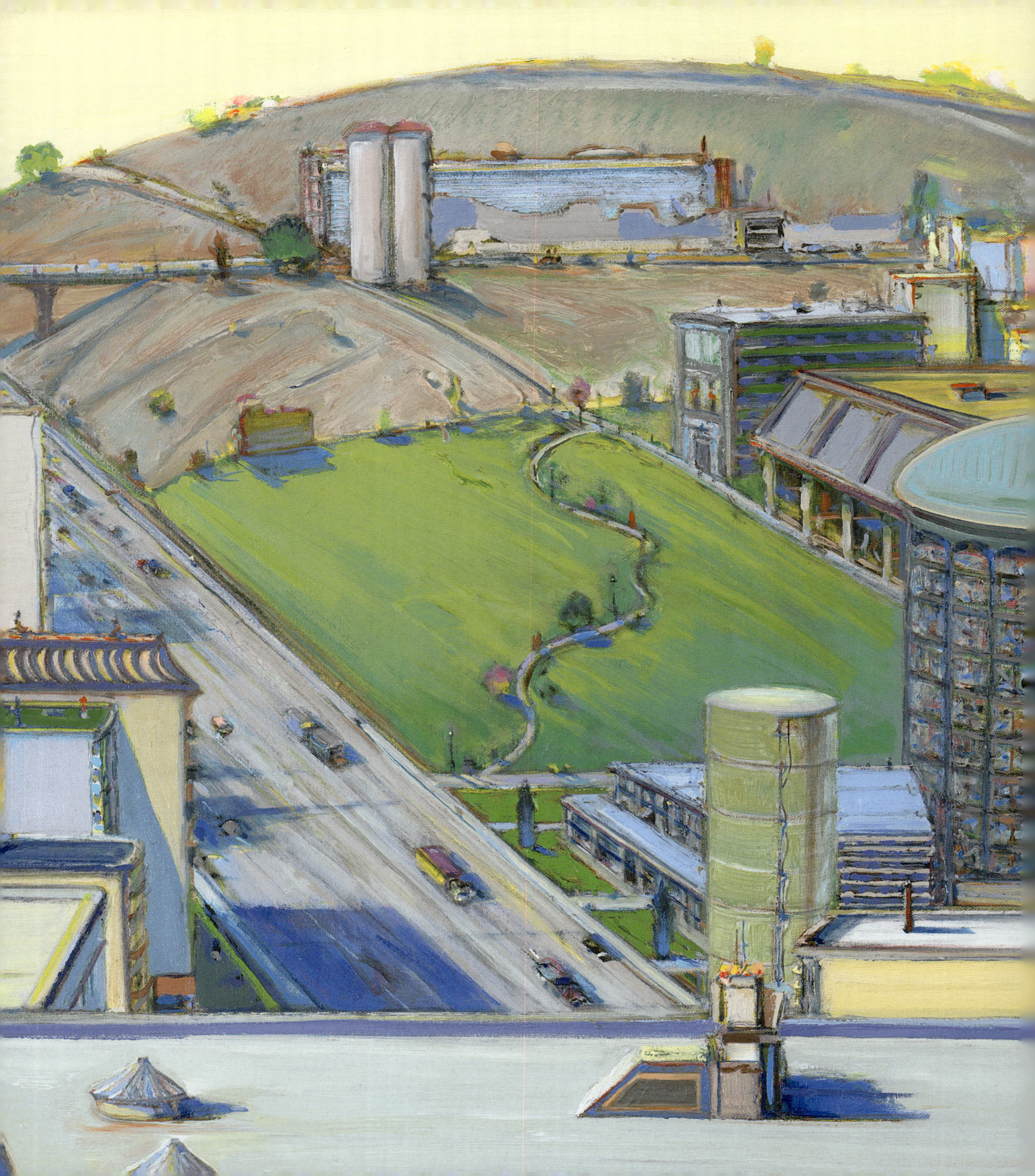

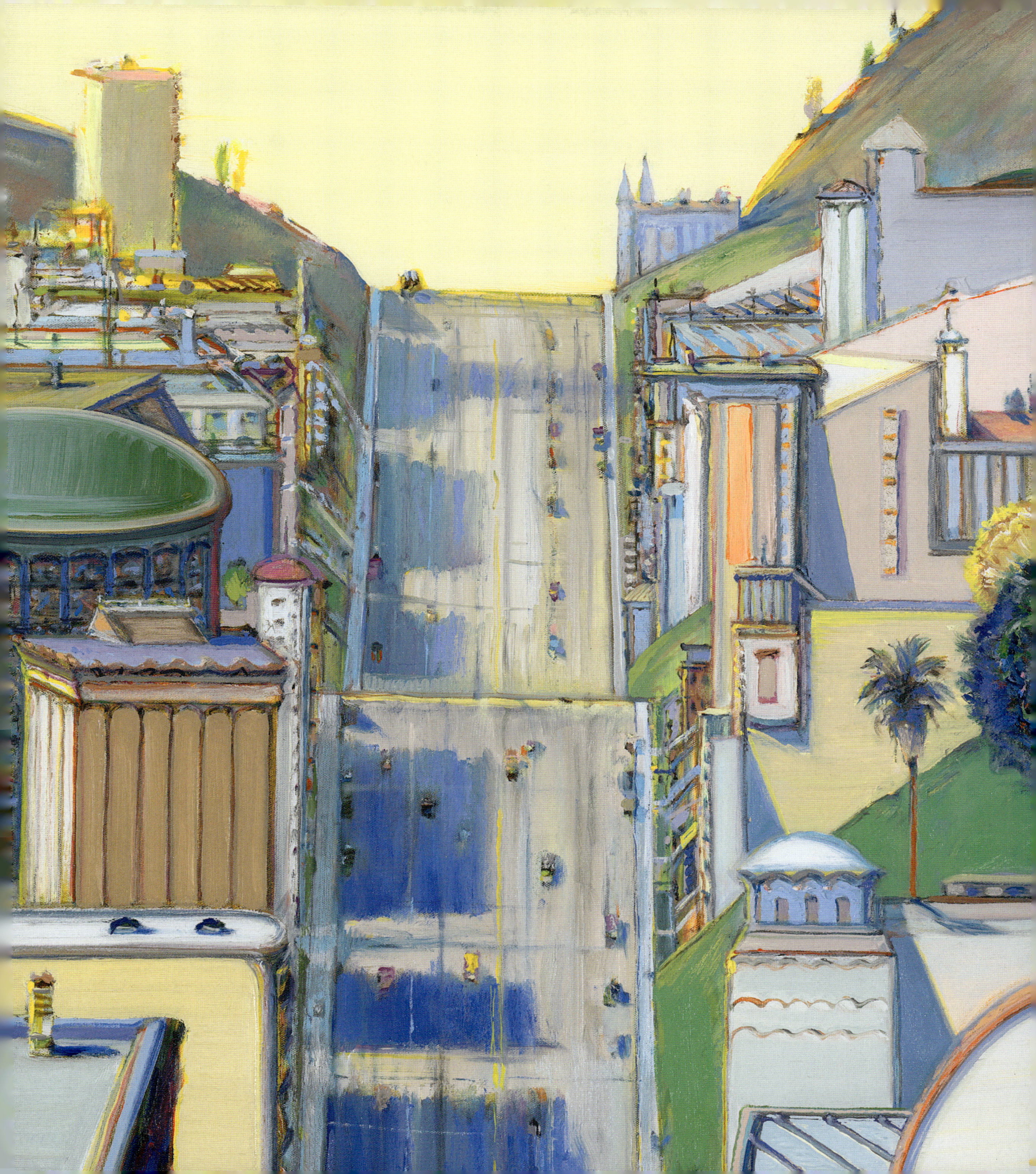

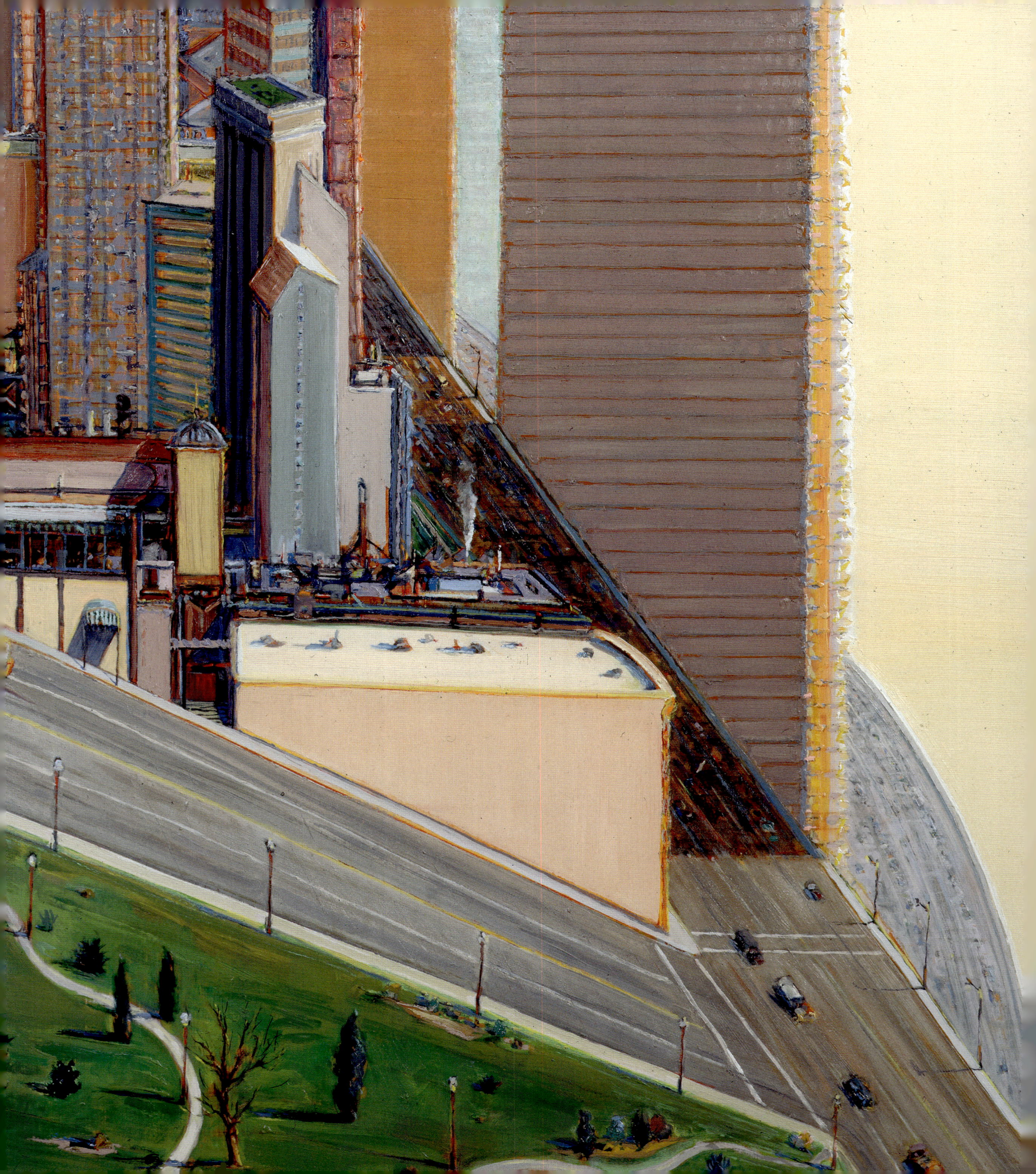

# Things Are Also as They Seem: Wayne Thiebaud and the World

Peter Frank

Wayne Thiebaud, **Uphill Streets** (detail), 1992–94

Rather early in his long career, Wayne Thiebaud had already entered the history books—above the footnotes. The pastries and other food items Thiebaud rendered with such lucid pathos, determining a one-man subgenre of still life painting, assured him a berth in 1960s American art—a berth that discomfited him mightily. Further, the earmarks of this painterly mirror held up to American consumerism displayed qualities of subject and of style associated with the West Coast of the United States—leading some to brand Thiebaud a kind of neo-regionalist, again to his chagrin. Thiebaud deeply valued the historic discourse around art, but in it found himself, by his own measure, deeply misunderstood. As he would have it, he wasn't a "Pop artist" and he wasn't a "California artist." Indeed, he wasn't (merely) a still life painter, either.

Thiebaud was in part all these things, in fact, and wholly none of them. If there is a category—especially one particular to his generation—appropriate to Thiebaud's oeuvre, it would be "radical realism." He worked in all three major modern genres—still life, figure, and landscape. He devised ways of changing and expanding these genres, modifying them not only to personal preference but according to strategies that play upon the audience's expectations and perceptions. No matter what he did, Thiebaud did things with his subjects and media that, for all their clearly articulated historical predecession, hadn't been done before.

Thiebaud bore the Pop imprimatur in its heyday thanks both to the nature of his subject matter and to his visual treatment of it. He painted the inert as it had rarely if ever been painted before—stylized, regimented, close up, devoid of narrative context, the result not of nature but of manufacture. Further, he suppressed, even eliminated, any nuanced illumination, so that the various edibles and their fussy displays were limned with an illustrator's dry precision and a caricaturist's simplification—rendered, with further irony, in rich, creamy pigments more tantalizing than the whipped cream they described. These mechanical meals certainly belonged in an exhibition titled *New Painting of Common Objects*. They portrayed objects; these objects were common to their audience (but not regarded heretofore as worthy of an artist's attention); they were painted and relied on qualities of paint for their incongruous sensuousness; and boy, were they new.

But they did not flatten into Pop art's emblematic presentation of modern life. They tweaked expectations by bending the rules rather than breaking them—by maintaining tonal values even while distorting them, by keeping the subjects in recessional space (even when only inferred), by retaining easel-size as the default proportion for making paintings. Thiebaud logically considered these isolated cake slices and prodigious display counters as the next step beyond Edward Hopper's in describing America's social landscape, still curdling in the postwar years with abiding anomie and a diminishing sense of poetic solitude. Thiebaud's style in his still lifes could be reduced to a formula, perhaps justifying the Pop label; but the meaning and spirit of his pictures were more removed from Pop art itself than were those of, say, Abstract Expressionism.

Thiebaud turned to figural subjects in part to shake the Pop-adjacent "common objects" attribution. In some ways, though, this move brought him yet closer to other artists labeled Pop. The human figure, stylized in myriad manners, ran rampant through the movement. But so did an underlying humanism that compelled artists as diverse as Ed Ruscha and Roy Lichtenstein, Mel Ramos and George Segal to think of their images as examinations of the human condition. The human presence in Thiebaud's still lifes was implied, but in a certain sense the implication sustained into the figures themselves. The people in Thiebaud's figural paintings, at least at this crucial time, were painted as if they themselves were still lifes, frozen in action or posed to conform to a pictorial fixity as motionless as a photographic studio portrait and (yet) as "normal" as a family album snapshot. It was easy enough for observers to regard Thiebaud's chilly, standardized images of women in bathing suits and organization men as critiques of American social and cultural vacuity. But, as opposed to his "fellow" Pop artists, Thiebaud's images were driven less by irony than by curiosity, by an ongoing dialogue with art history that engaged the effects of mid-century only as a prop.

What finally enabled Thiebaud to escape both the Pop rubric and the still life ghetto was his turn to the landscape. Or, rather, his return. He had always taken an interest in the landscape, certainly the natural and urban spaces he grew up with in various parts of California. Landscape studies and smaller paintings are among his earliest mature works, investigations of the relationship of form to space, color to atmosphere that require no neutralizing or amplifying pretext. By 1972, when he and his wife, Betty Jean, took a pied-à-terre in San Francisco, Thiebaud had embarked on a veritable embrace of the local terrain, urban and rural, wringing from it an infinitude of visual tactics that lasted him the rest of his life. Through his practice alone Thiebaud finally elided the labels critics were still trying to pin on him—although art history itself wasn't quite so yielding.

Thiebaud's landscapes and cityscapes, certainly after the '60s, rode the same illogic that his still lifes and figures did, but to opposite effect. While he grounded the other subject matter in a kind of bare-bones compositional structure, eliminating anything that wasn't integral to the image itself, Thiebaud made of the landscape figure *and* ground—optical space, its contents, and its bounds. His renditions of spaces are renditions of *places*, credibly enterable (or at least mappable) ambiances delineated by buildings and streets, fields and waterways. Their distance from our everyday experience of such subjects is indisputable; these vertiginous drops and maplike patterns improvise wildly on the sites they connote. But in their very distortion these roller-coaster topographies appeal to a sense of familiarity we keep at least partly buried in our dreams.

In his landscape work, finally comprising an oeuvre at least as imposing as anything else he ever did, Thiebaud exited the notion of observed reality and entered the notion of invented, or reinvented, reality. The cityscapes and landscapes do not record what the eye sees but what the body senses and/or what the mind invents. In their plummeting perspectives and halated colors the cityscapes and landscapes, mountainous and aqueous by turns, propose that ordinary life can be quite a ride. To be sure, these paintings reverently celebrate (primus inter pares) San Francisco's hills and the lush lagoons of the Sacramento River delta, and their exaggerations underscore the uniqueness of these Northern California landmarks. But in Thiebaud's hands the city and the delta, the swooping trajectories and the boundless patternings, become ambitious flights of imagination, bird's-eye abstractions that anticipated drone photography by decades.

Thiebaud's acceptance, nay exploitation, of unreal conditions providing uncanny views does not square with what Americans, at least, consider "realism." "Surrealism" is more like it. By the time he moved his practice entirely to dreamscapes, the topical sterility of Thiebaud's still lifes and isolated figures had been taken over by post-Pop painters working in a photorealistic or otherwise hyperrealistic mode. (I don't think it an accident that some of the earliest and best Photorealist artists such as Robert Bechtle and Howard Hack were situated in the Bay Area.) Likewise, I think it significant that by this time Thiebaud considered Richard Diebenkorn, a master of landscape-derived abstraction, a close friend, and that his circle of friends and colleagues in Sacramento and Davis included Funk artists such as William T. Wiley, Roy De Forest, and Robert Hudson. When Thiebaud turned to land- and cityscape, it was indeed to get out-of-doors, but it was also to get out the door, to let the eye and heart and mind all take flight, to proclaim that the ordinary could be not only extraordinary, but unlikely. A case can be made that Thiebaud achieved his most innovative and exalting work in his land/cityscapes. The early still lifes may be historically more important, but the scapes are the most rewarding, and most affecting, in his body of work.

Through all this, what we see conistently in Thiebaud's oeuvre is a California attitude toward California light and space (as it were). The crisp delineations of his still life and figure subjects are given to them by that merciless yet elusive Pacific sunshine, the one flecked with fog even as it throws the desert back at us. In the scapes, the brilliance and ephemerality of that sunshine throw everything into dazzling color and exaggerated contour, so that there is no edge to the picture, only a place where life escapes gravity, Potrero Hill becomes as steep as El Capitan, and the delta fills with lush tapestries.

Thiebaud was nothing if not a "regional" painter. As he insisted, he wasn't a "regionalist," with all the ideological freight that term carried for a child of the Depression years; but his styles and strategies, subjects and solutions all rely upon an intimate experience of coastal California cities and unique agrarian formulations inland. If he was touched by Funk, he was a California artist. If he saw landscapes in abstract terms, as Diebenkorn and other Bay Area Figurative painters did, he was a California artist. If he realized early success in New York through one of New York's leading galleries and yet chose to stay put, he was a California artist. Wayne Thiebaud was one of California's greatest painters—and one of American art's greatest Californians.

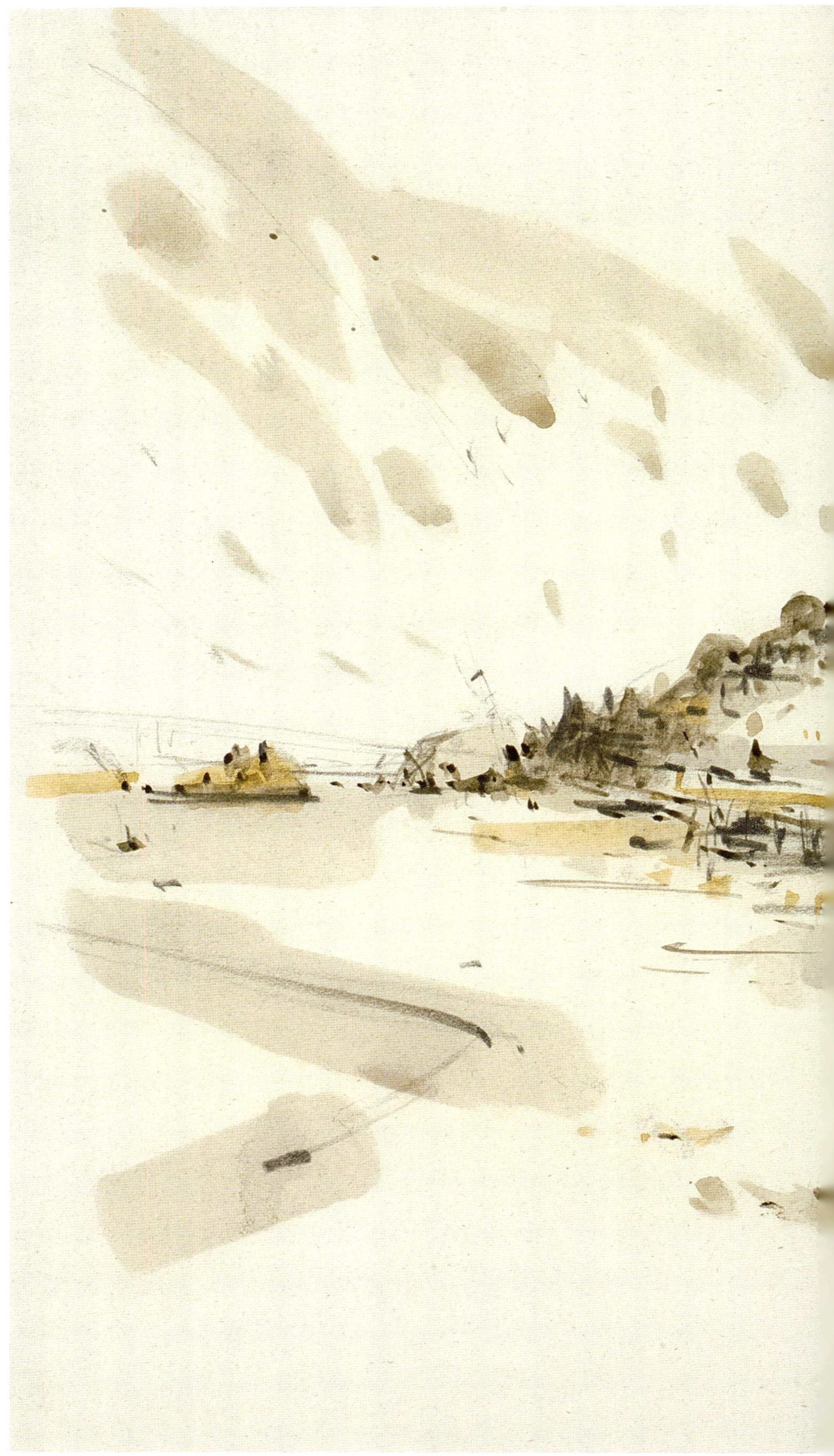

Wayne Thiebaud
**Sausalito**, 1954
Watercolor and pencil on paper
12 ¼ × 19 ⅛ in.
Private Collection

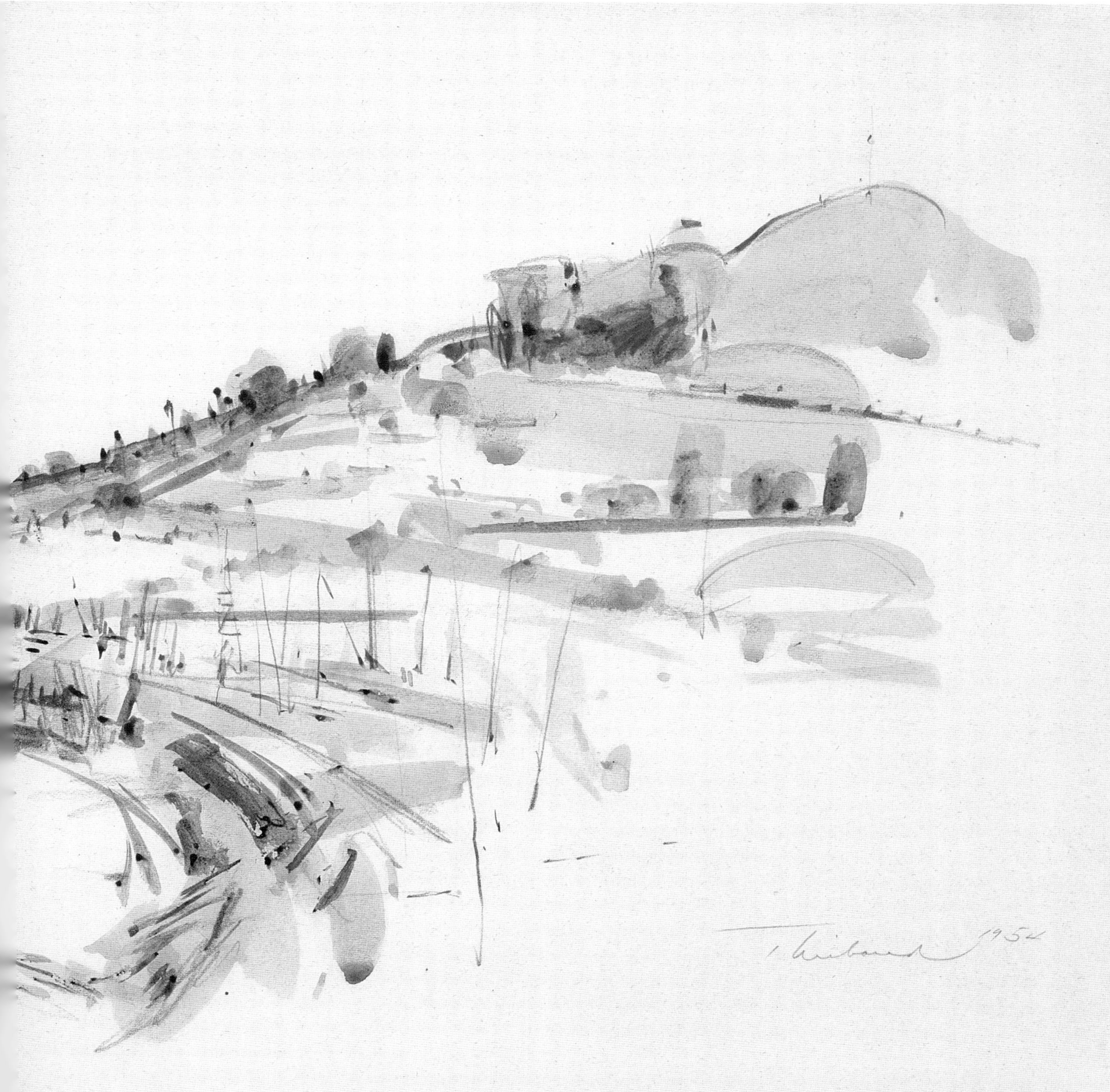

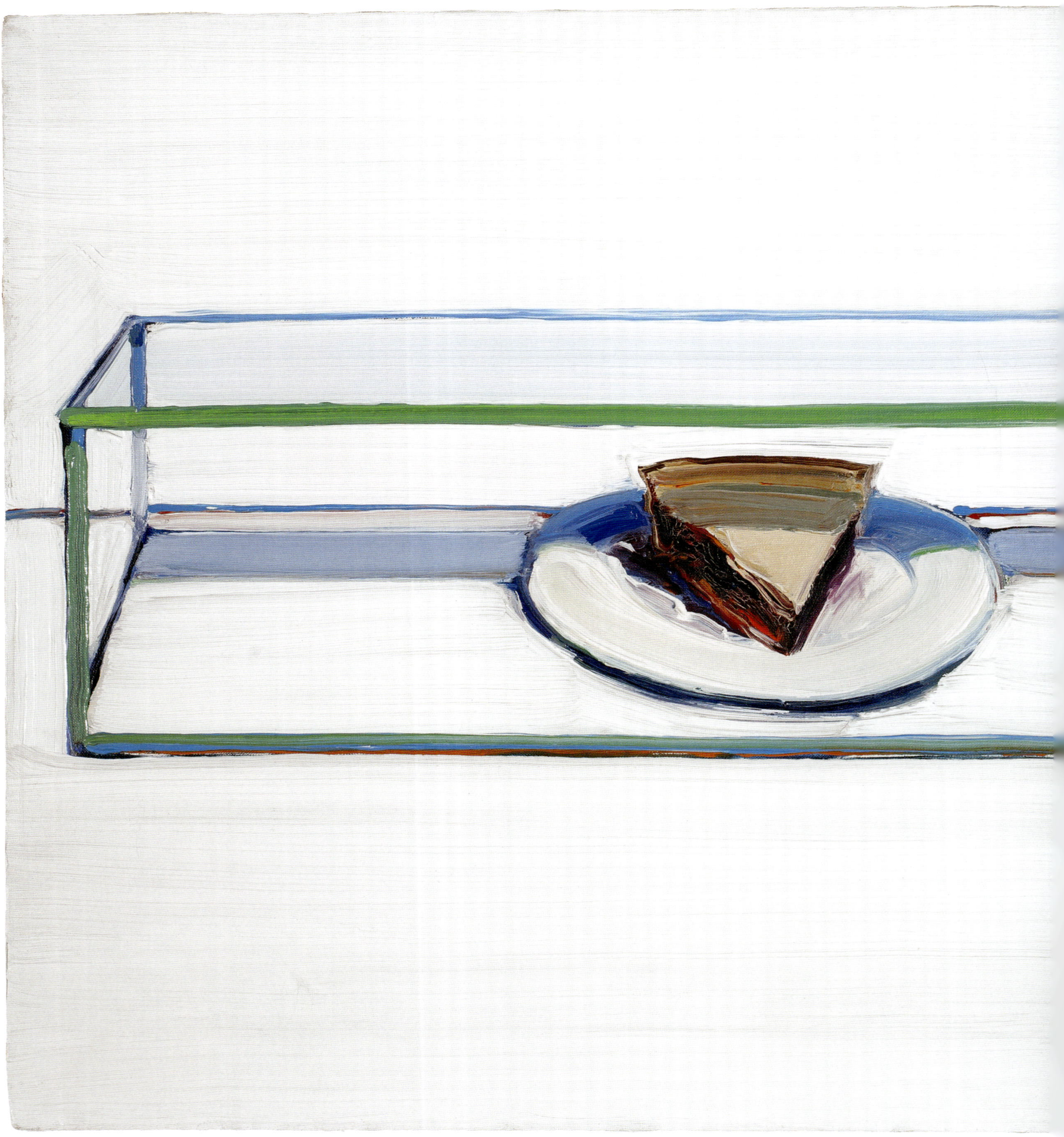

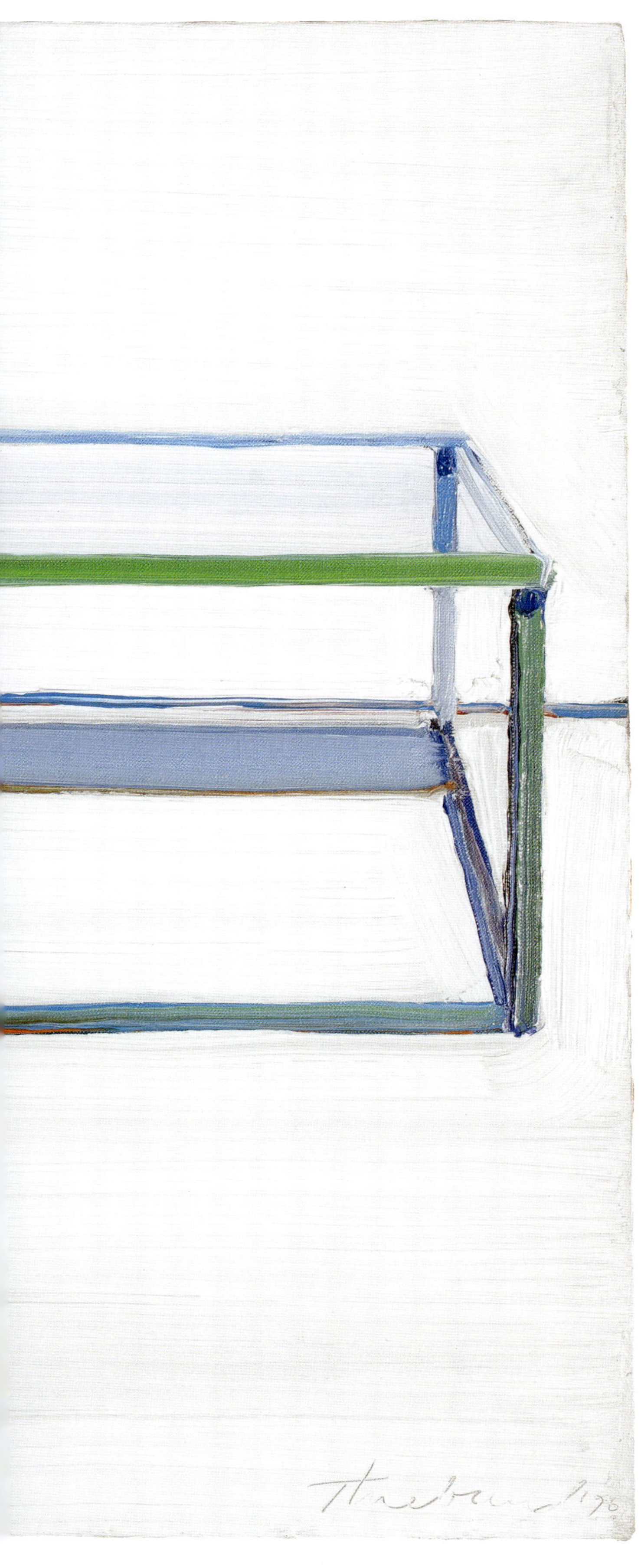



Wayne Thiebaud
**Caged Pie**, 1962
Oil on canvas
20 ⅛ × 28 ⅛ in.
San Diego Museum of Art
Museum purchase through the Earle W. Grant Acquisition Fund

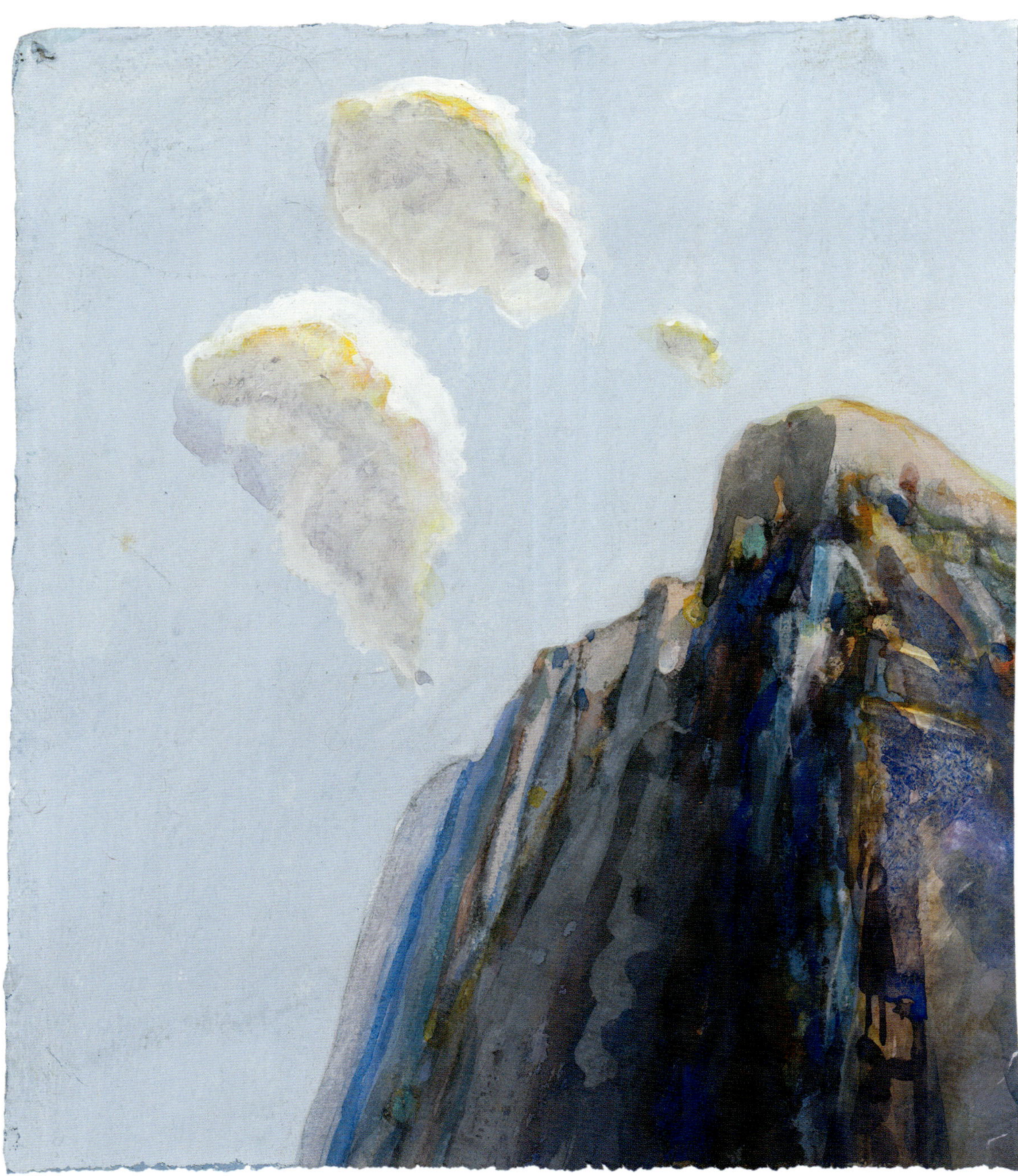

Wayne Thiebaud
**Untitled (Mountain and Clouds)**, 1965
Gouache and watercolor on paper
7 ½ × 6 ¾ in.
San Francisco Museum of Modern Art
Gift of the Thiebaud Family

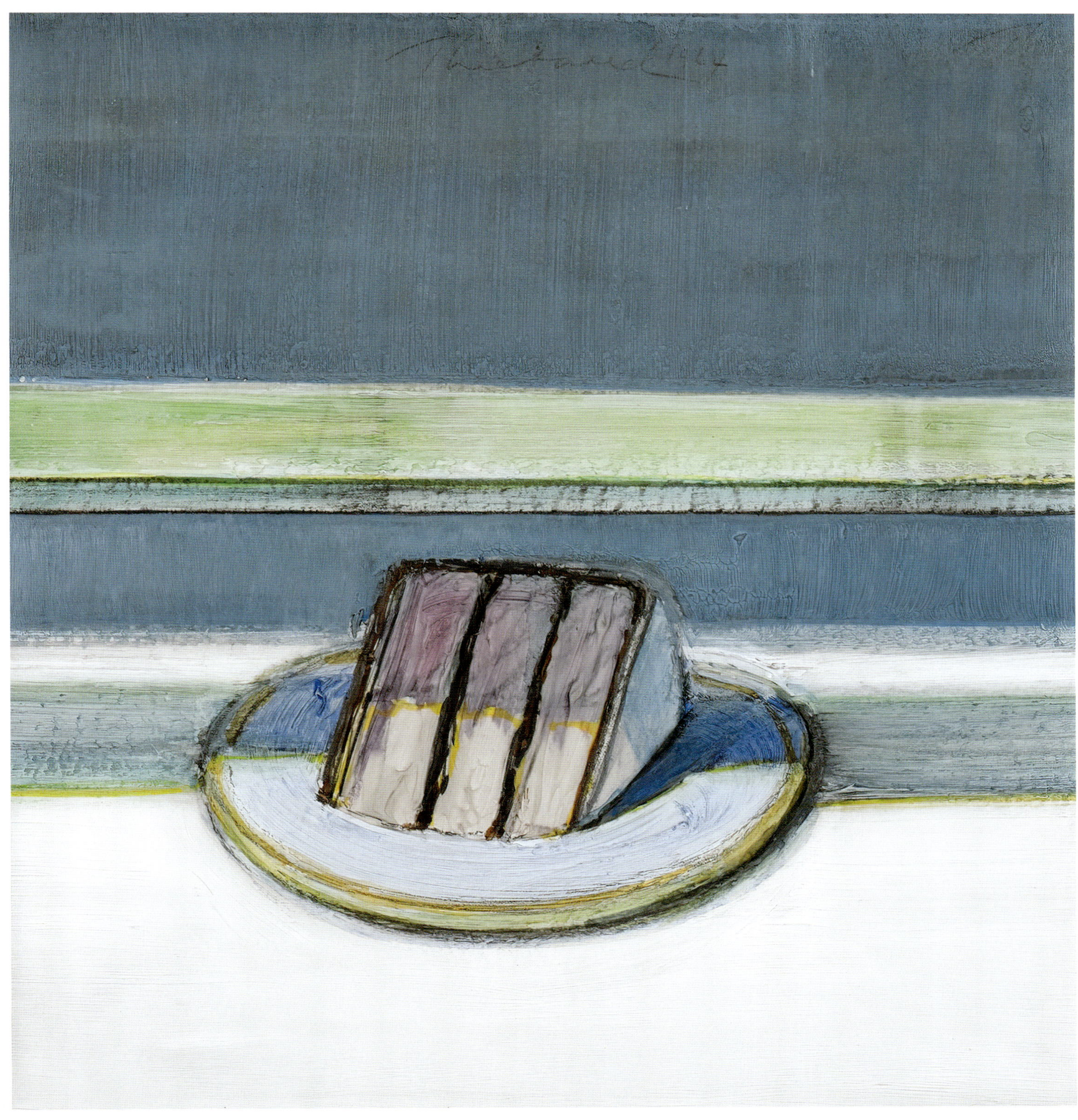



Wayne Thiebaud
**Cake Slice**, 1964
Mixed media (including oil) on illustration board on wood
15 ⅛ × 14 ¾ in.
Private Collection

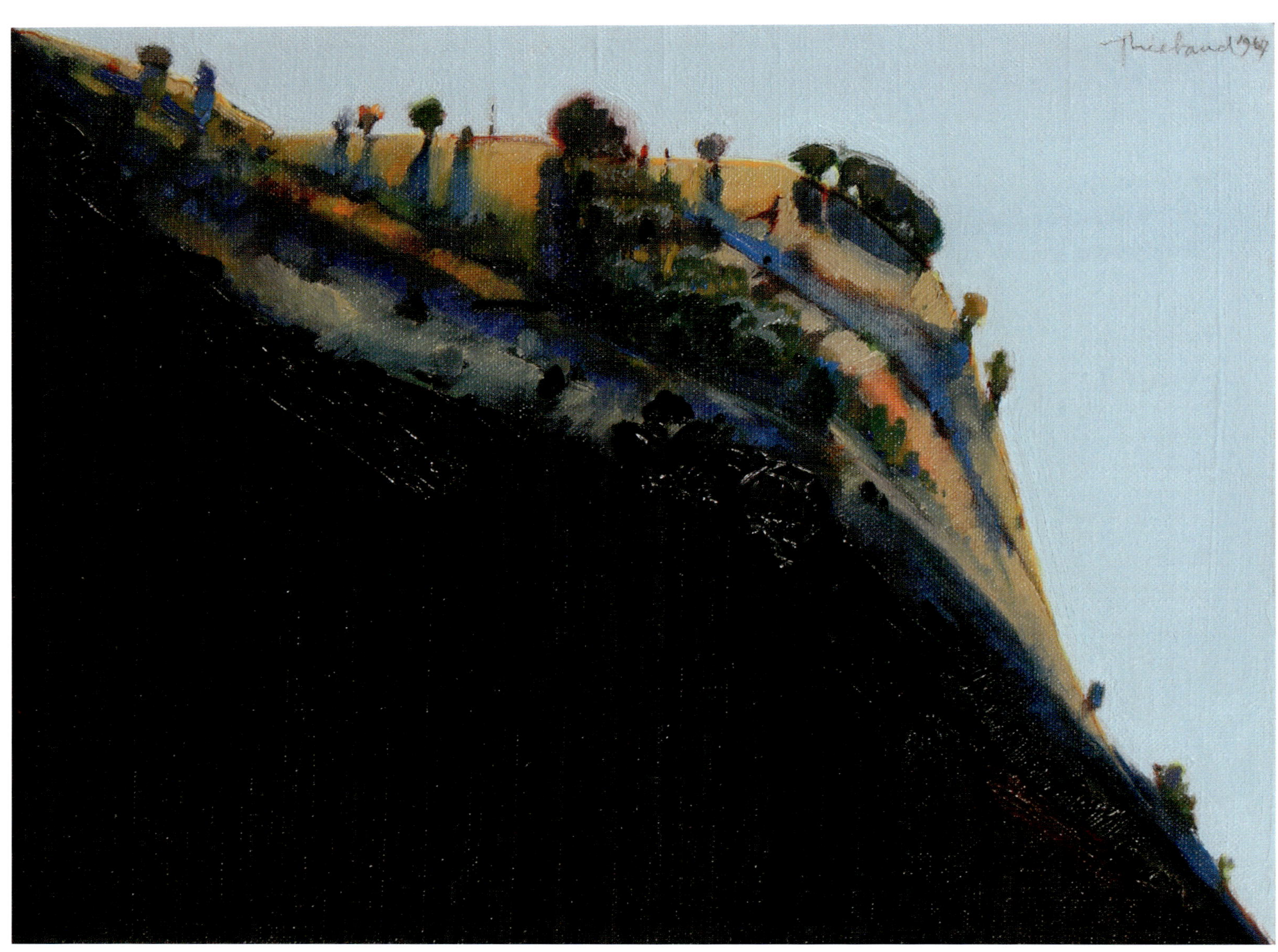

Wayne Thiebaud
**Coloma Ridge Study**, 1967
Oil on canvas
8 ⅞ × 12 ⅛ in.
Collection of Matt and Maria Bult

Wayne Thiebaud
**Landscape**, 1968
Oil on canvas
36 × 36 in.
Private Collection

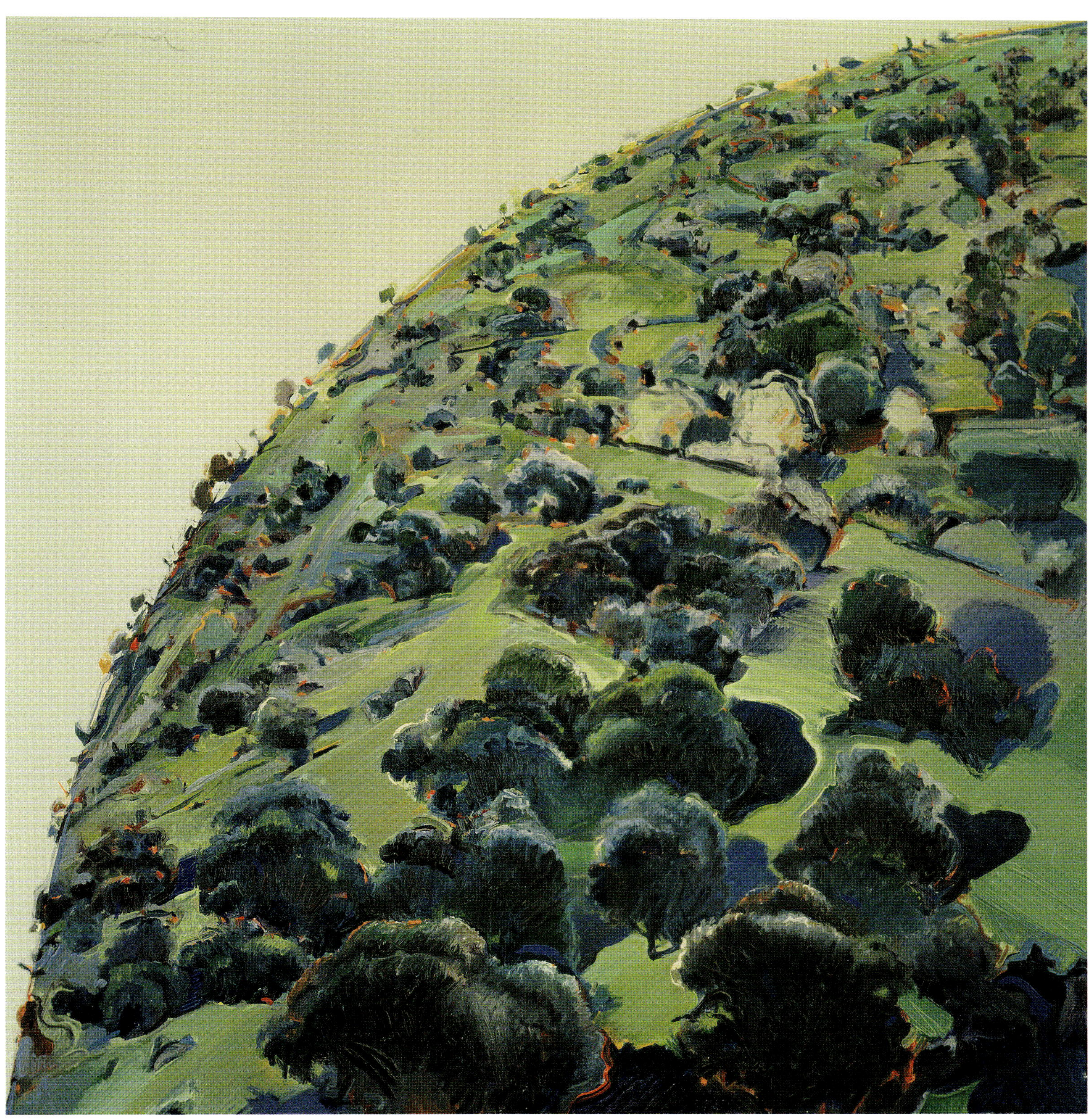

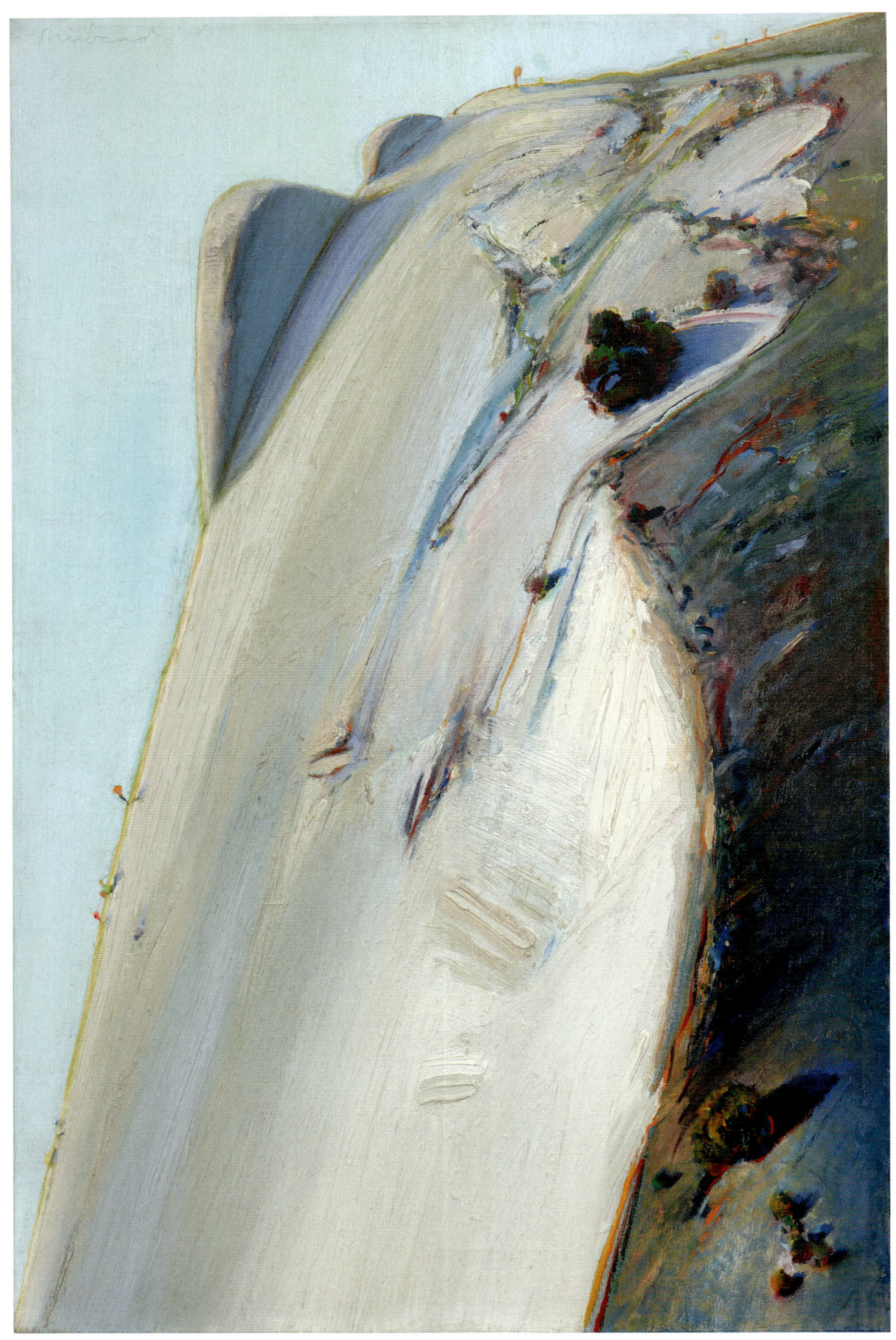

Wayne Thiebaud
**White Ridge**, 1969
Oil on canvas
36 × 24 in.
Fine Arts Museums of San Francisco

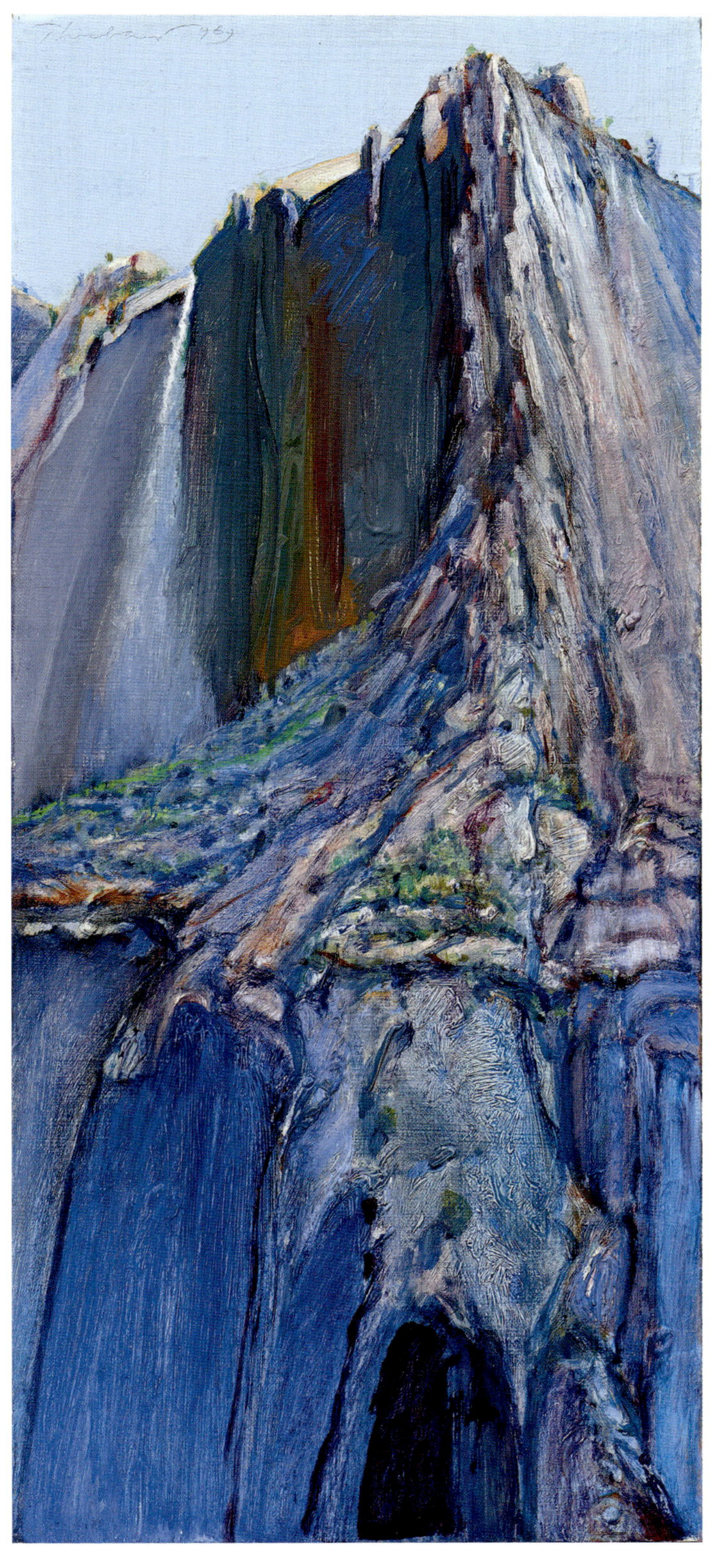

Wayne Thiebaud
**Yosemite**, 1969/2010
Oil on linen
21 ⅞ × 9 ⅞ in.
Fine Arts Collection, Jan Shrem and Maria Manetti
Shrem Museum of Art, University of California, Davis
Gift of Wayne Thiebaud Foundation

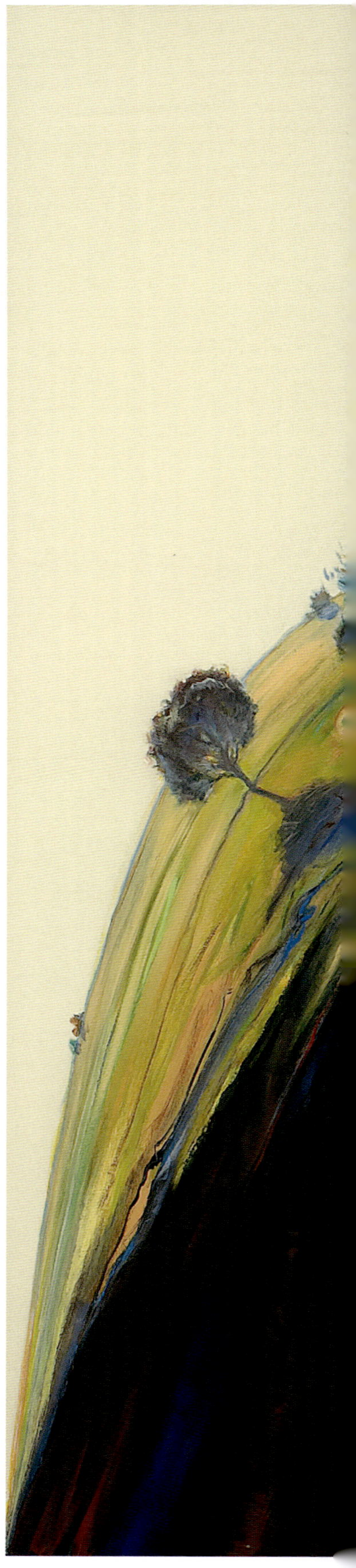

Wayne Thiebaud
**Estate**, 1969–96
Oil on canvas
60 × 72 in.
Private Collection

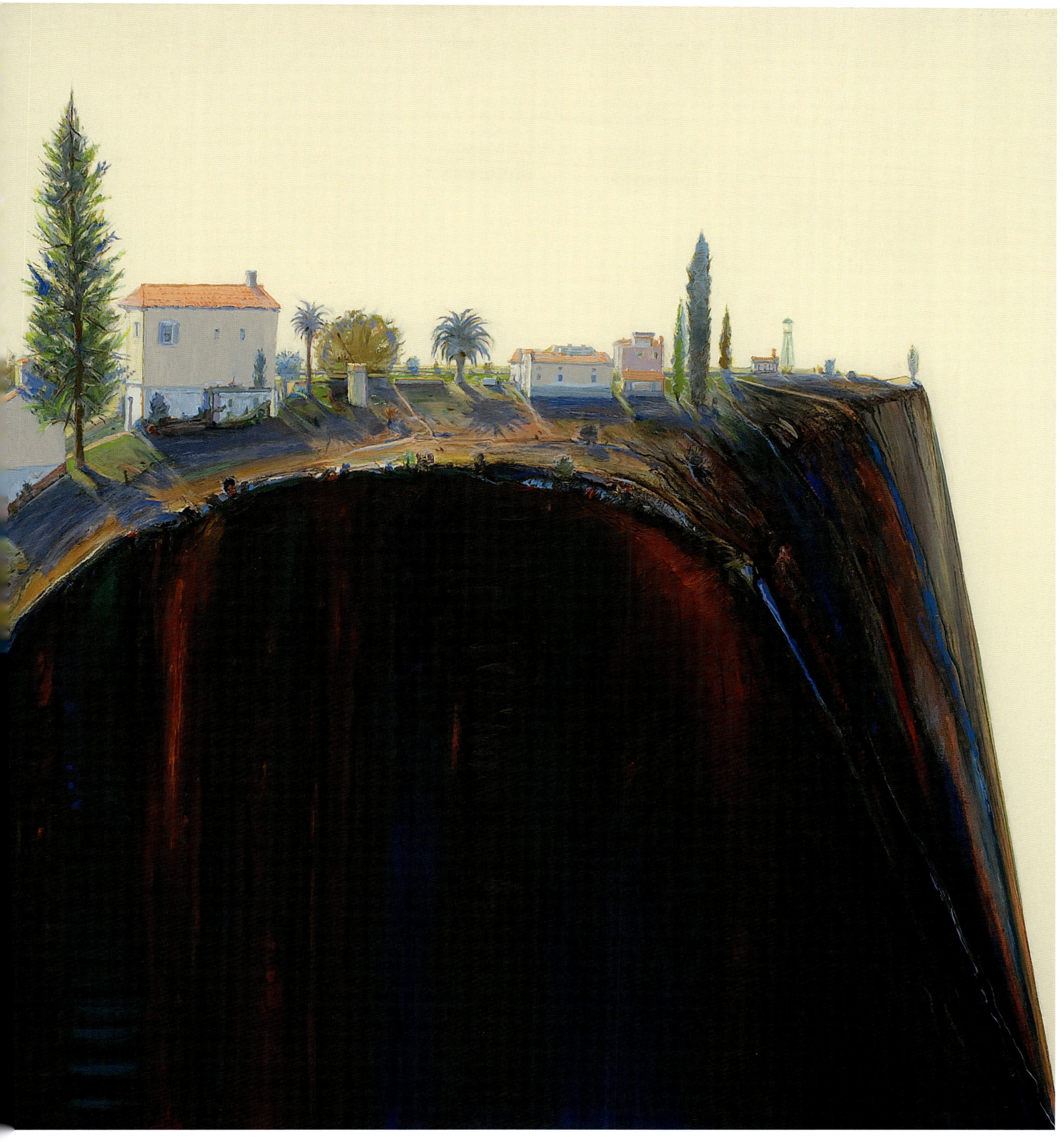

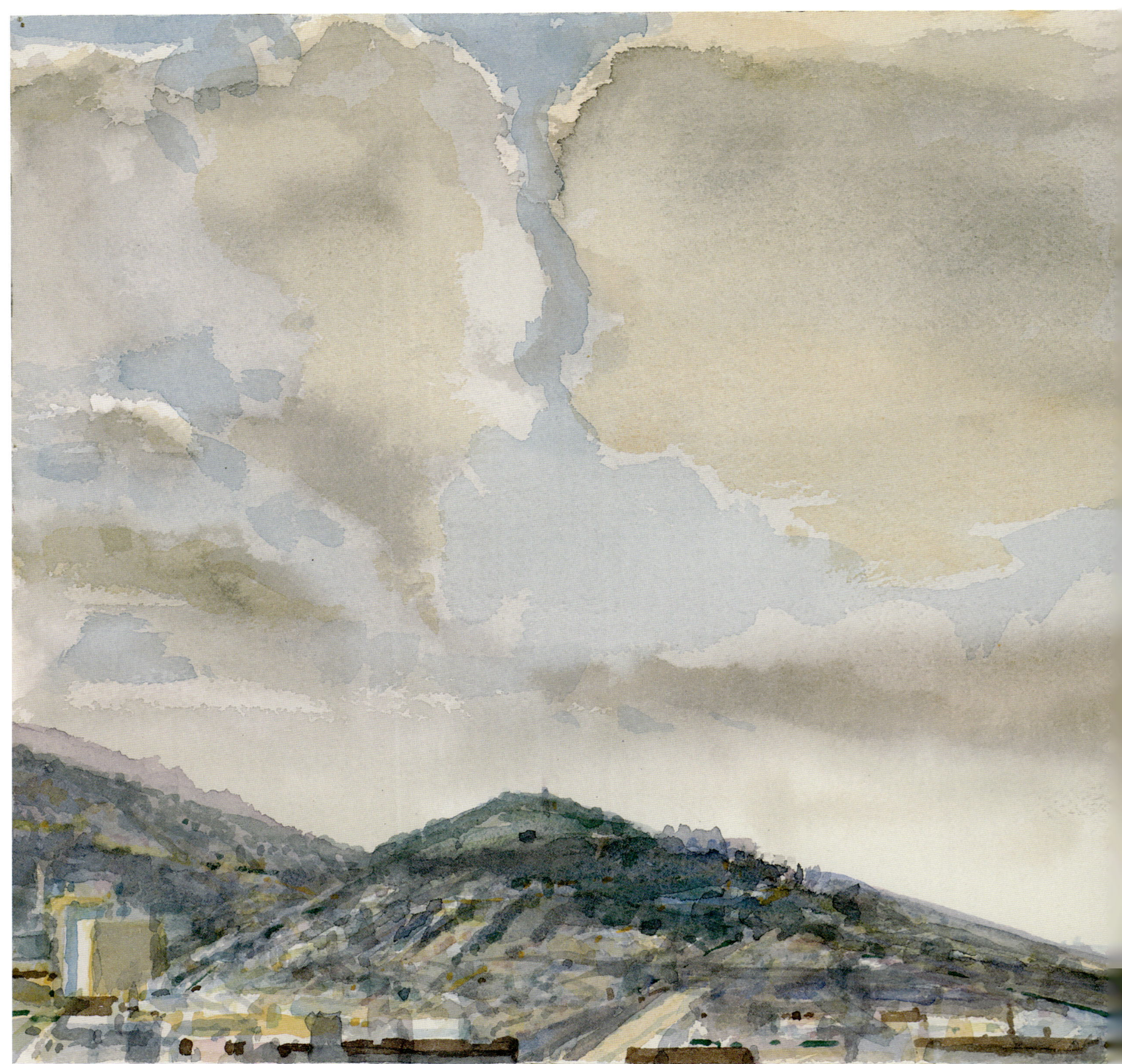

Wayne Thiebaud
**Towards Twin Peaks from 538 Utah (Back Window)**, 1975
Watercolor on paper
10 ¼ × 14 $\frac{3}{16}$ in.
Fine Arts Museums of San Francisco
Gift of Glenna and Charles Campbell

Wayne Thiebaud
**Yosemite Rock Ridge**, 1975–2013
Oil on canvas
36 × 36 in.
Collection of Matt and Maria Bult

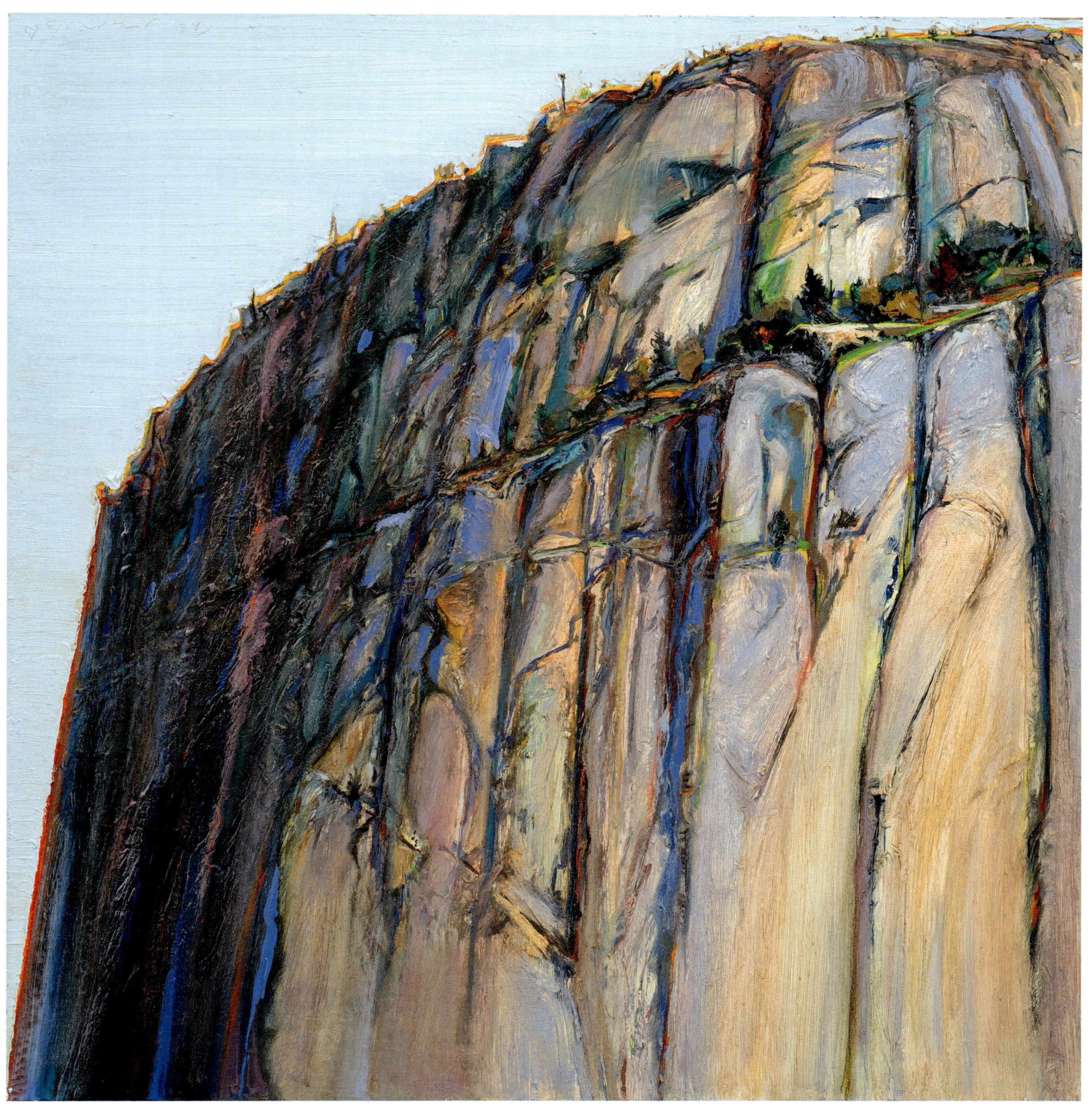

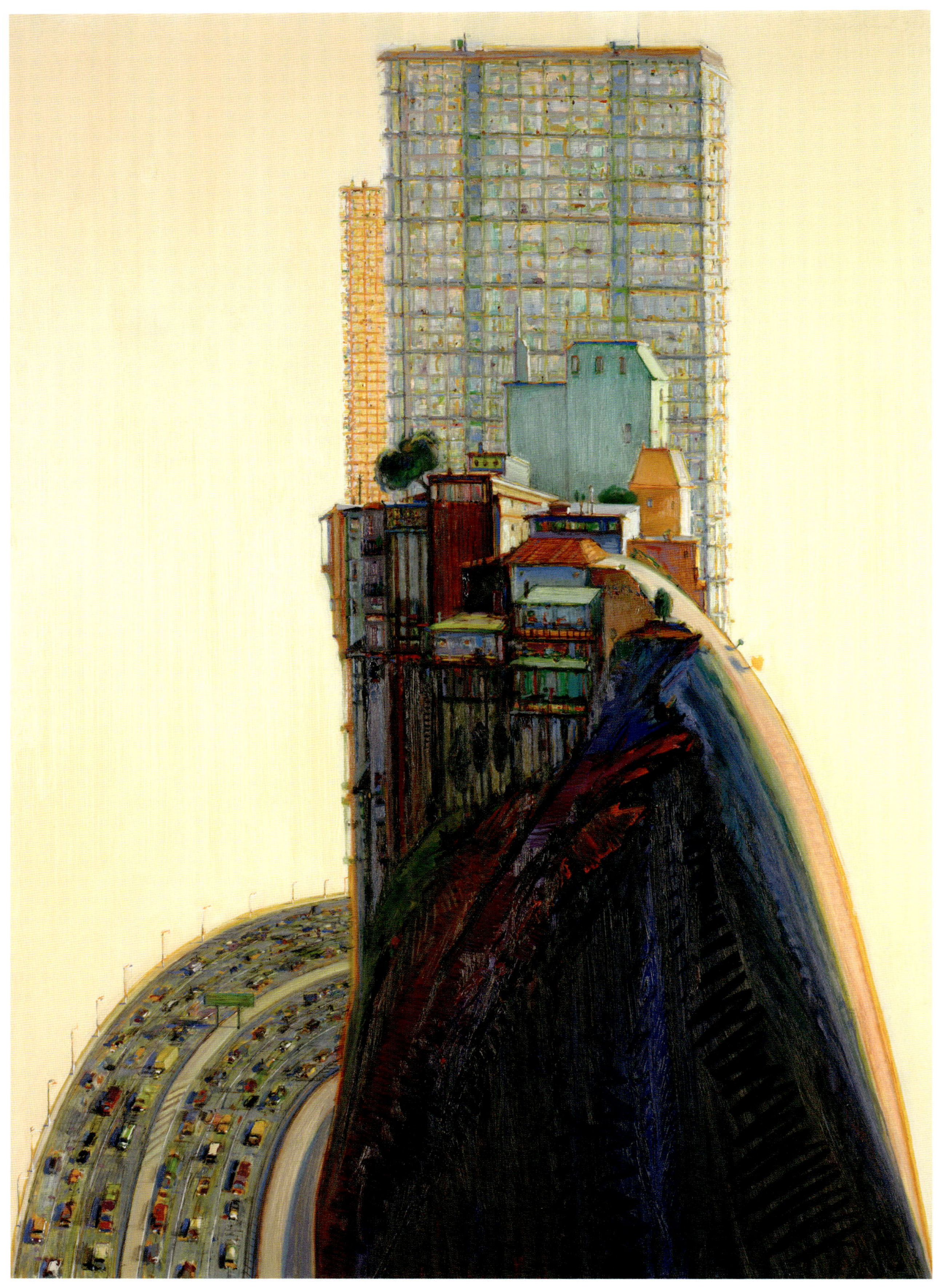

57

Wayne Thiebaud
**Apartment Hill**, 1980
Oil on linen
65 × 48 in.
Nelson-Atkins Museum of Art
Object Number F86-4
Acquired through the generosity of the Friends of Art and the Nelson Gallery Foundation

58

Wayne Thiebaud
**Street and Shadow**, 1982–83/1996
Oil on linen
35 ¾ × 23 ¾ in.
Crocker Art Museum
Gift of the artist's family, 1996.3

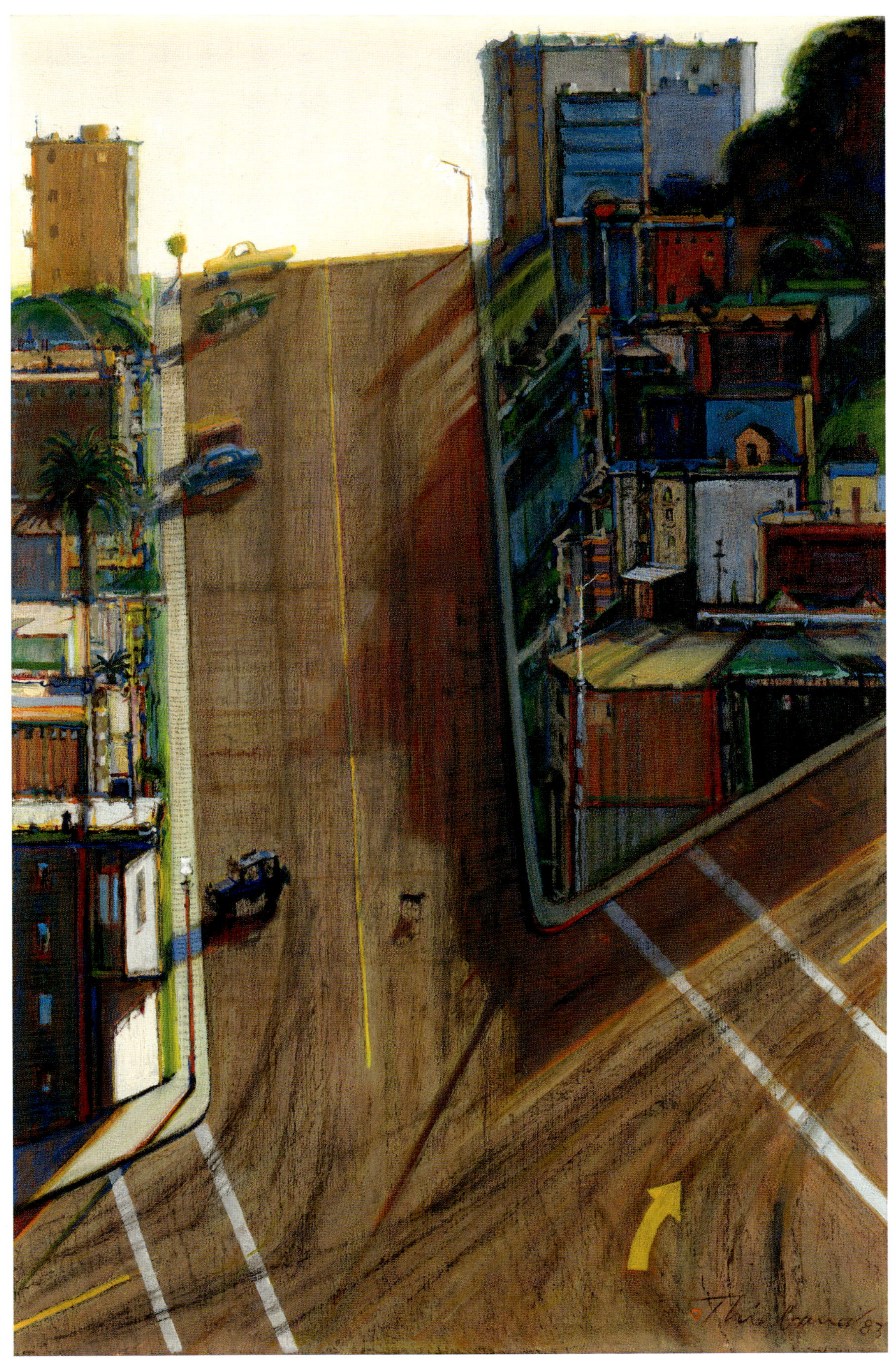

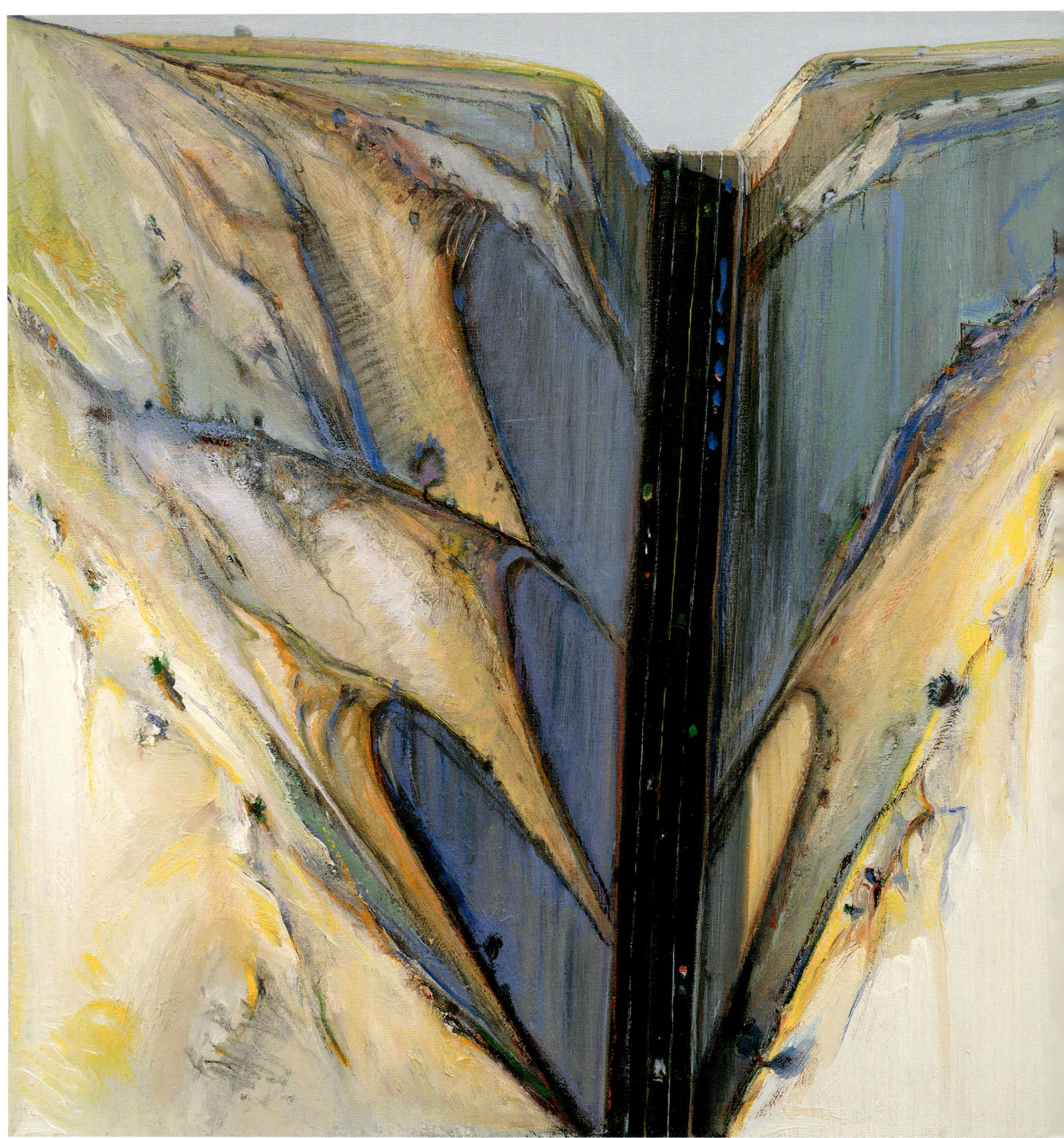

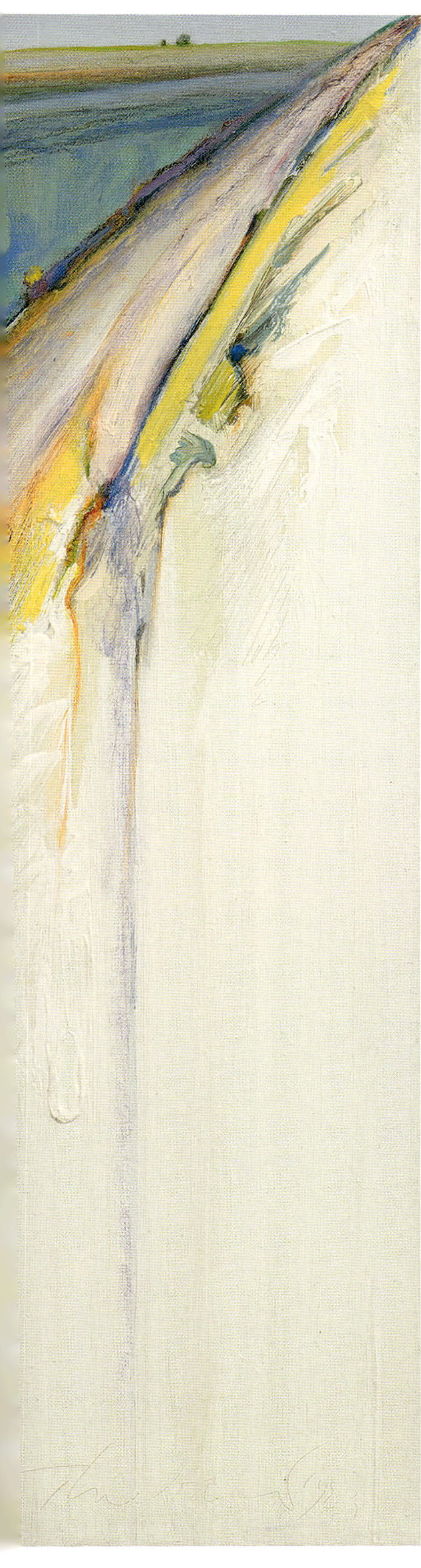



Wayne Thiebaud
**Road Through**, 1983
Oil on canvas
24 ⅞ × 30 in.
Private Collection

62

Wayne Thiebaud
**Sunset Streets**, 1985
Oil on canvas
48 × 35 ¾ in.
San Francisco Museum of Modern Art
Purchase with the aid of funds from public subscription, William L. Gerstle Fund, Fund of the '80s, Clinton Walker Fund, and Thomas W. Weisel

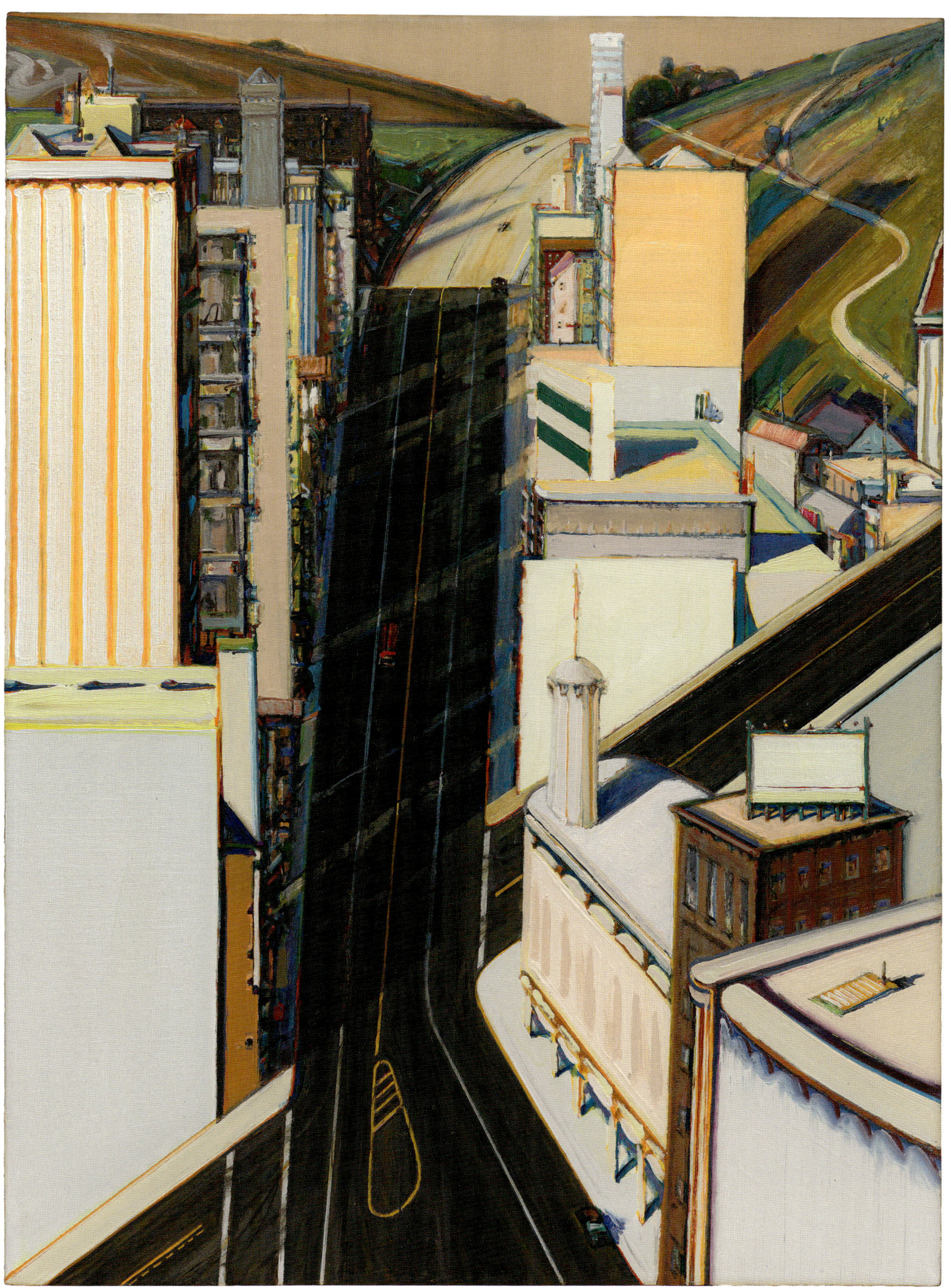

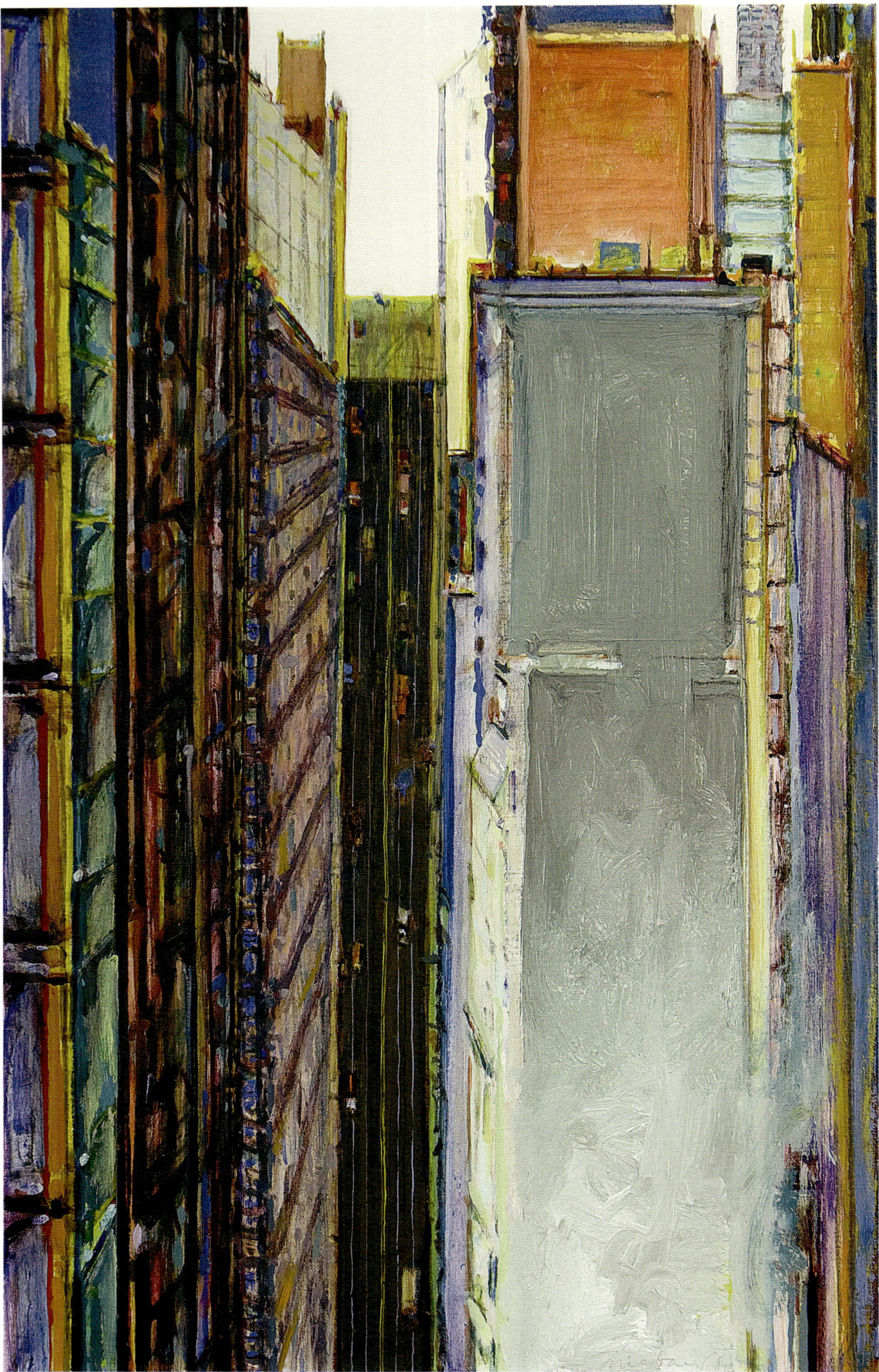

Wayne Thiebaud
**Untitled**, 1986
Oil on canvas
28 × 18 in.
Private Collection

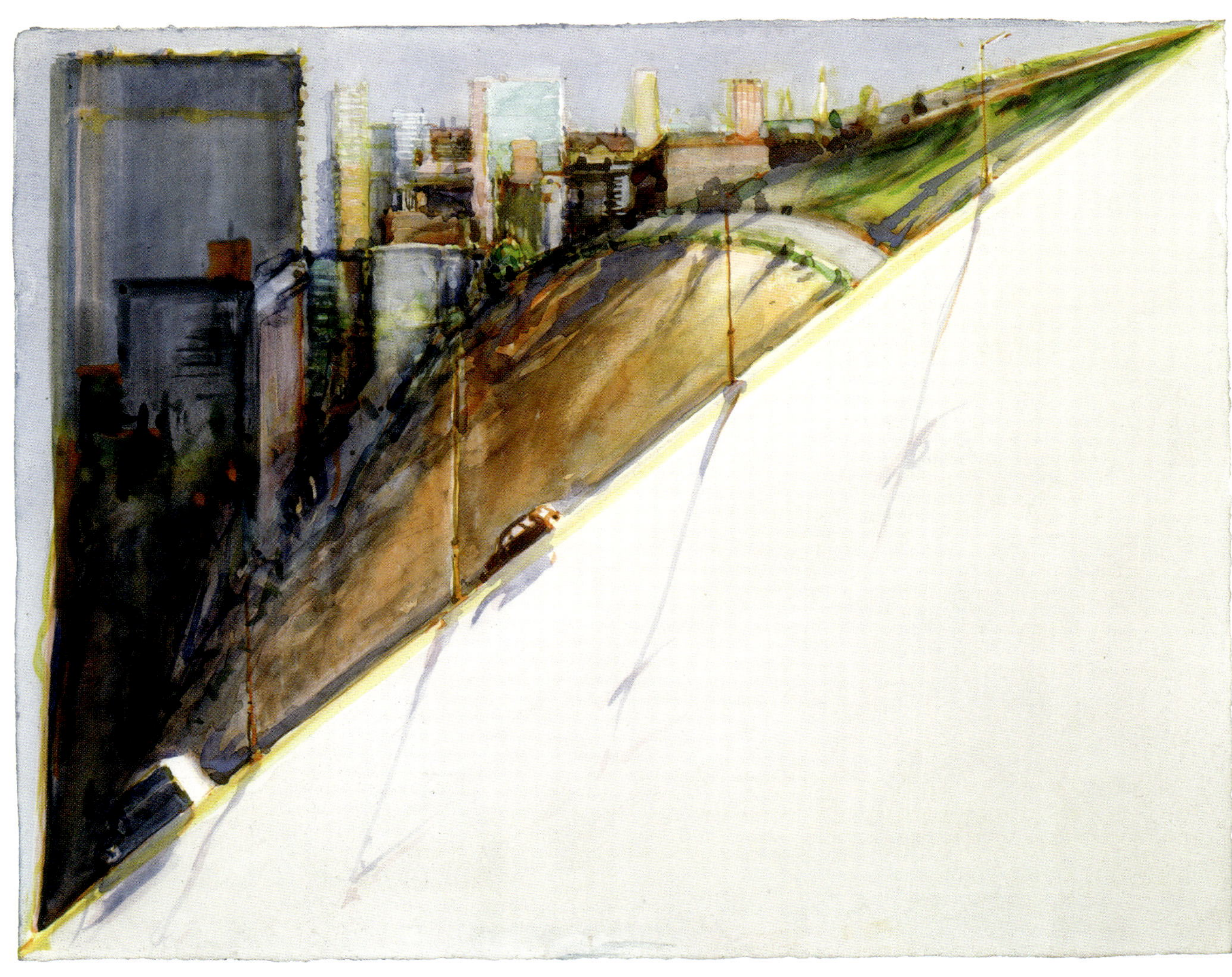



Wayne Thiebaud
**Diagonal Ridge**, 1987
Watercolor on paper
11 ½ × 14 ⅞ in.
Private Collection

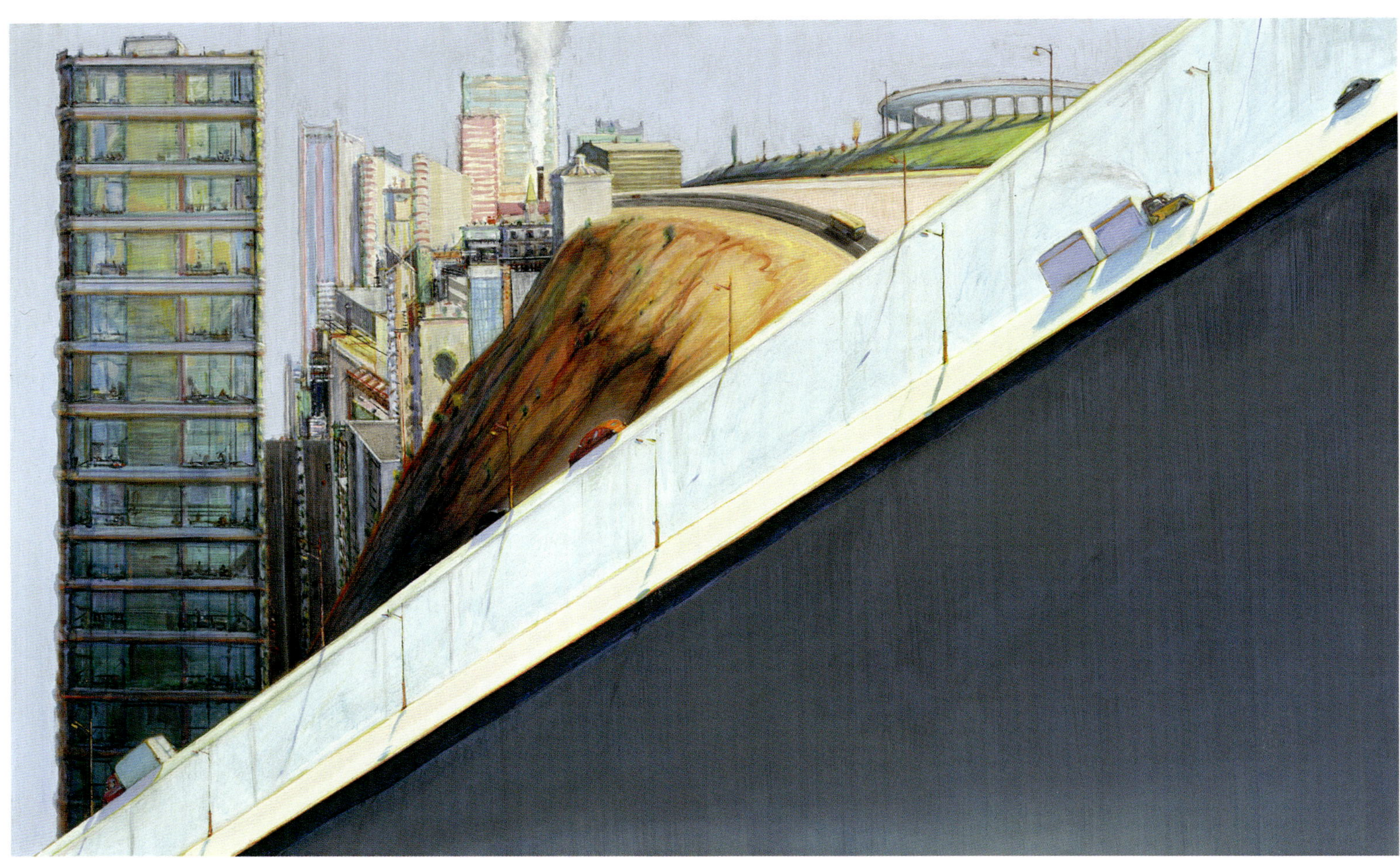



ABOVE
Wayne Thiebaud
**Diagonal Freeway**, 1993
Acrylic on canvas
36 × 60 in.
Fine Arts Museums of San Francisco

OPPOSITE
Wayne Thiebaud
**Uphill Streets**, 1992–94
Oil on canvas
60 ¼ × 48 ¼ in.
Private Collection

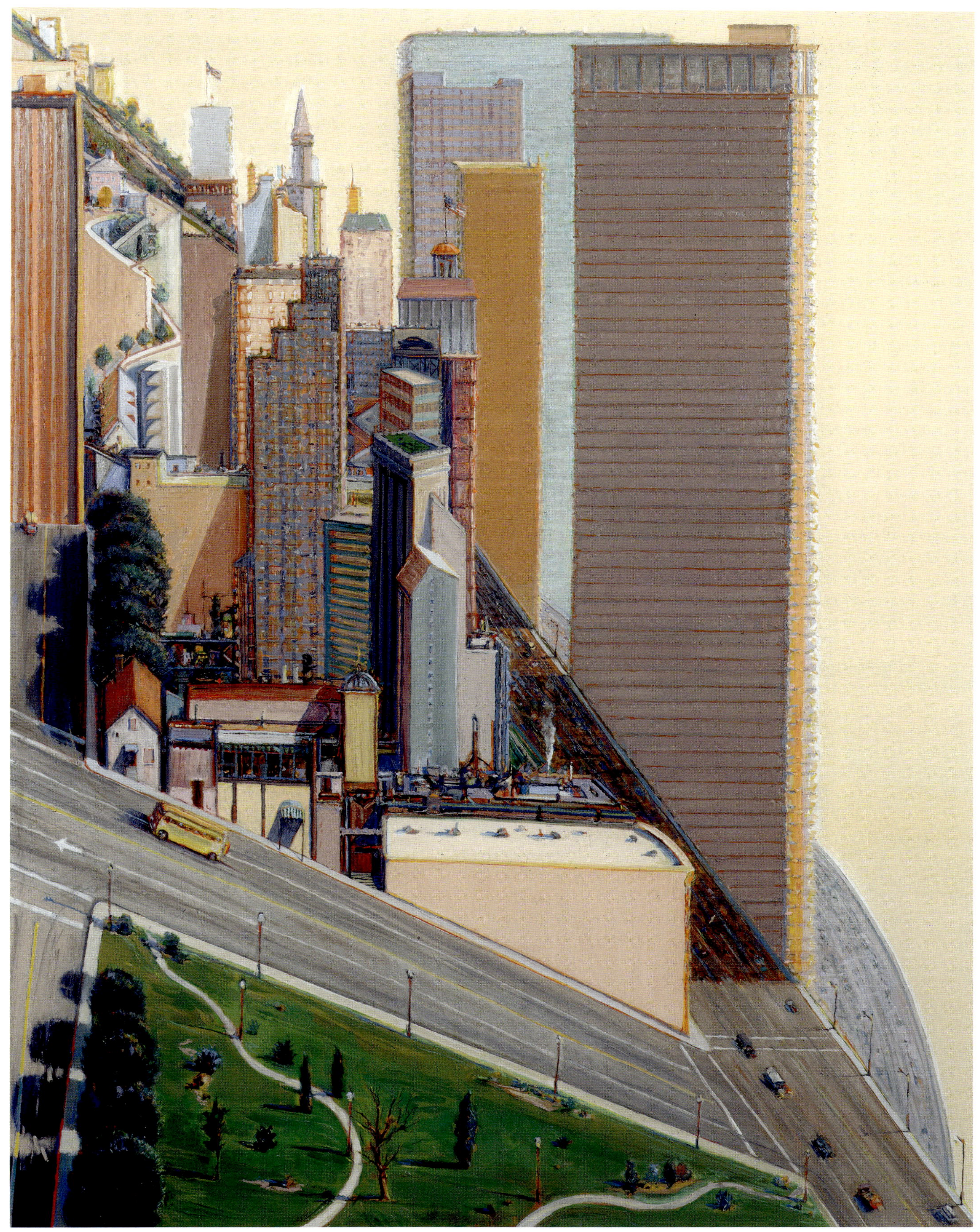

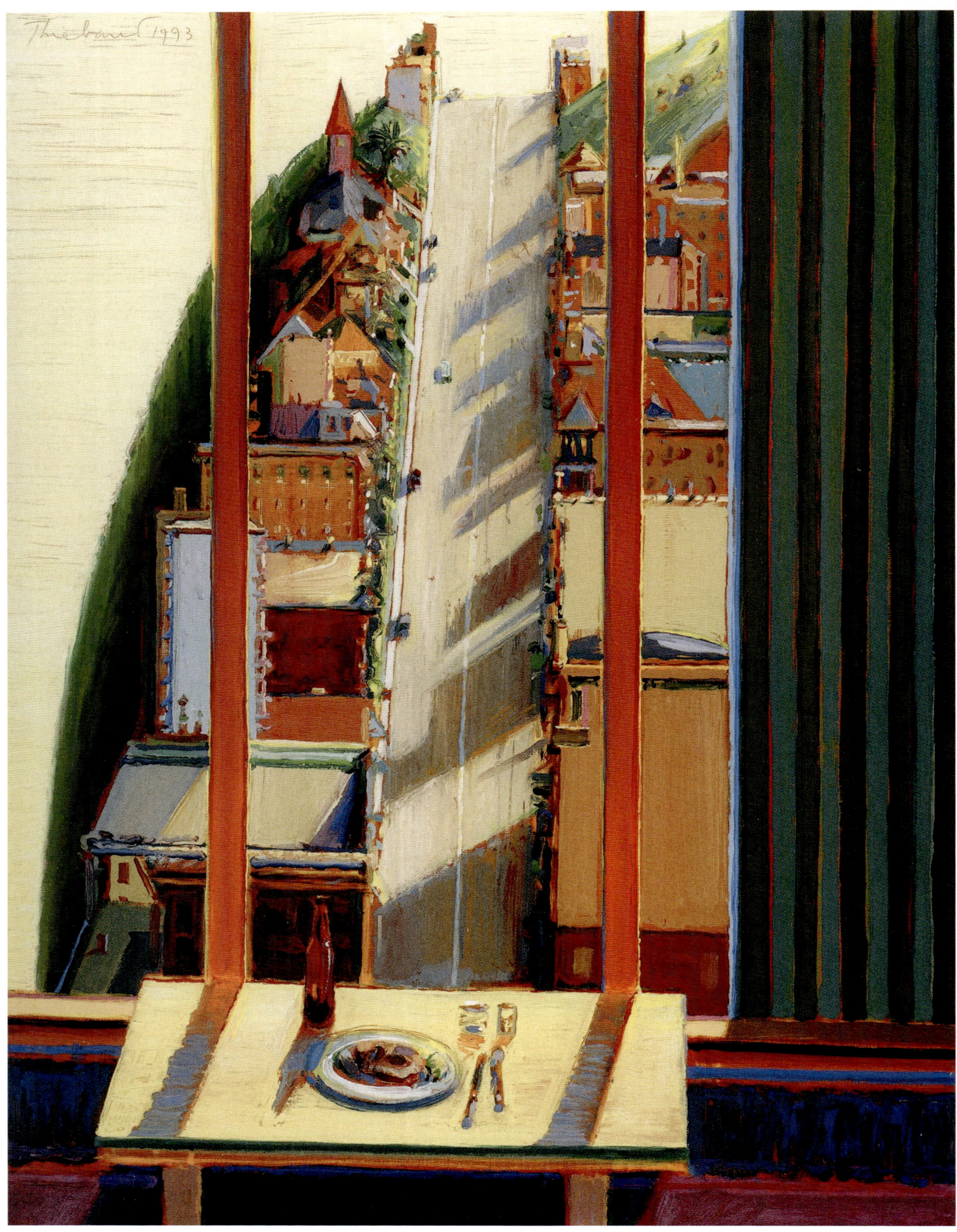
Thiebaud 1993

69

Wayne Thiebaud
**Apartment View**, 1993
Oil on canvas
60 × 48 ¼ in.
Private Collection

Wayne Thiebaud
**Park Place**, 1995
Color etching handworked with watercolor, gouache, colored pencil, graphite, and pastel
29 $\frac{9}{16}$ × 20 ¾ in.
Crocker Art Museum, Gift of the artist's family, 1995.9.50

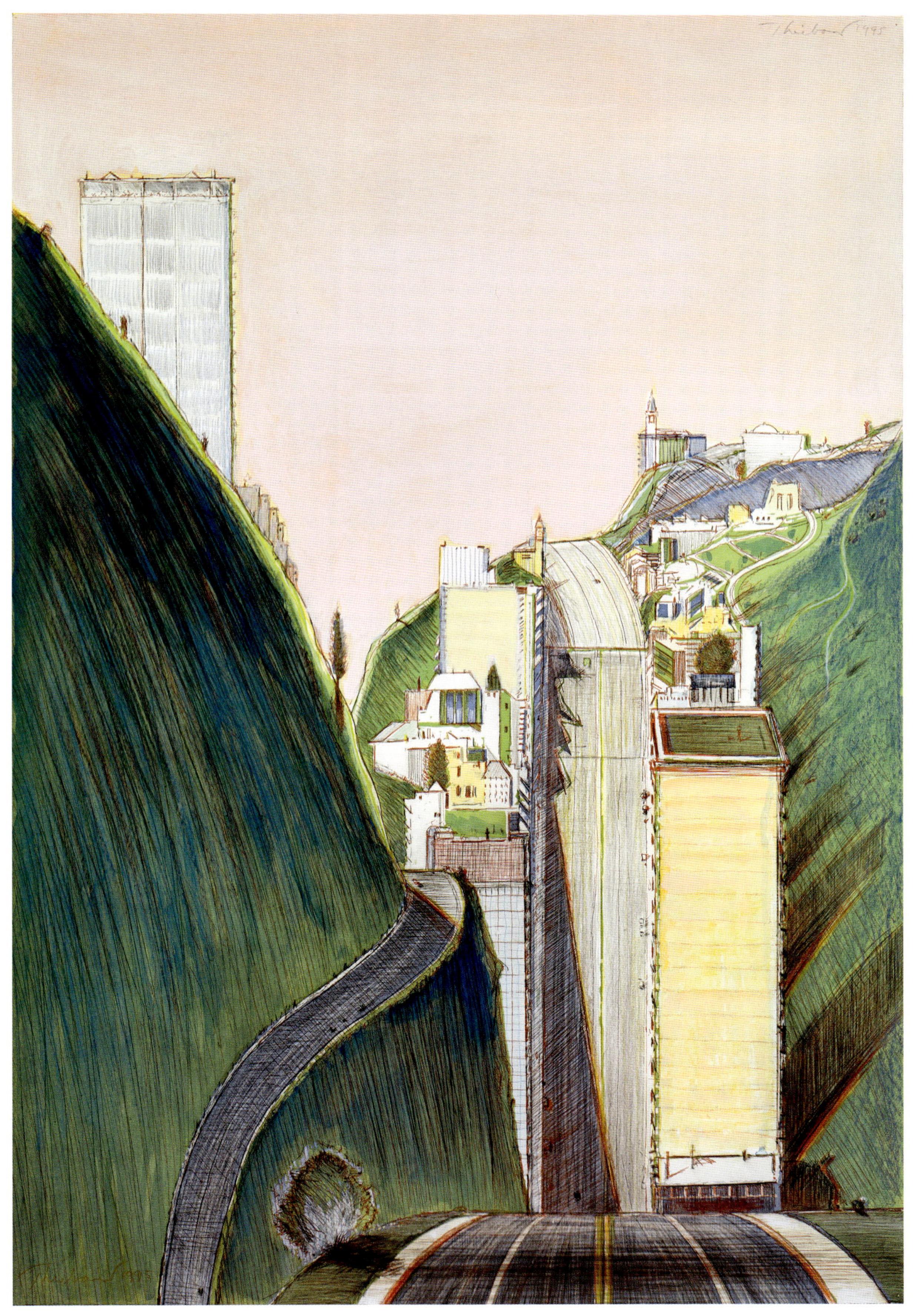

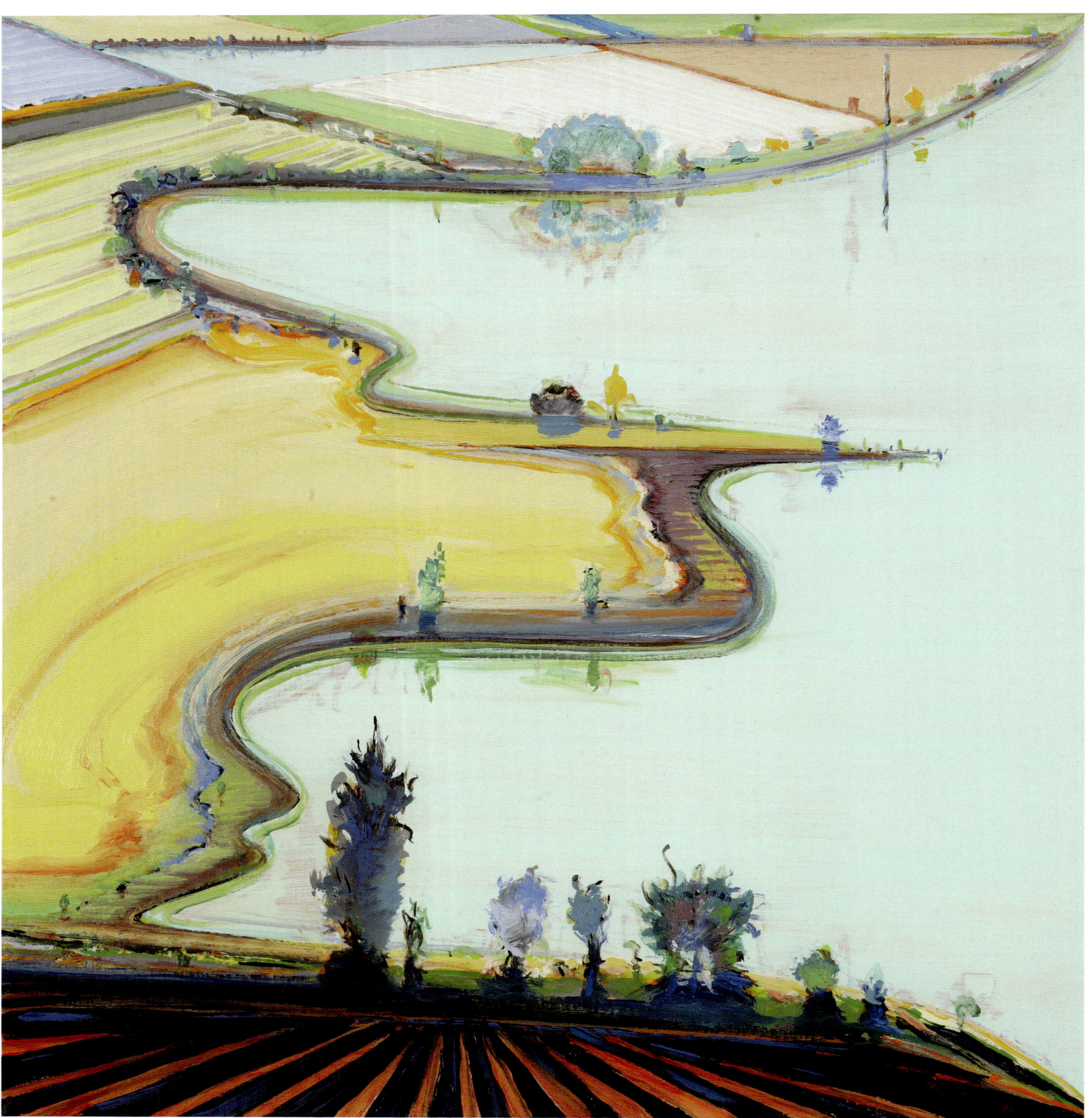

73

Wayne Thiebaud
**Coastal Farms**, 1997
Oil on canvas
24 × 24 in.
Fine Arts Museums of San Francisco
Gift of Jacqueline Hoefer

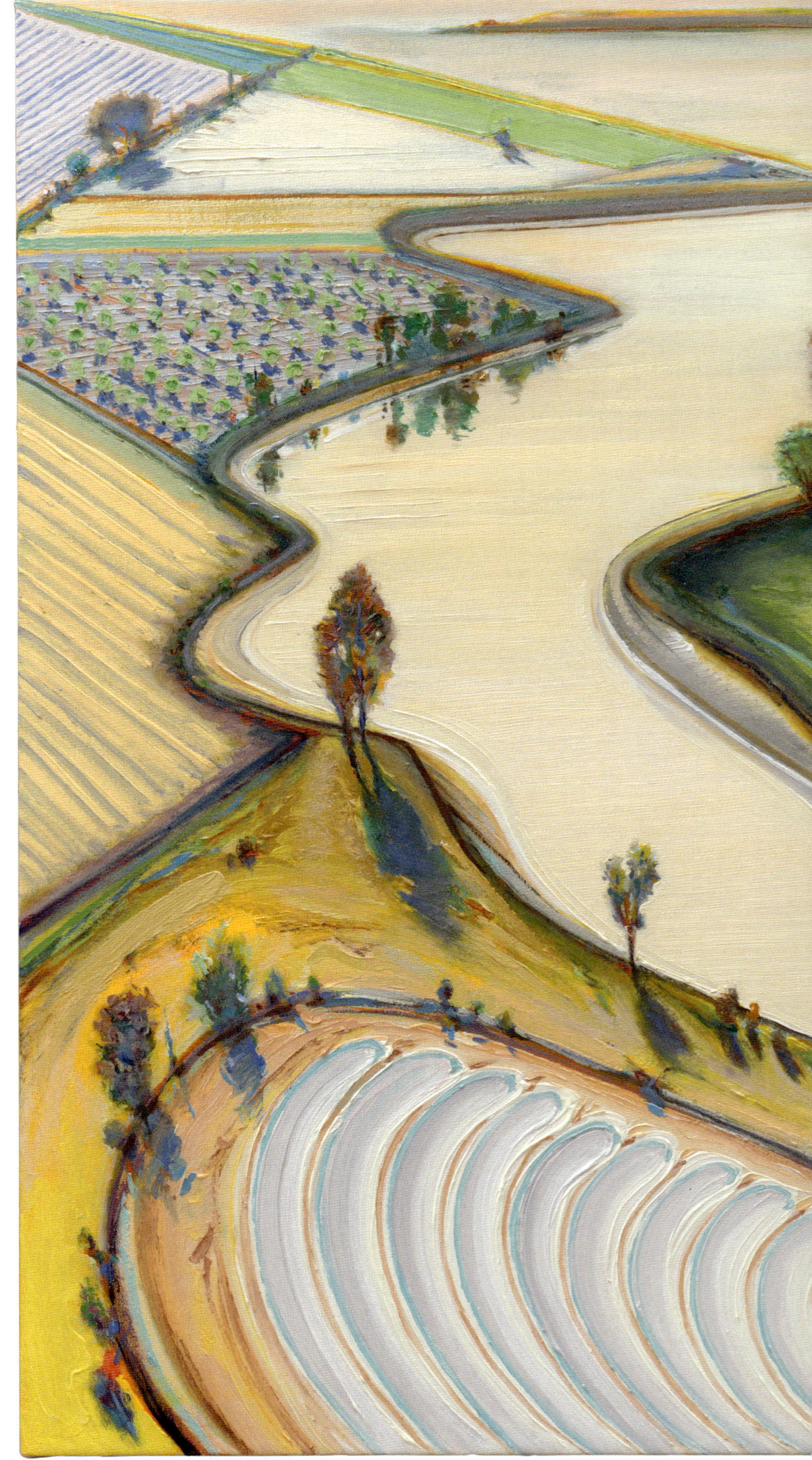

Wayne Thiebaud
**Flatland River**, 1997
Oil on canvas
38 × 58 in.
San Francisco Museum of Modern Art
Purchase through a gift of Phyllis C. Wattis

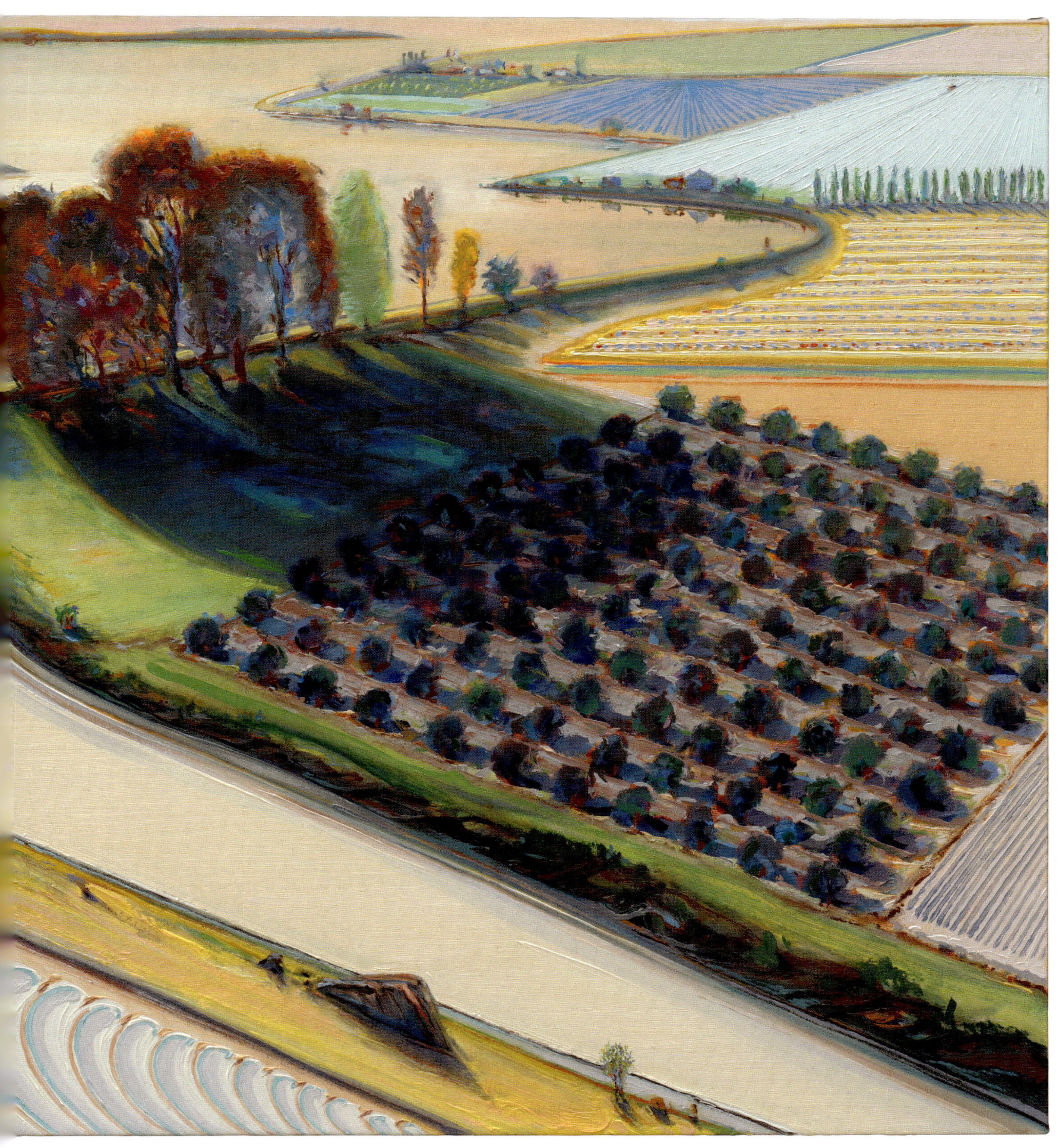

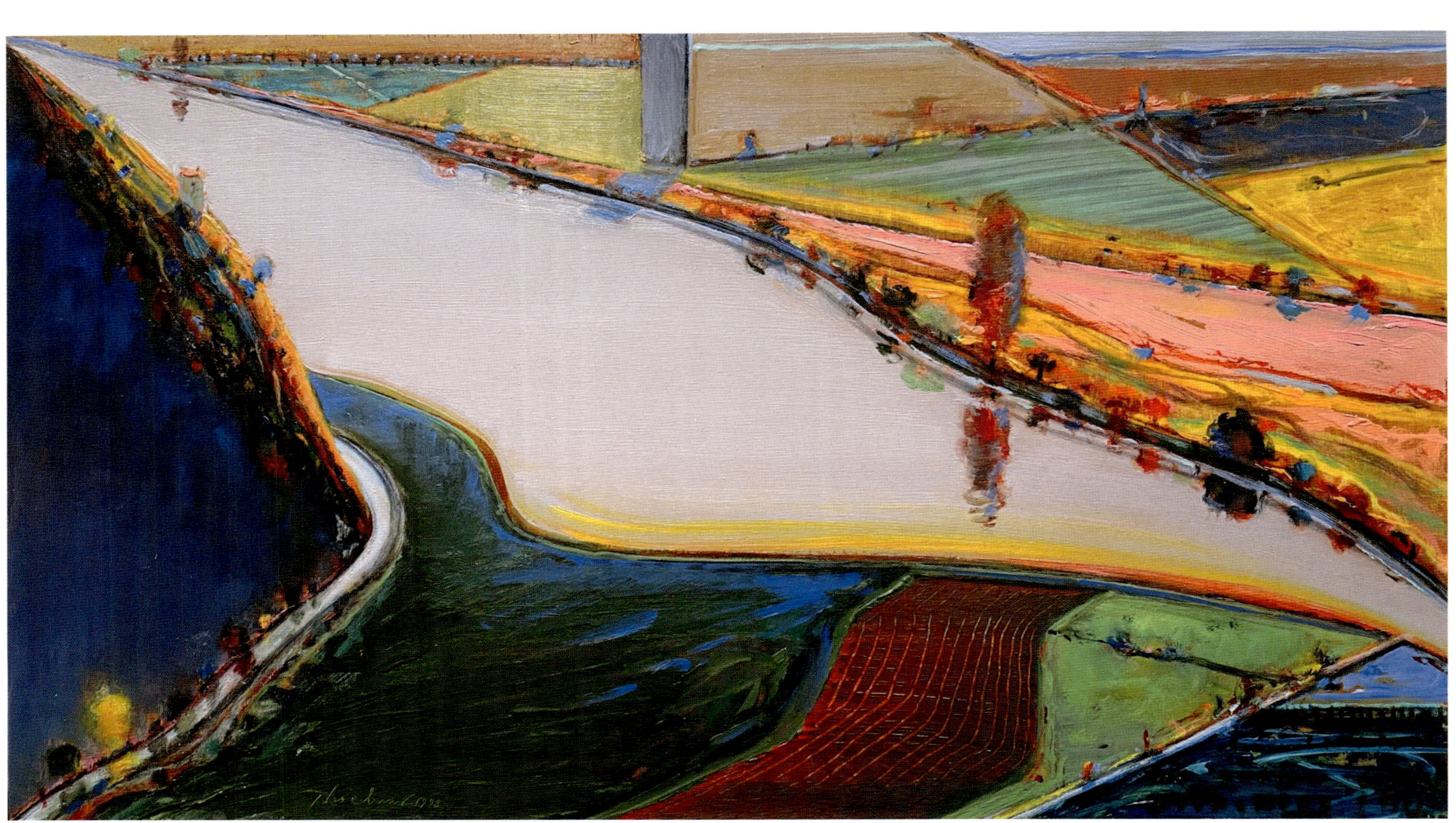



Wayne Thiebaud
**Hill River**, 1998
Oil on wood
12 × 22 ½ in.
Private Collection

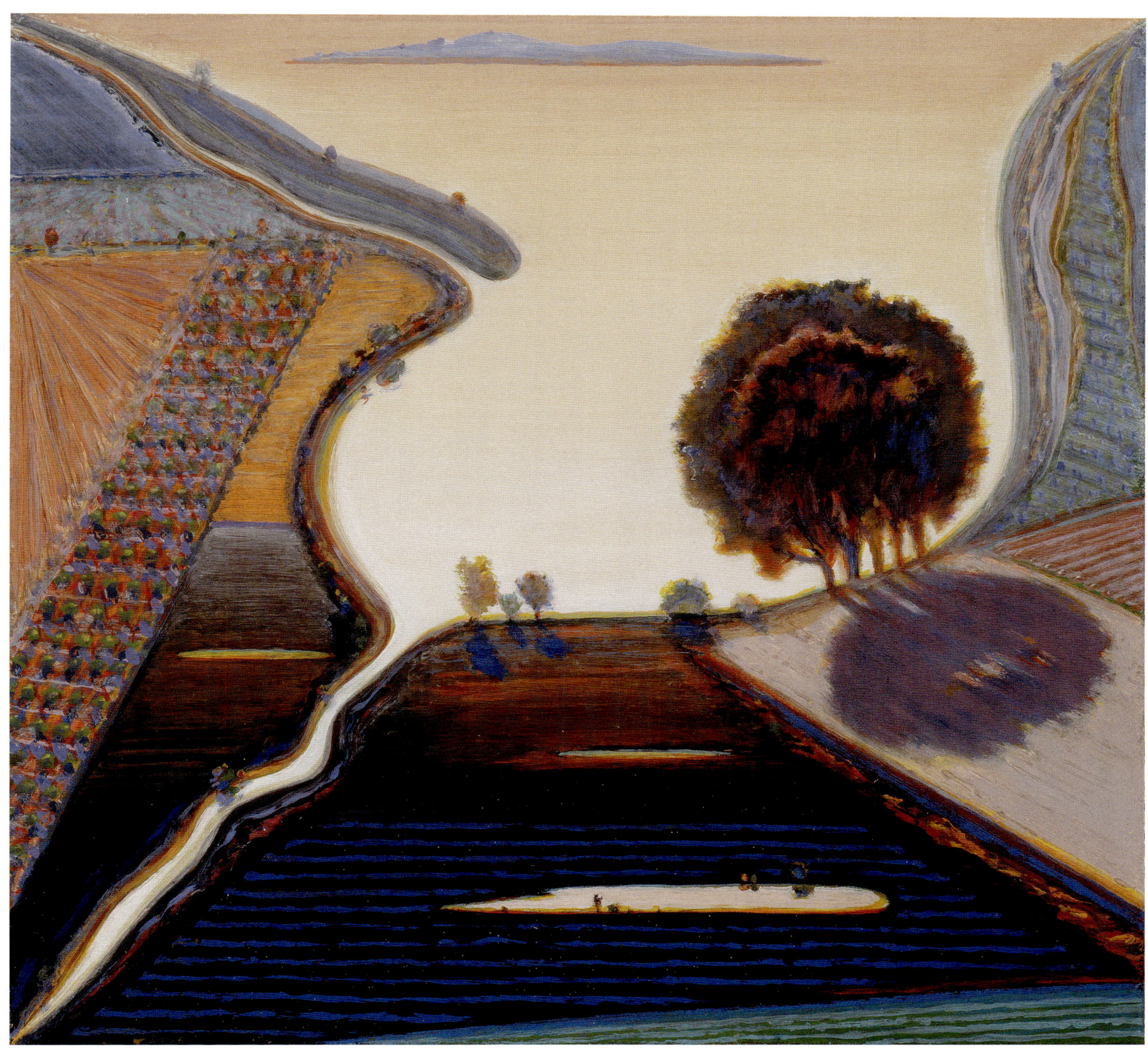



Wayne Thiebaud
**River Ponds Study**, 1998
Oil on wood
17 × 18 in.
Private Collection

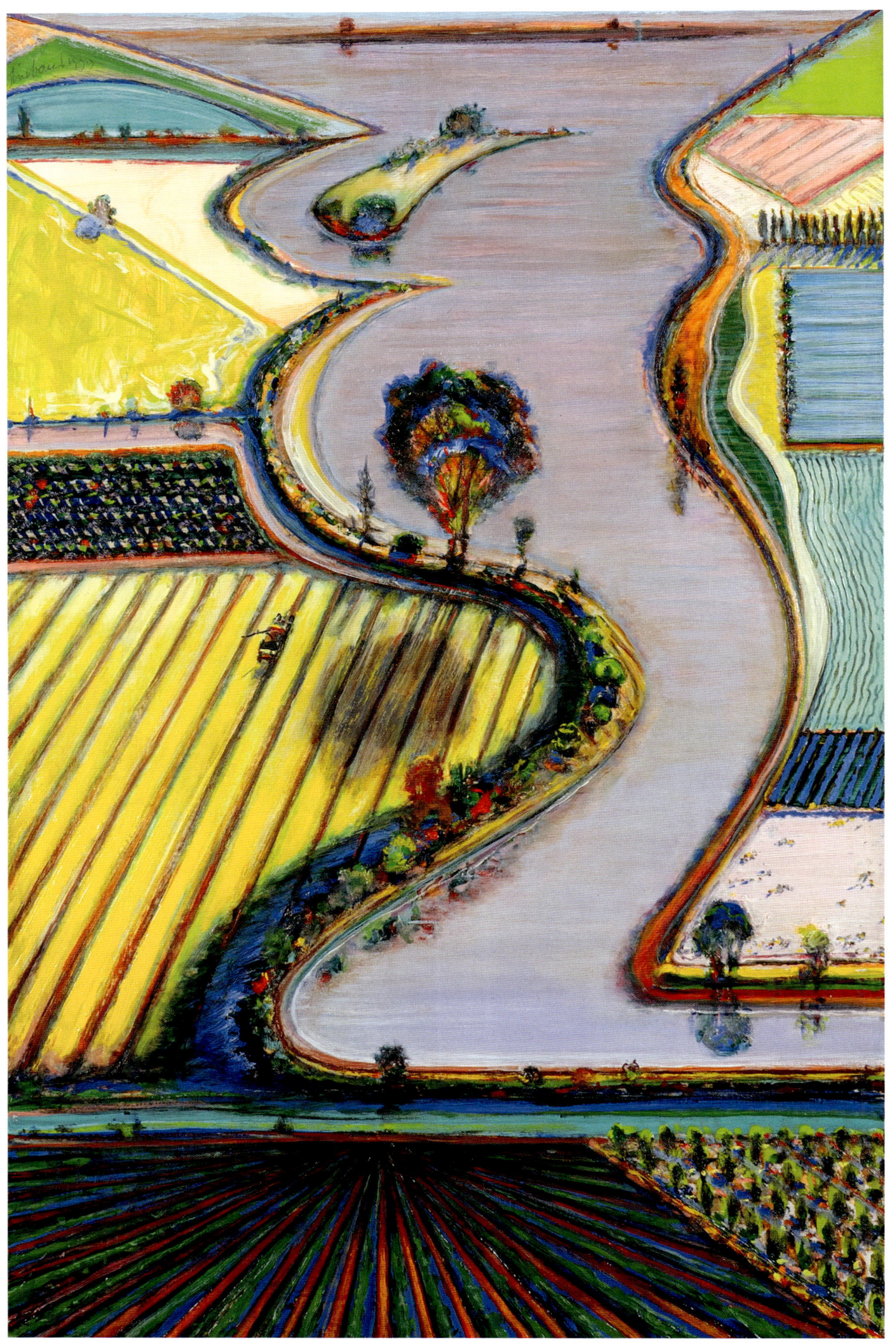

79

Wayne Thiebaud
**Purple River**, 1999
Oil on canvas
36 × 24 in.
Private Collection

Wayne Thiebaud
**Dark City**, 1999
Oil on canvas
72 × 55 in.
Collection of Wayne Thiebaud Foundation

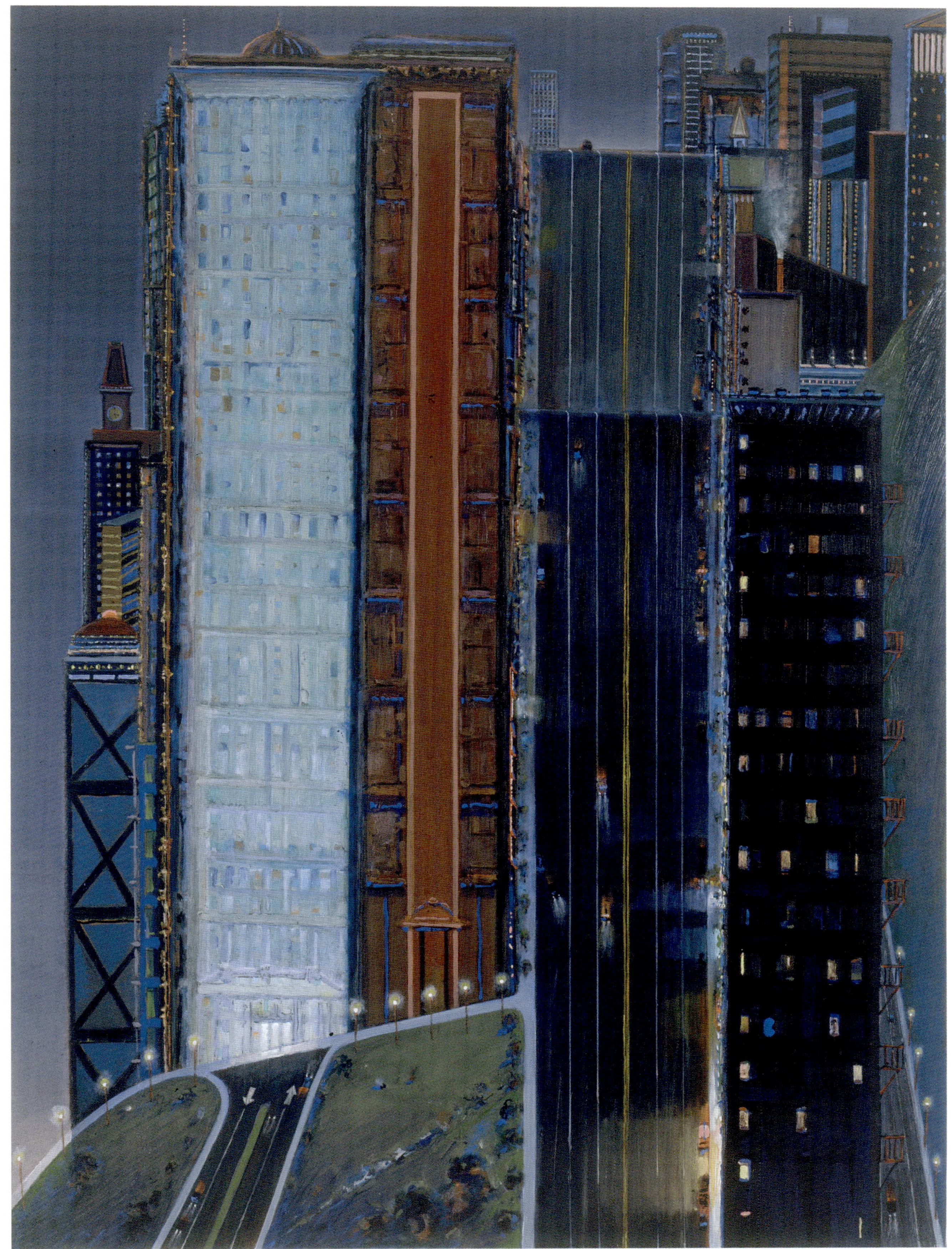

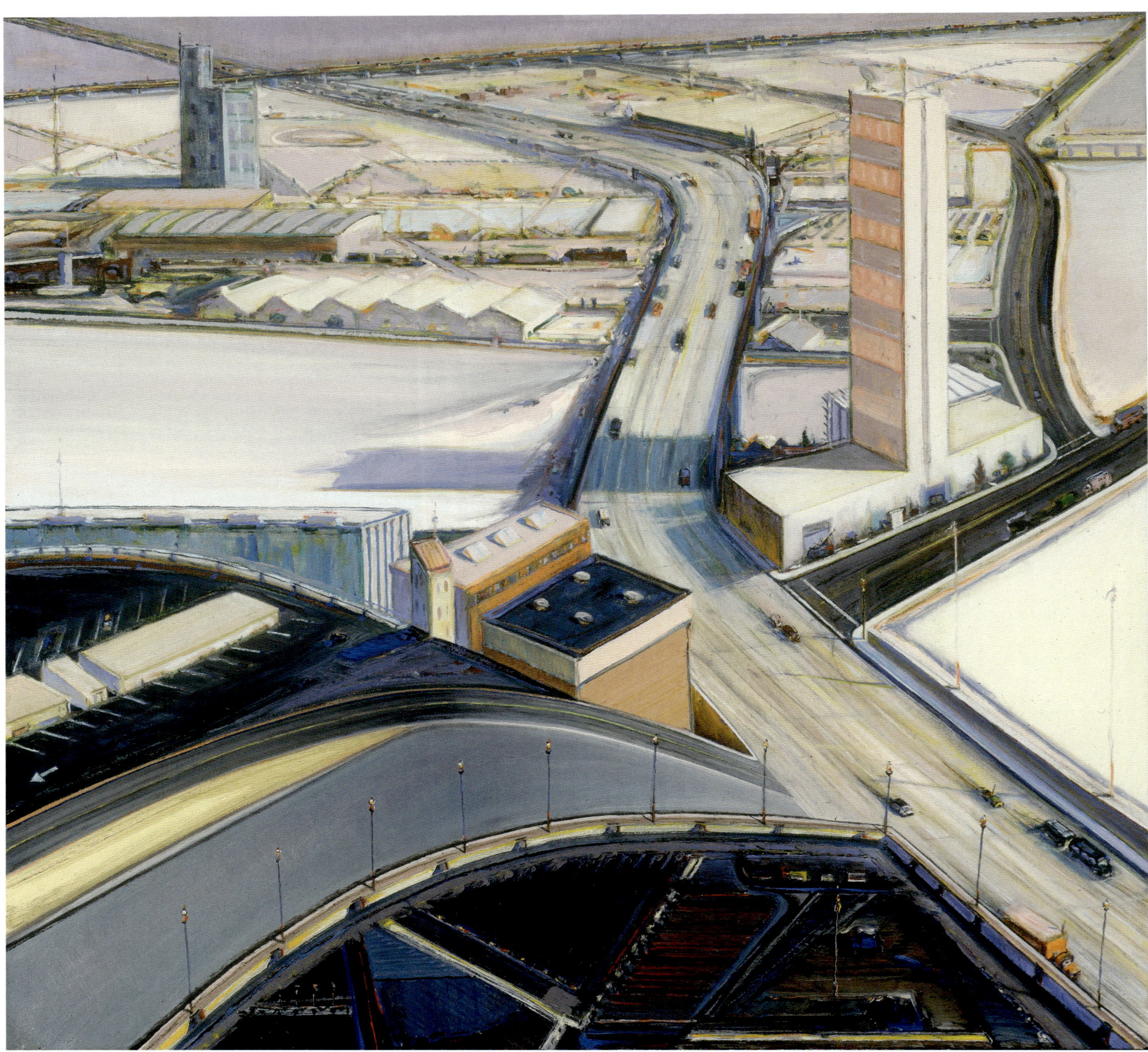

83

Wayne Thiebaud
**Towards 280**, 1999–2000
Acrylic on canvas
54 × 60 in.
Collection of Wayne Thiebaud Foundation

Wayne Thiebaud
**Canyon Mountains**, 2011–12
Oil on canvas
66 ⅛ × 54 ⅛ in.
San Francisco Museum of Modern Art
Purchase, by exchange, through
fractional gifts of Gretchen and John
Berggruen and Madeleine Haas Russell,
and gift of the Thiebaud family

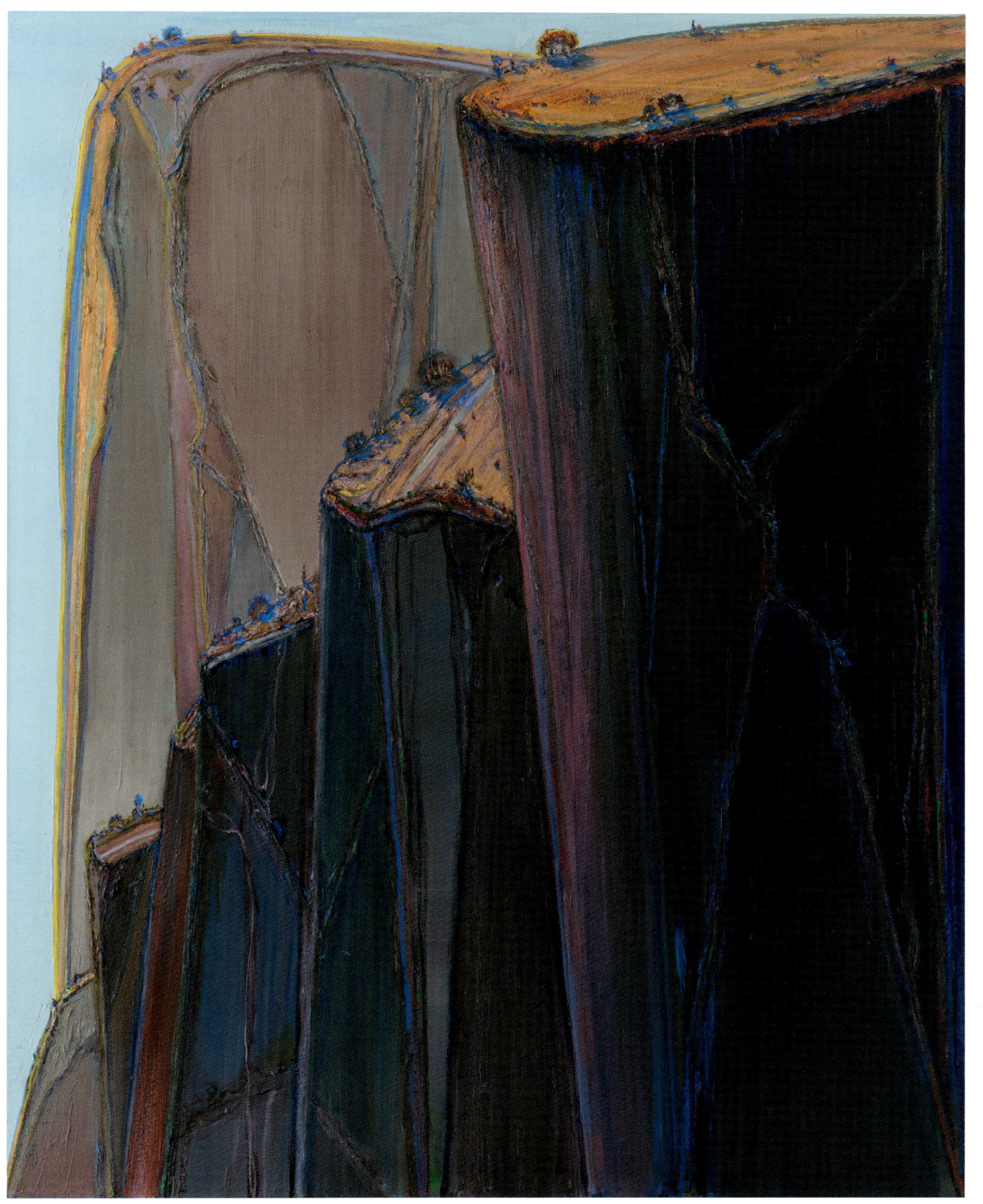

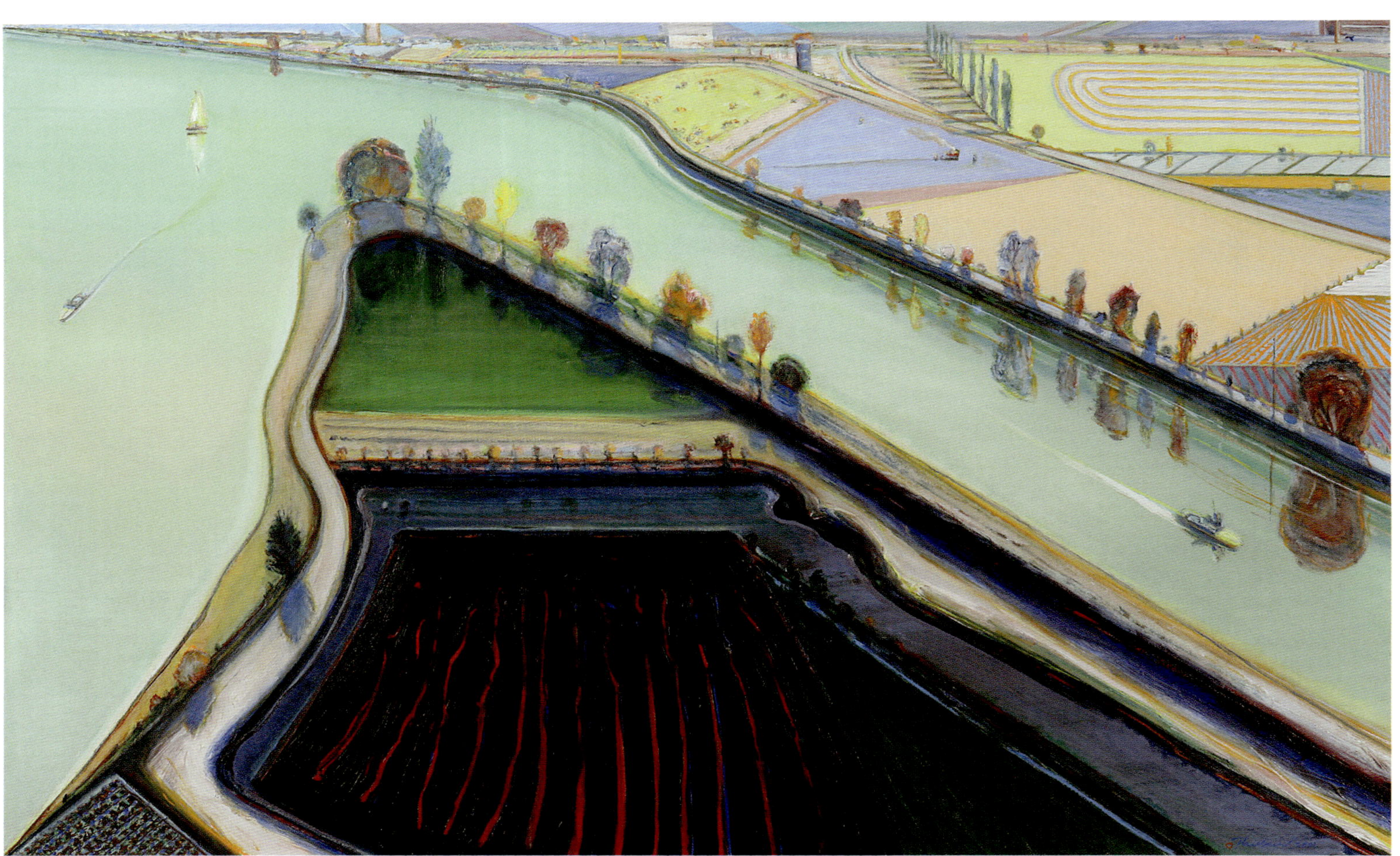



ABOVE
Wayne Thiebaud
**River Boats**, 2001
Oil on canvas
36 × 60 in.
Private Collection

OPPOSITE
Wayne Thiebaud
**Ponds and Streams**, 2001
Acrylic on canvas
72 × 60 in.
Fine Arts Museums of San Francisco
Museum purchase, gift of Richard N. Goldman
2001.168

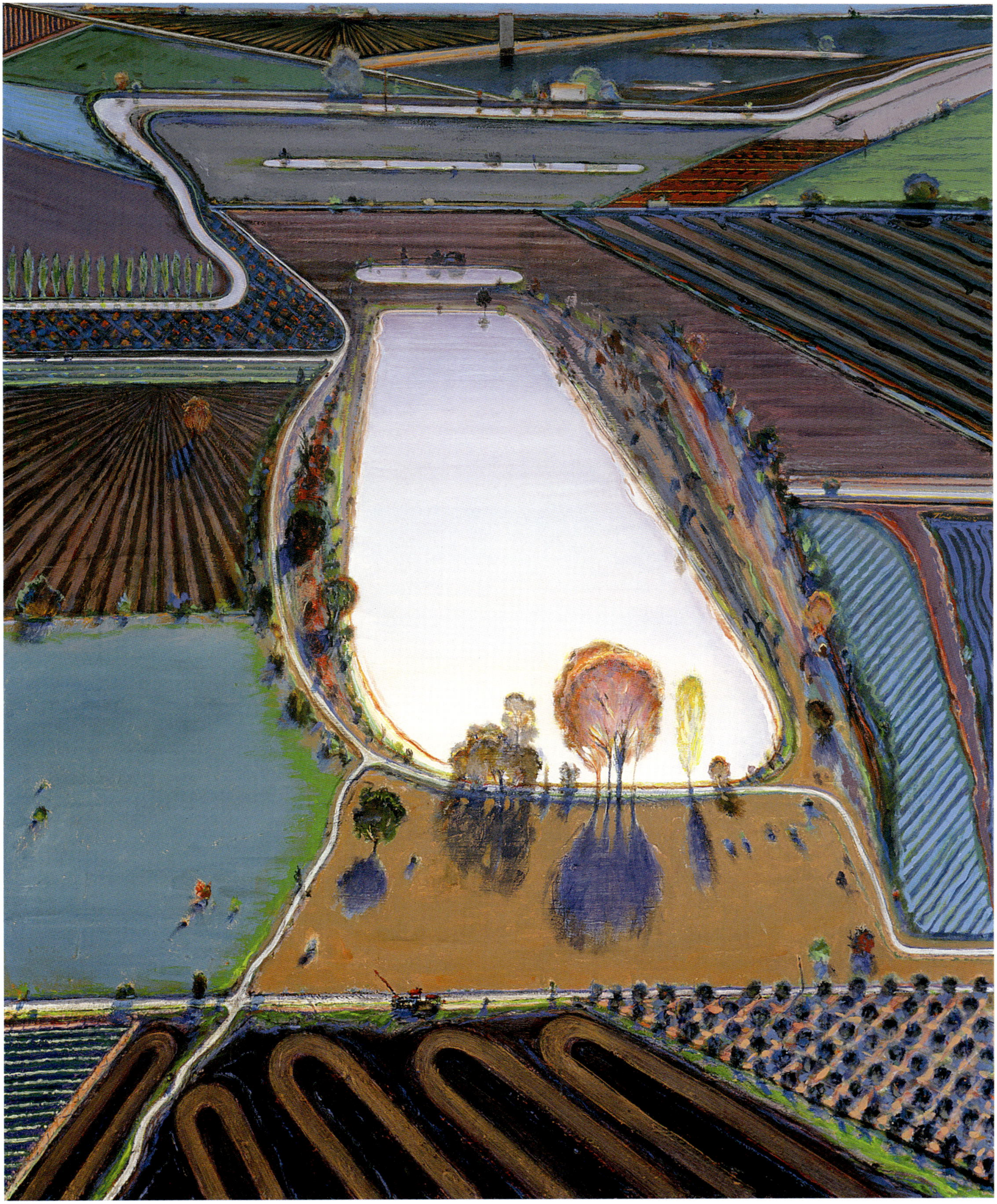

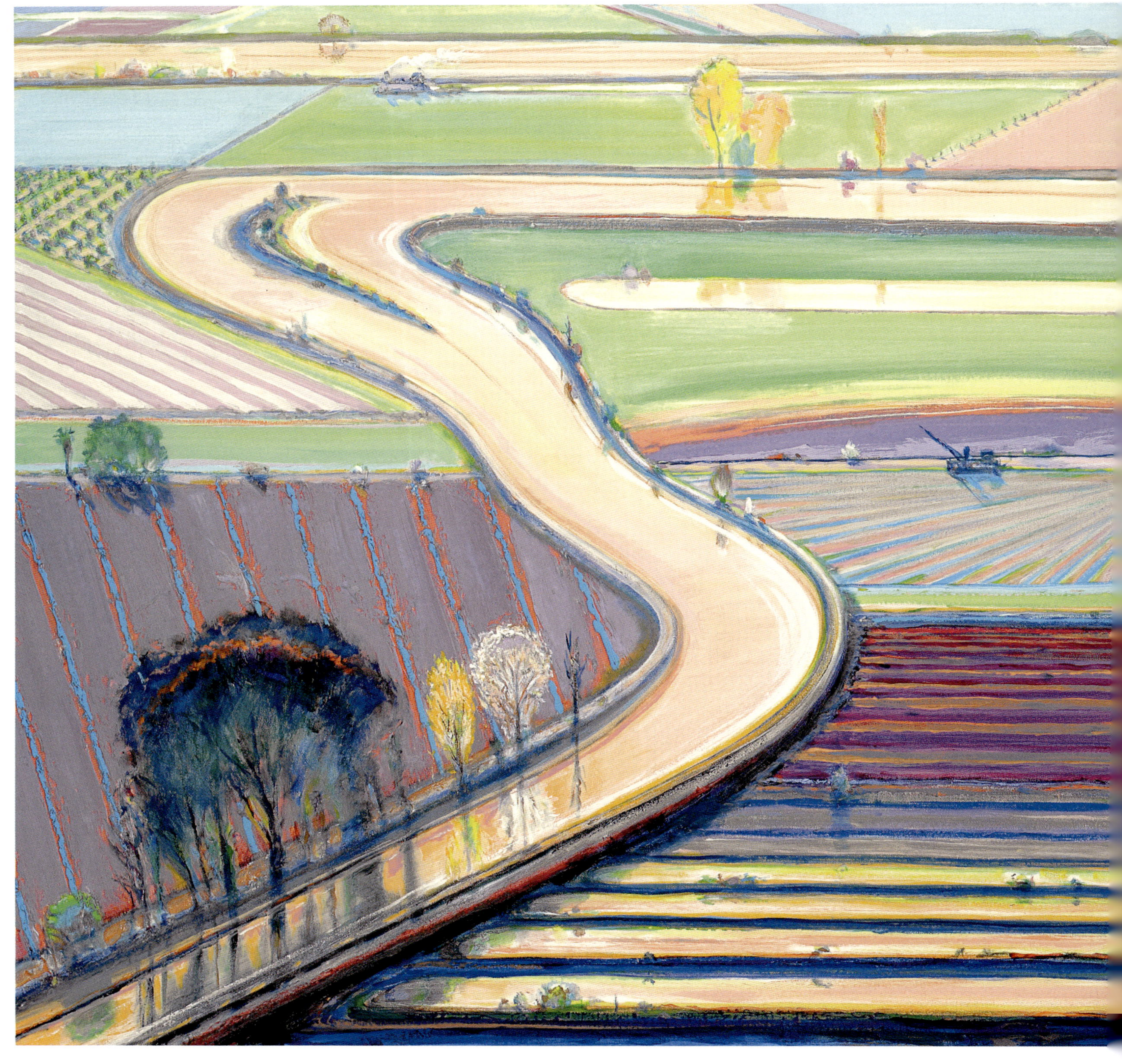

Wayne Thiebaud
**River Channels**, 2003
Oil on canvas
36 × 72 in.
Private Collection

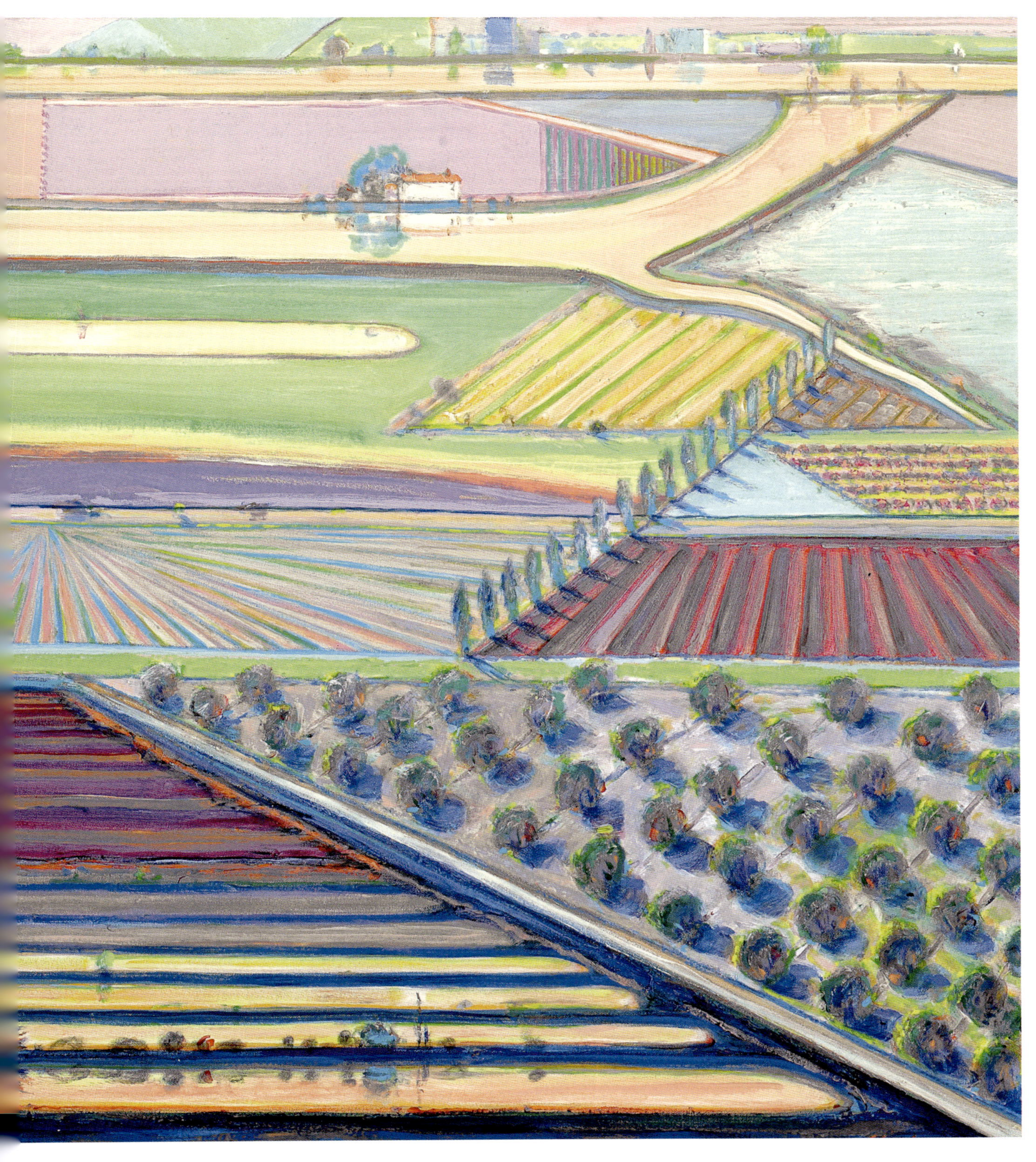

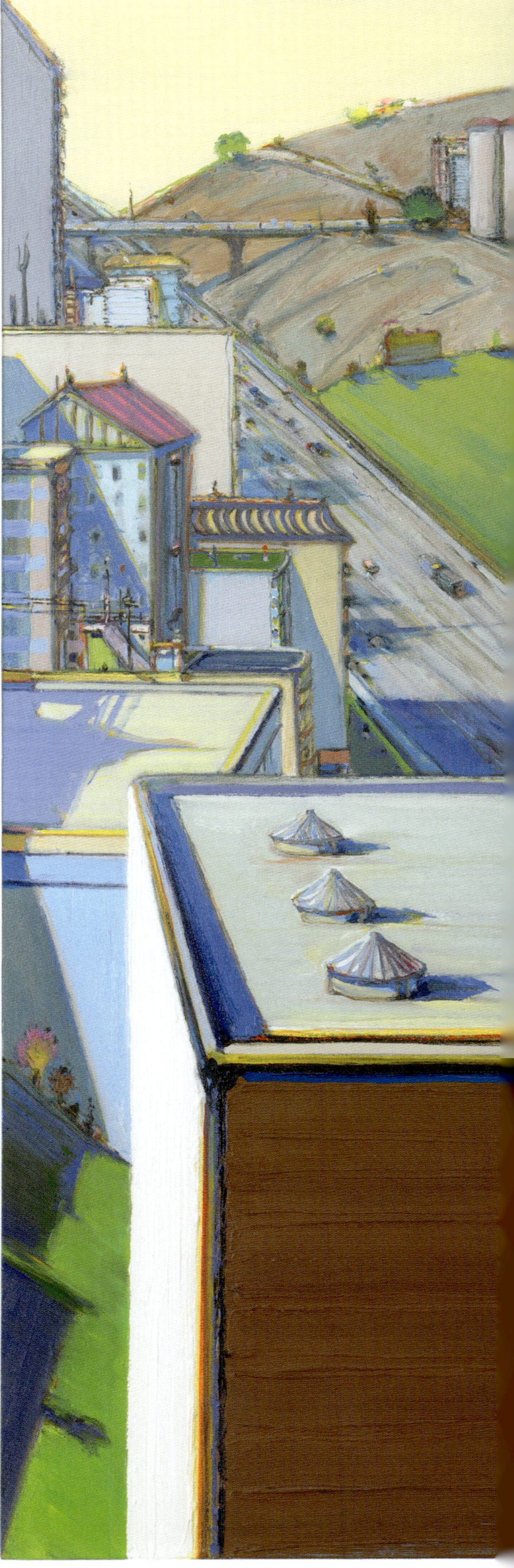

Wayne Thiebaud
**Valley Streets**, 2003
Oil on canvas
48 × 60 in.
San Francisco Museum of Modern Art
The Doris and Donald Fisher Collection

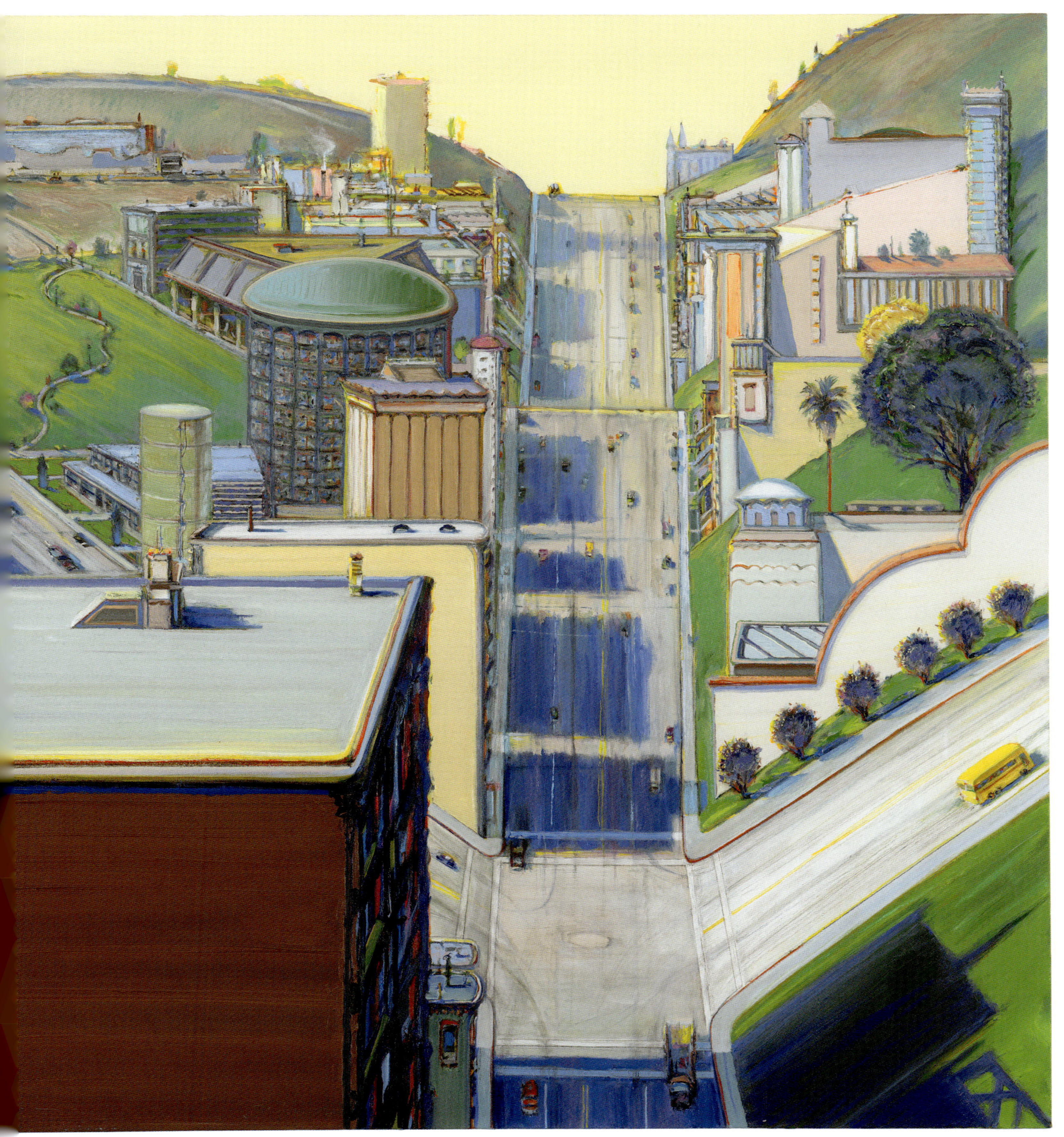

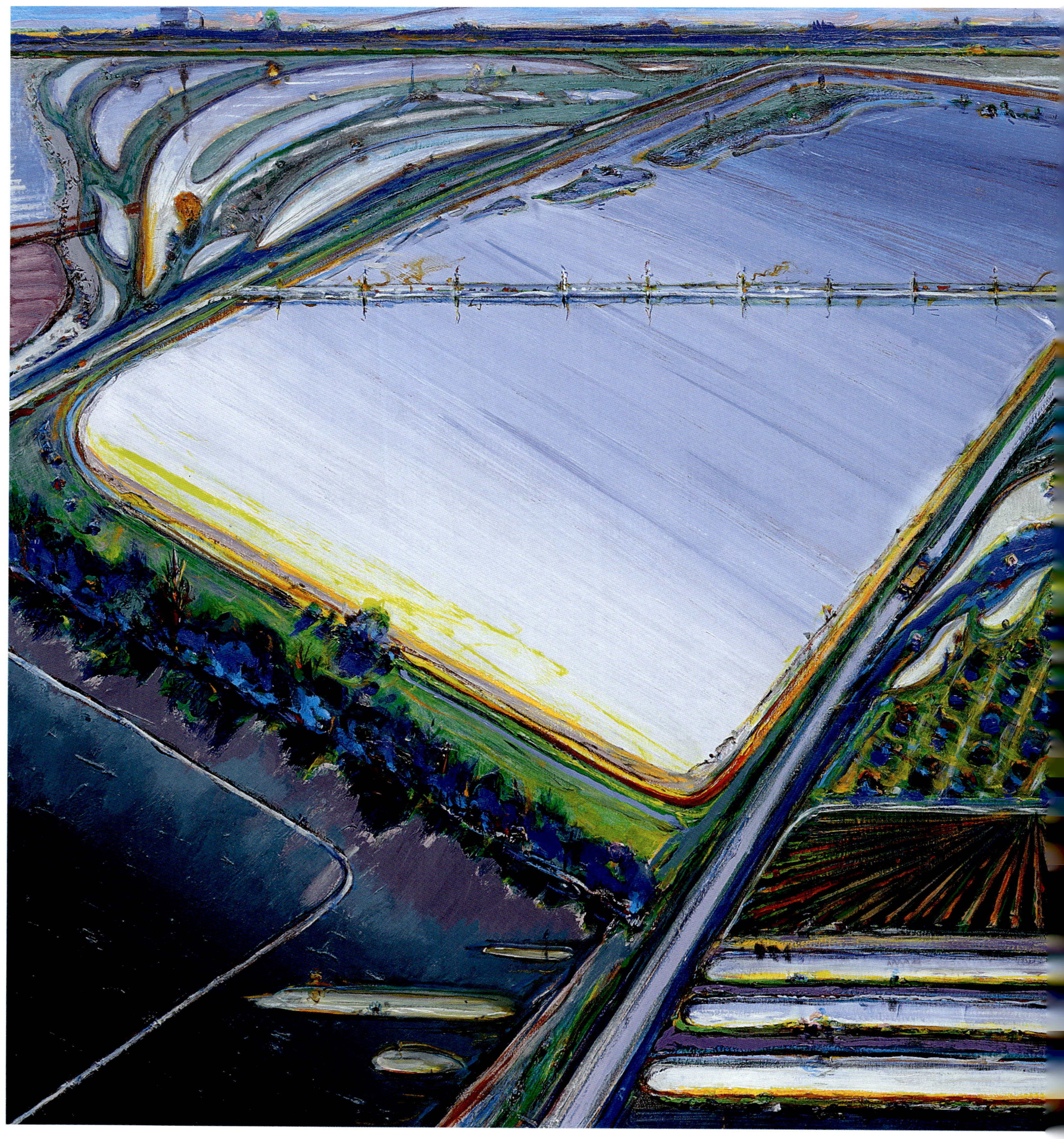

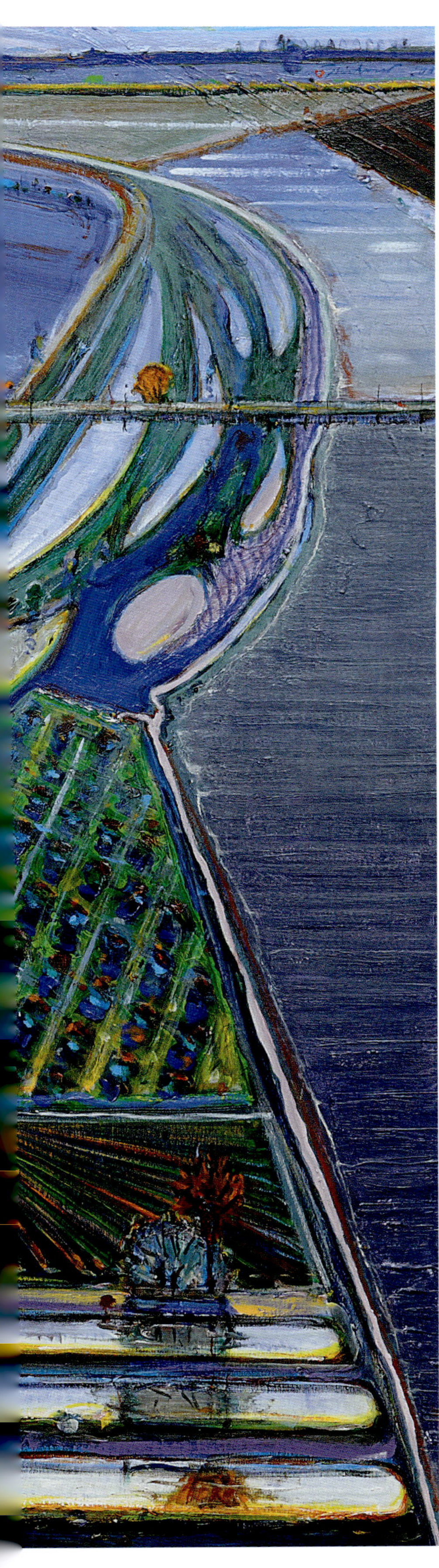



Wayne Thiebaud
**Flood Waters**, 2006
Oil on canvas
48 × 60 in.
Private Collection

Wayne Thiebaud
**Ocean City**, 2006–7
Oil on canvas
48 × 36 in.
Private Collection

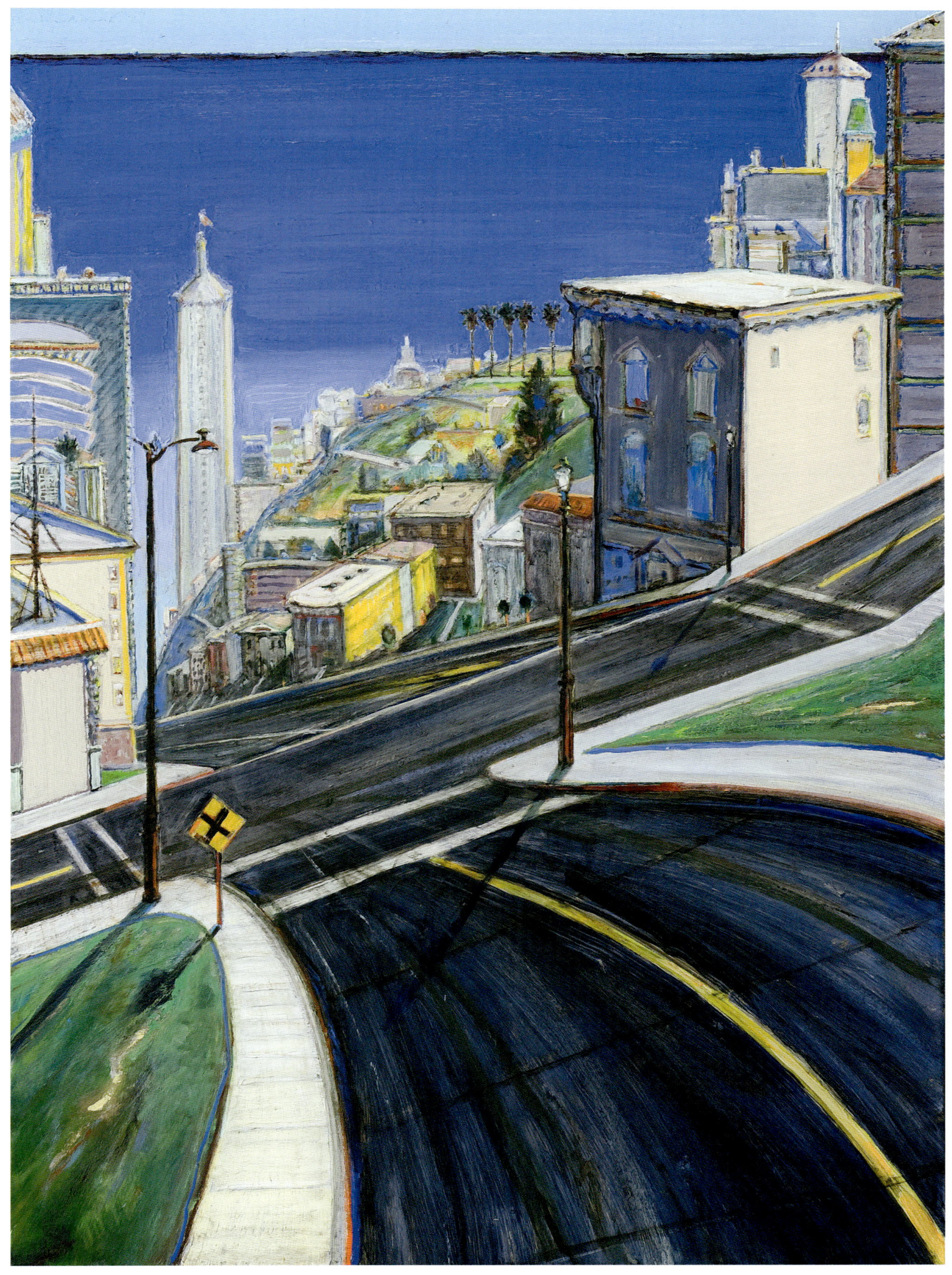

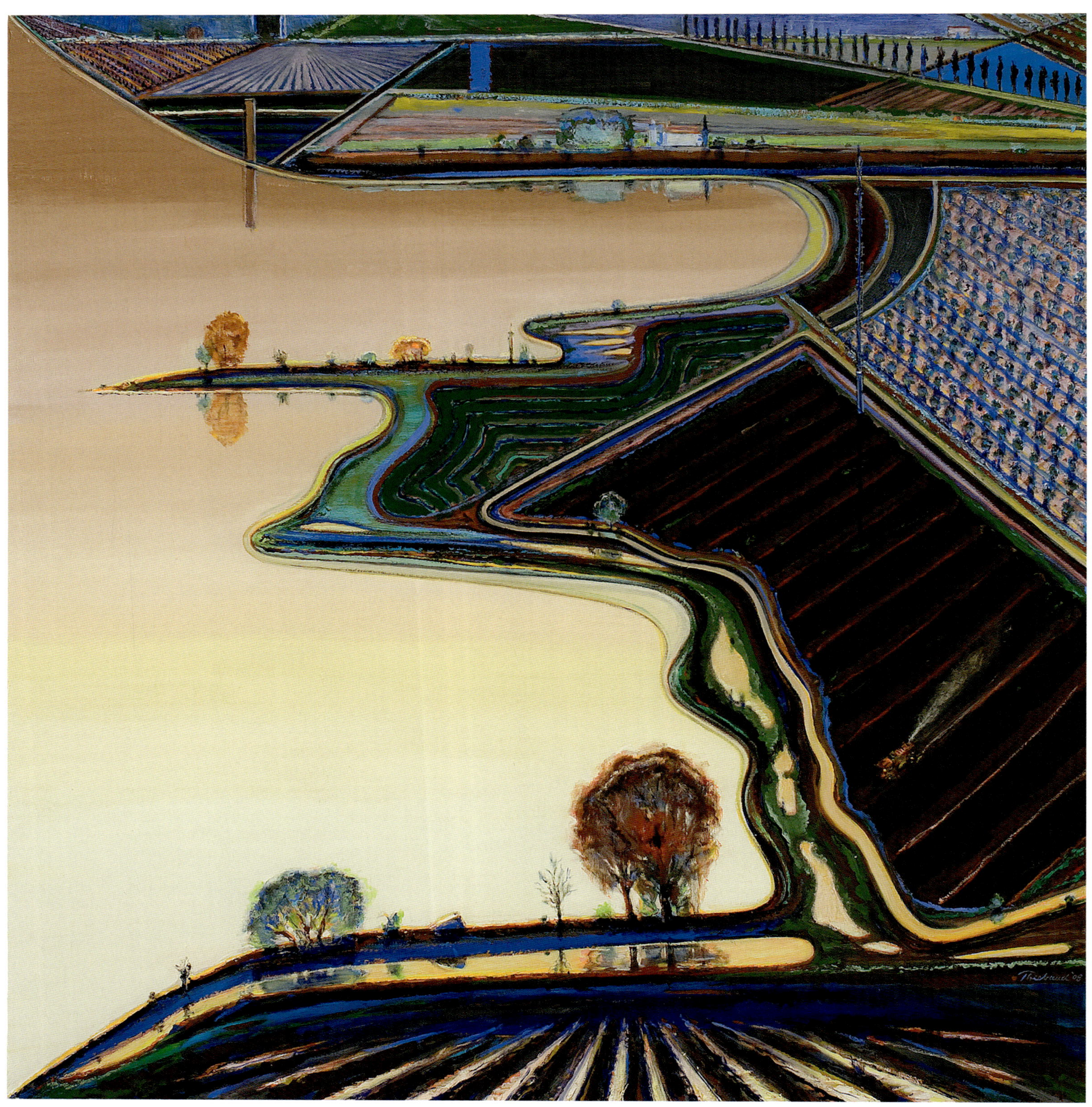
Thiebaud '08

Wayne Thiebaud
**River Lake**, 2008
Oil on canvas
60 × 60 in.
Private Collection

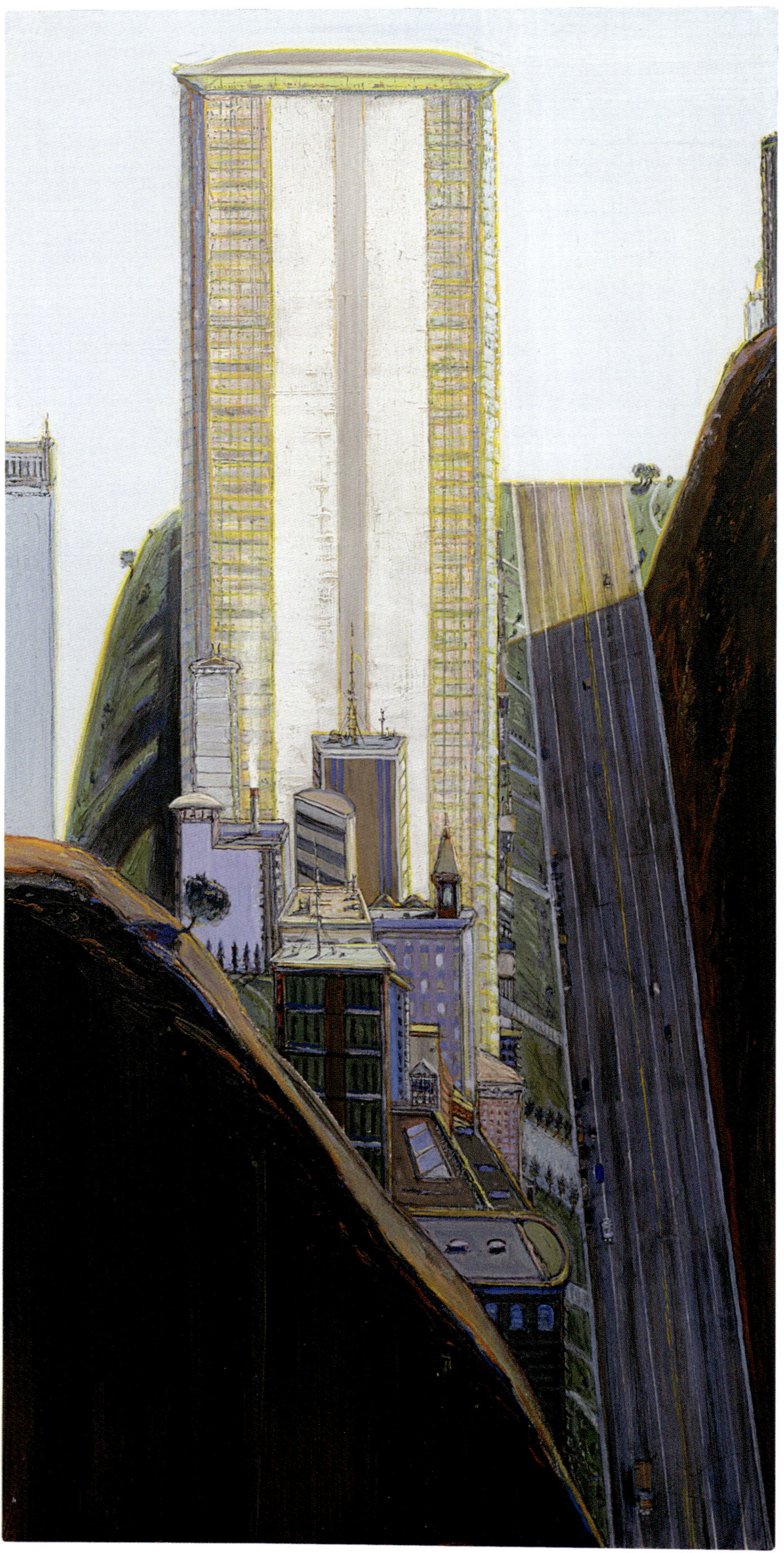

Wayne Thiebaud
**Big Condominium**, 2008
Oil on canvas
72 × 26 in.
Private Collection

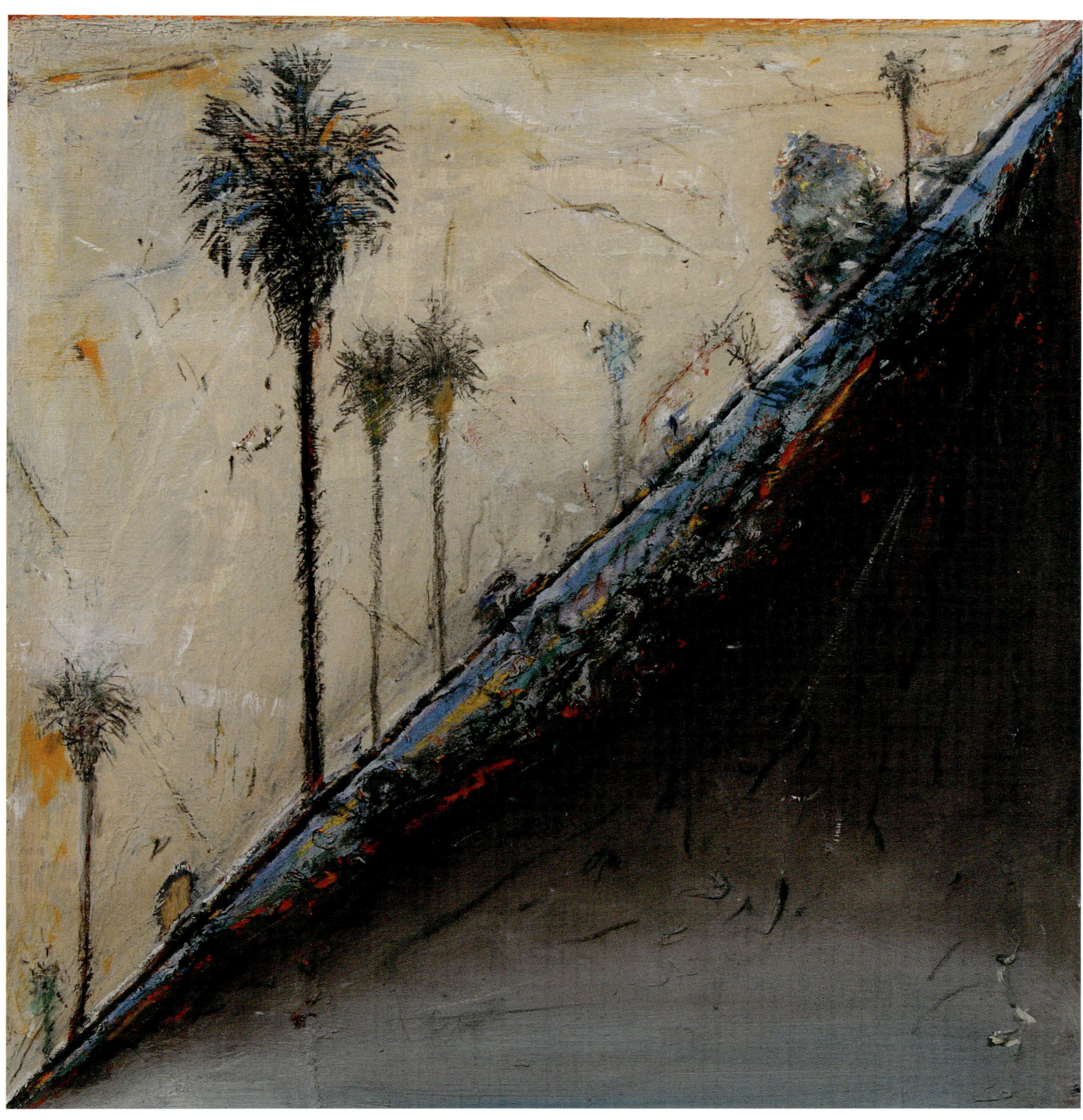



Wayne Thiebaud
**Dark Ridge**, 2010/2012/2019
Oil and charcoal on board
24 ¼ × 24 ¼ in.
Collection of Wayne Thiebaud Foundation

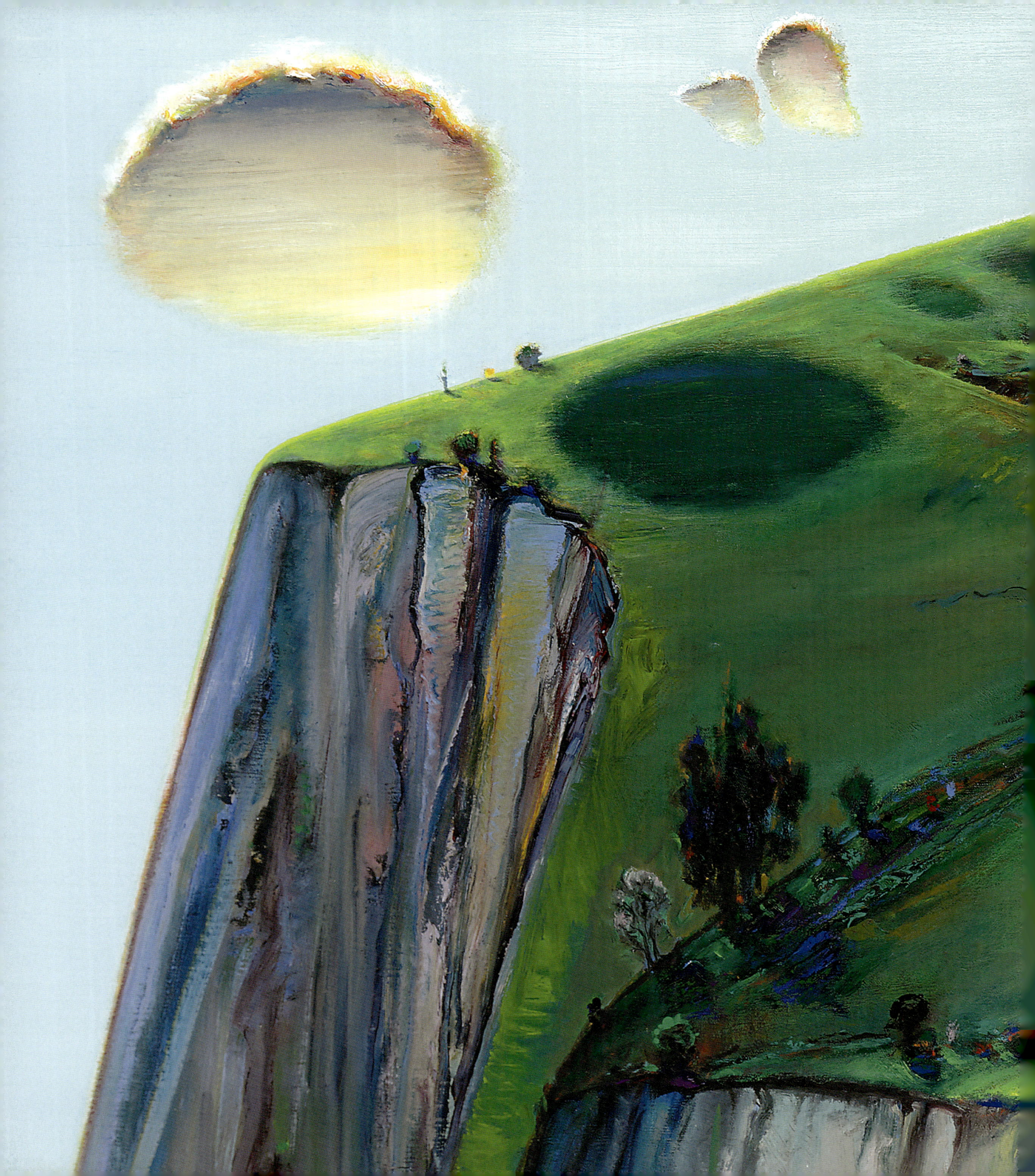

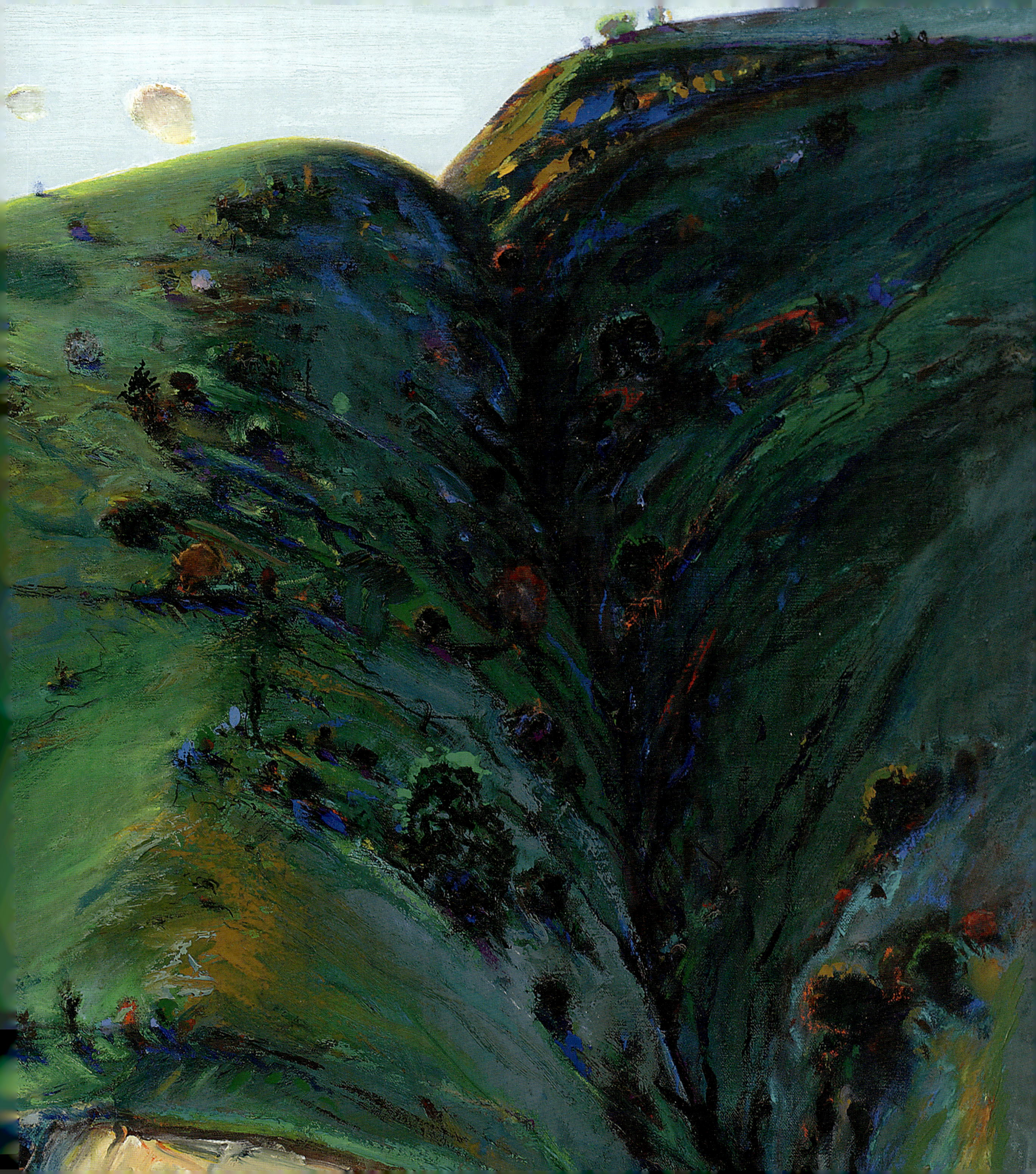

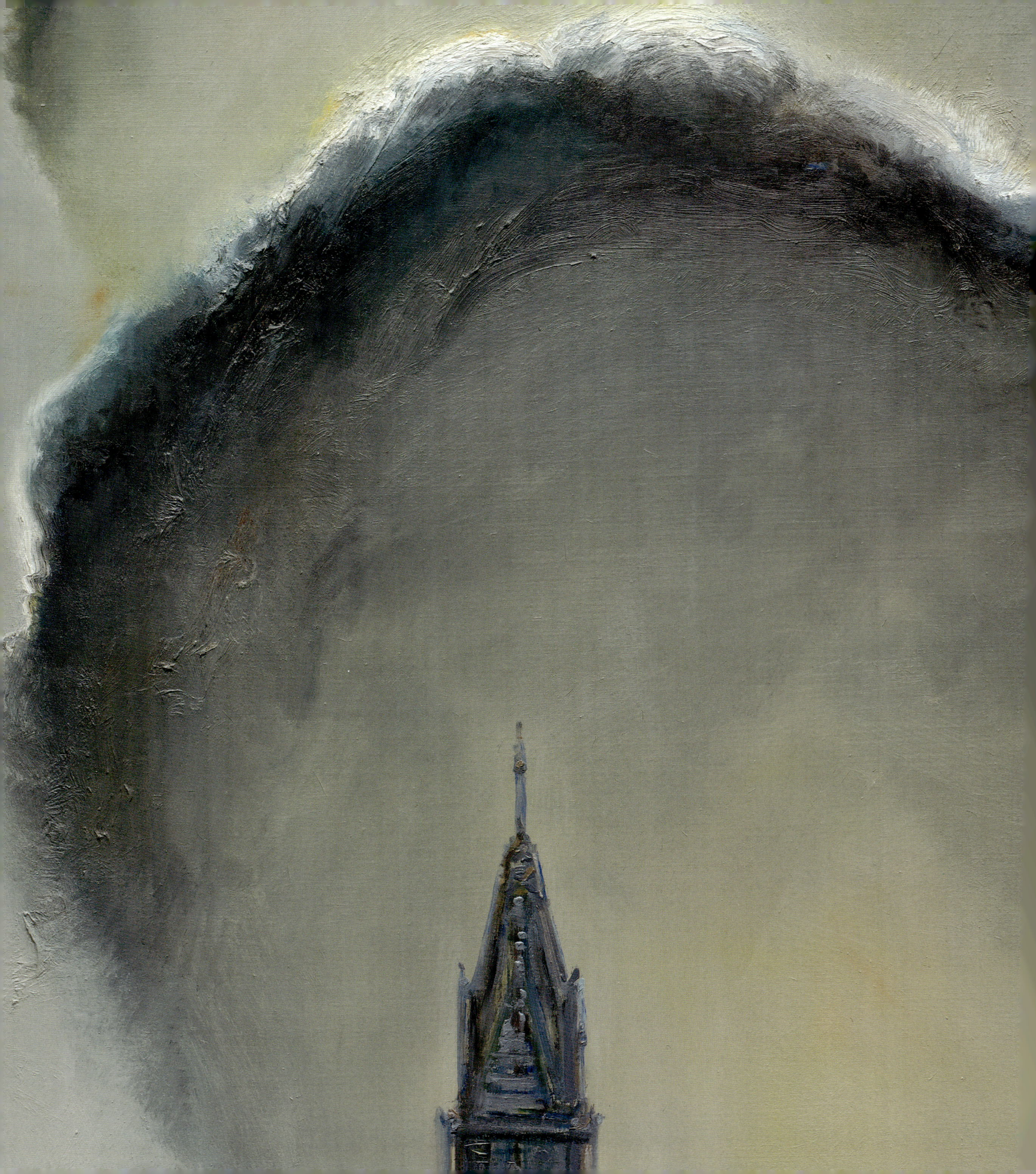

# Cloud City

Rachel Teagle

Wayne Thiebaud, **Cloud City** (detail), 1993–94

How do you know if a painting is special? Does the subject make it special? Is it the color palette, or maybe the painting's history? Is it just a feeling? Wayne Thiebaud's *Cloud City* (1993–94), an exceptional painting in every aspect (P. 105), affirms each of these questions and so much more. As both a daring experiment and the culmination of more than a decade of rigorous exploration of San Francisco's unique urban qualities, the work assumes special status in the painter's career. Moreover, Thiebaud treasured this particular painting, so much so that just three years after selling it, he bought it back so that he could work from it again, one more time, before he released it back into the world.

*Cloud City*'s story begins in 1993 when Thiebaud started to work on the painting, one among many canvases in his studio. Typically, he would work across several paintings at the same time. Stopping, looking, painting, turning it against the wall for a time, and then looking again. Thiebaud liked to think of each painting as a problem to be solved. Was he even asking the right questions? Thiebaud believed good painters assure their every painting poses a question. Great painters, he liked to assert, are deeply critical of their questions.

Thiebaud had a landmark year in 1993. He exhibited for the first time in his son Paul's newly established Campbell-Thiebaud Gallery in San Francisco. For this auspicious debut they decided to focus on the painter's San Francisco cityscapes, a then relatively unknown body of work. Some of Thiebaud's cityscapes had introduced the public to the genre in 1985, when the San Francisco Museum of Modern Art celebrated its fiftieth anniversary with a Thiebaud retrospective. While his favorite city was a new subject of his paintings, landscapes could be found on his easel as far back and as frequently as pies and ice cream. In fact, paintings of Sacramento's rivers and bridges long predate the confections that garnered so much acclaim in the early 1960s. Likewise, Thiebaud had always painted mountain landscapes, often sketching *en plein air* from the Sierra Nevadas to the Vaca Range in Napa Valley.



It was only in the 1970s that Thiebaud began to sketch the streets of San Francisco. His journals from this period are filled with faithful renderings of the city's distinctive topography. The sheer number of drawings are a clear indication of the artist's fascination. In 1972, he and his wife, Betty Jean, bought a home on Potrero Hill, and living in the city resulted in a profusion of paintings. Like his first drawings, these early city paintings portray recognizable vistas. For example, *24th Street Intersection* from 1977 (PP. 106–7) is a straightforward depiction of a place, the corner of 24th and Mariposa Streets. On second look, however, the viewer sees the painting as a disorienting intersection of lines, angles, and vertical planes. It almost falls into abstraction, but not quite. Thiebaud loved such visual complication, and it would continue to predominate his attention for another decade. Fittingly, *24th Street Intersection* hung at the conclusion of Thiebaud's retrospective; and just like that, at the age of sixty-five, the artist announced a major new body of work.

In the catalogue that accompanied his 1993 gallery exhibition, Thiebaud reflected on his early, more literal takes on the city: "I felt none of them were very successful." He went on to explain, "The reason for not feeling that they were delivering on what I had hoped for had to do with some sort of dramatic feeling in this peculiar San Francisco landscape." He wanted his cityscapes to achieve more than mere likeness; he sought "a visual and physical feeling" that was "closer to the idea of San Francisco." Later in the same interview, he described what he was looking for as "a feeling of gravitational pull."[1] Following more than twenty years of painting the city, Thiebaud was ready in 1993 to present his cityscapes in a stand-alone exhibition. At last he had found a way to paint San Francisco's vertiginous pleasures that met his own highest standards.

*Cloud City* was not included in this momentous exhibition. We know from the dates on the painting's stretcher that Thiebaud was working on it at the time of the show, but he held it back. In November 1993, when the exhibition opened, he could already see that this particular painting was becoming something truly special, an apex, the culmination of his cityscapes. But it was not quite ready, not yet.



The painting stands alone among Thiebaud's cityscapes. At five by three feet, it is large for him, occupying a scale he reserved for projects ("problems") reaching resolution. He chose a canvas in proportion to his aspirations. Moreover, *Cloud City* looks different from others in this series. It is a dark painting with cloudy skies that shroud the city in shadow. For a painter best known for images bathed in bright white light, especially when painting the out-of-doors, it is a statement of difference. However, the painting is not a nocturne like, for instance, his *Night City* from 1980; instead, it celebrates San Francisco's unique light, where California's bright sunlight could be held at bay by billowing clouds or fog blowing in off the Pacific. Here we are looking out from Potrero Hill toward the Pacific with clouds backlit by the setting sun.

Like the city it depicts, *Cloud City* is a study in contrasts. Thiebaud thrust light against dark. The cloud's bright edges encompass a dark center. Amplifying this effect, flecks of light fall along all the edges of the painting. The artist gives us ample evidence of the sun's intensity, making this a painting about light obscured, Thiebaud's fastidious and fantastic orchestration of the play of light and dark across a single canvas. The extreme dynamic range in this painting is one of the most successfully dramatic in the painter's career. Known as a painter of light, Thiebaud achieves one of his greatest essays on light with *Cloud City*.

In Thiebaud's only cityscape to feature clouds, there is not much city in *Cloud City* and a whole lot of cloud. Thiebaud delighted in rendering clouds' evanescent form. *Cloud Ridge* (1967) is an early example of his ongoing fascination. *Mound and Cloud* (1972), *Half Dome and Cloud* (1975), *Napa Valley Ridge* (1986–97) (PP. 112–13), *Cloud Smoke* (1993), and *Passing Cloud* (2014/2019) are just a few among many examples of his cloud paintings. Clouds, like his signature icing, are tangible but ephemeral—a combination this artist found endlessly tantalizing.

It's not surprising that Thiebaud loved to paint clouds—made of light as much as water, shapeless and taking shape, refracting light into every color of the rainbow while also casting shadows. Clouds are the artist's perfect subject. They are as dynamic and also as overlooked as shadows, which are, of course, Thiebaud's

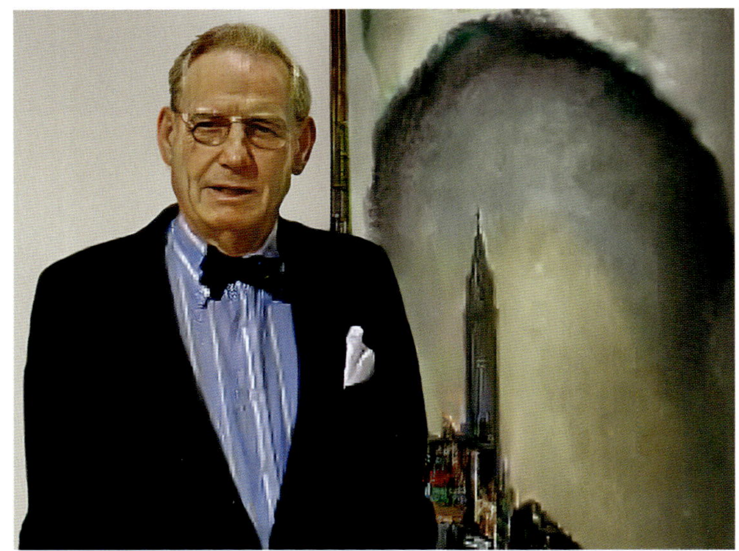

Wayne Thiebaud with **Cloud City** at Campbell-Thiebaud Gallery, San Francisco, ca. 1995–97

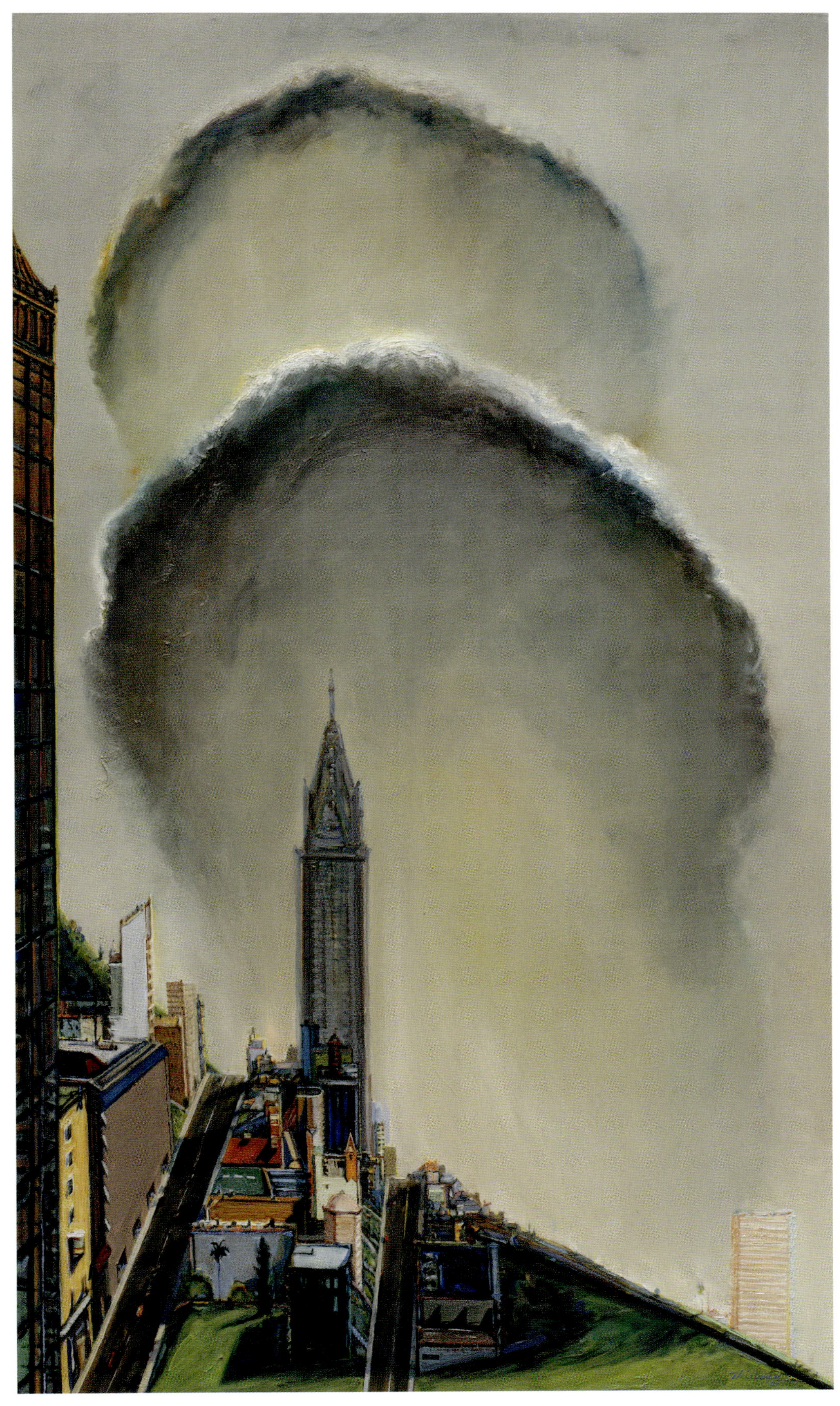

Wayne Thiebaud
**Cloud City**, 1993–94
Oil on canvas
60 × 36 in.
Private Collection

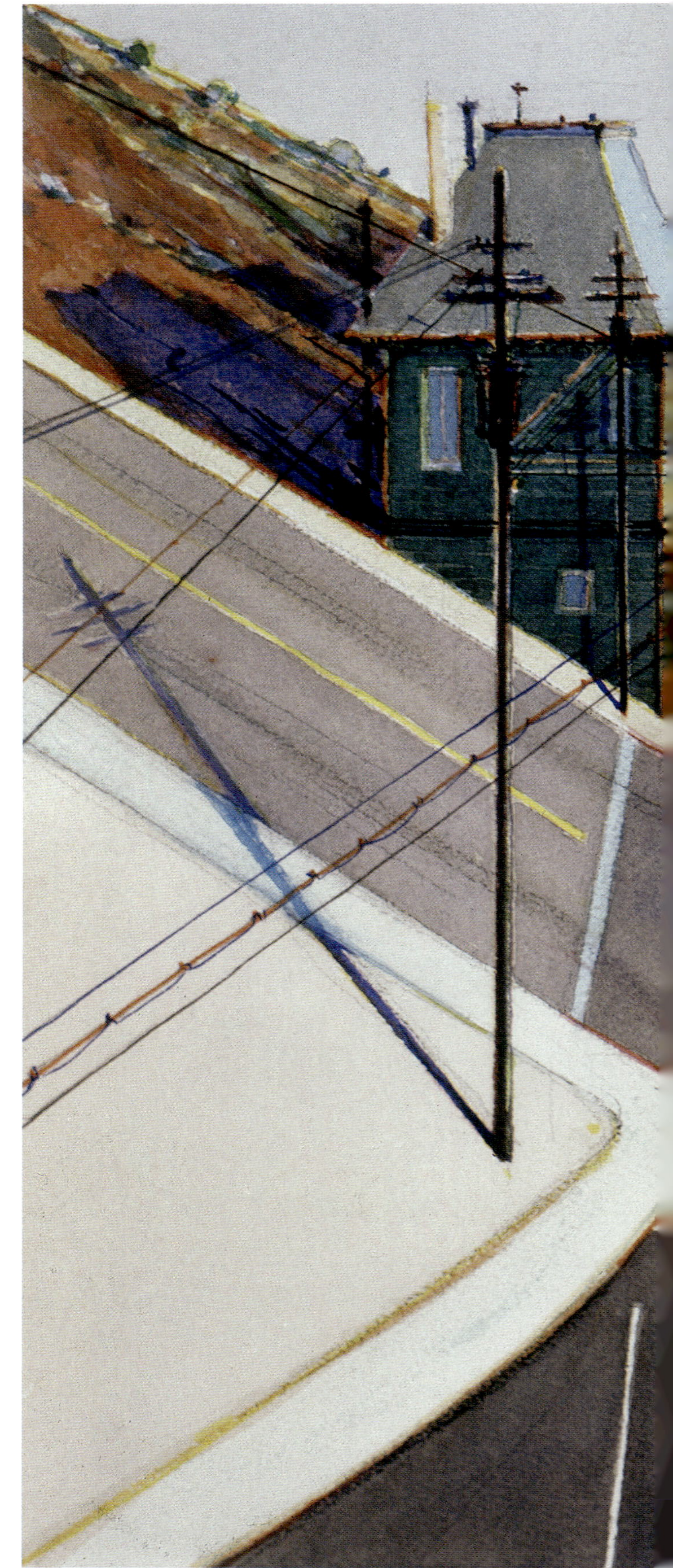

Wayne Thiebaud
**24th Street Intersection**, 1977
Oil on canvas
35 ½ × 48 in.
Private Collection

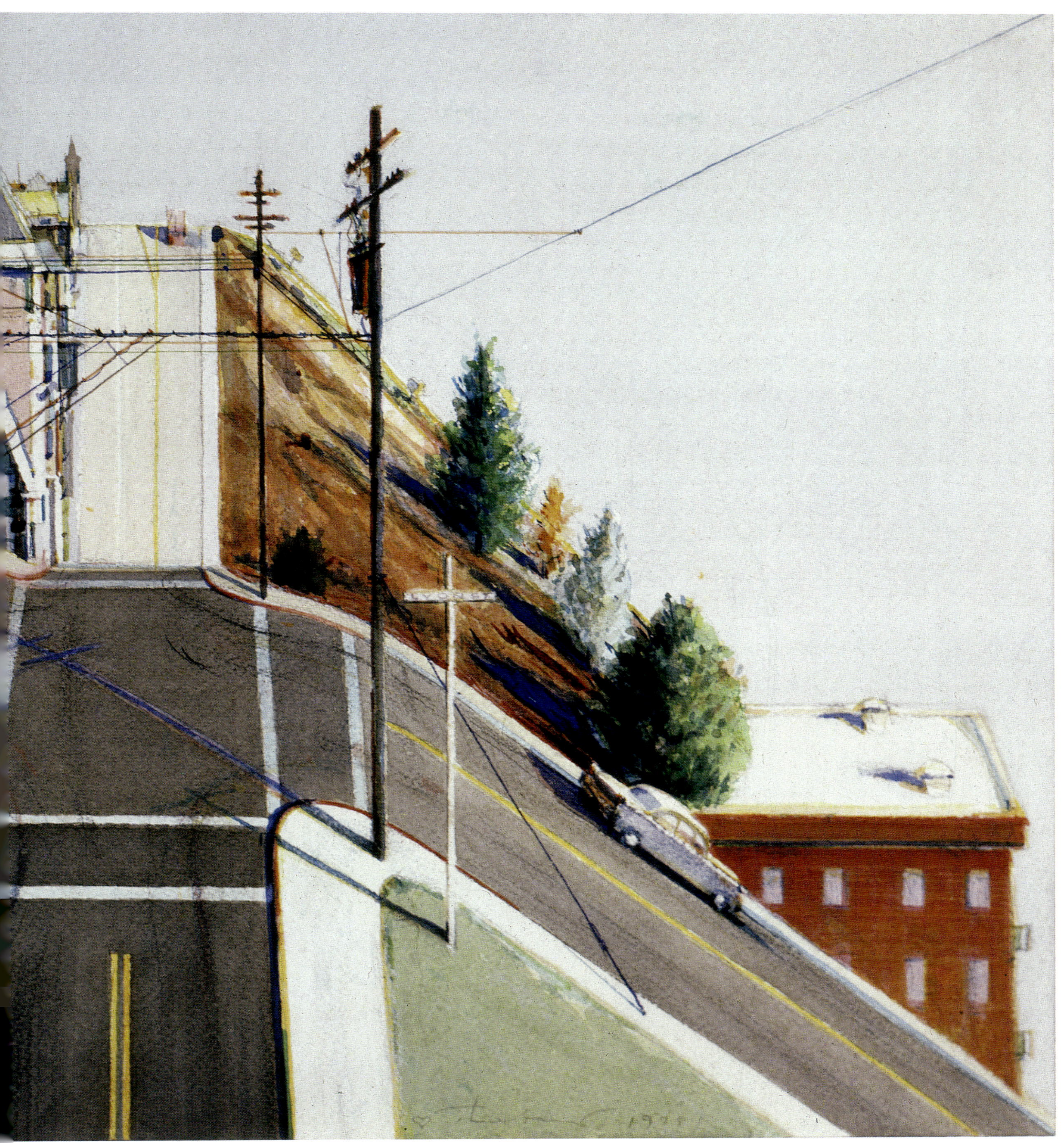

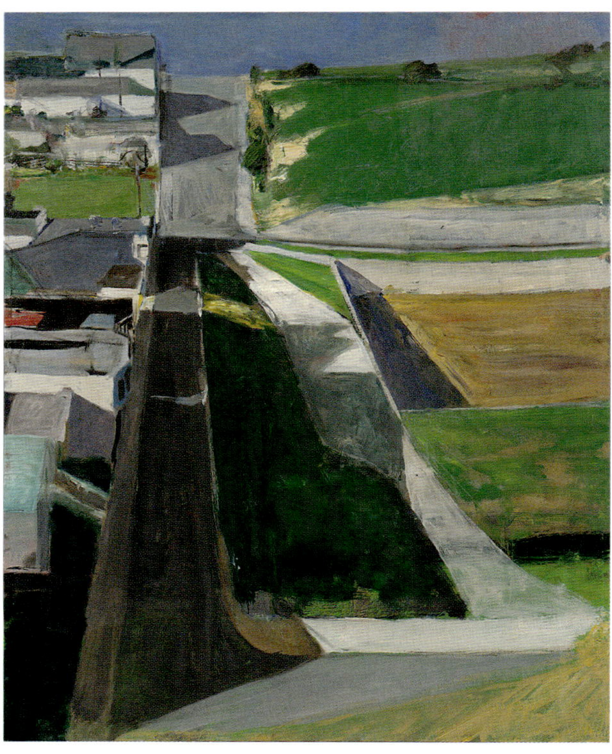

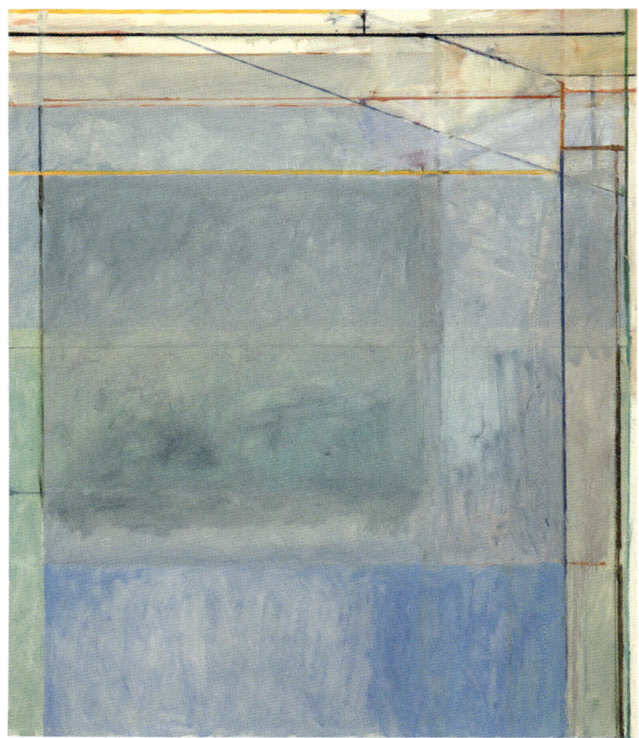



proprietary subject. He is known for his brilliant shadows, crafted to be more colorful, more charged, more exciting than the subjects that cast them. Thiebaud was always most interested in painting light and its effects.

In *Cloud City* his clouds are misty and diaphanous at their center, with heavily worked accumulations of paint along their edges. The doubled upper edges of the clouds, one stacked behind the other, are the center of painterly attention. Bright cerulean blue defines edges formed with bright white. Mustardy yellows and flecks of burnt sienna undergird grays that range from silver to the deepest flannel. Mustard migrates throughout the cloud, settling into a diffuse yellow center. Anyone who has spent a late afternoon in San Francisco as the marine layer blows in would recognize these clouds that both hold bright light and cast dark shadows. Their colorway is the palette of this city—warm blues, golds, and grays that turn cool as the day wears on. In terms of color, the painting repeats the tones and shades of *24th Street Intersection*, completed some sixteen years before. One is hard and linear, all about angles of intersection, and the other is soft and diffuse—two takes on the same light.

Capturing the city's distinctive light, *Cloud City* is Thiebaud's homage to Richard Diebenkorn's *Ocean Park* paintings (ABOVE LEFT AND RIGHT). Thiebaud held his mentor and friend in enormous esteem. Just as Diebenkorn painted the diffuse, abstracted light of coastal Los Angeles, a home adopted later in life, Thiebaud found a figurative means of painting San Francisco's distinctive play of light and shadow, in particular its shimmering golden grays.

You might think the buildings at the bottom of the painting comprise the portrait of the city, but all that architecture is fanciful. Is that the top of the Ferry Building at the end of the street? Of course not, it's just a piece of architecture that *feels* like San Francisco. It is the clouds in *Cloud City* that record the true experience of the city, what Thiebaud prized as "the idea of San Francisco." In its glorious glowing clouds, the painting is Thiebaud's consummate portrait of his beloved city.

As clouds take center stage, everything else falls under their shadow, miniature by comparison. Just a bit of city occupies the painting's foreground and left edge. Even the three skyscrapers are dwarfed by cloud. While *Cloud City* is the

LEFT
Richard Diebenkorn
**Cityscape #1**, 1963
Oil on canvas
60 ¼ × 50 ½ in.
San Francisco Museum of Modern Art
Purchase with funds from trustees and friends in memory of Hector Escobosa, Brayton Wilbur, and J. D. Zellerback


RIGHT
Richard Diebenkorn
**Ocean Park #60**, 1973
Oil on canvas
93 × 81 ¼ in.
Anderson Collection at Stanford University
Gift of Harry W. and Mary Margaret Anderson, and Mary Patricia Anderson Pence
2014.1.006

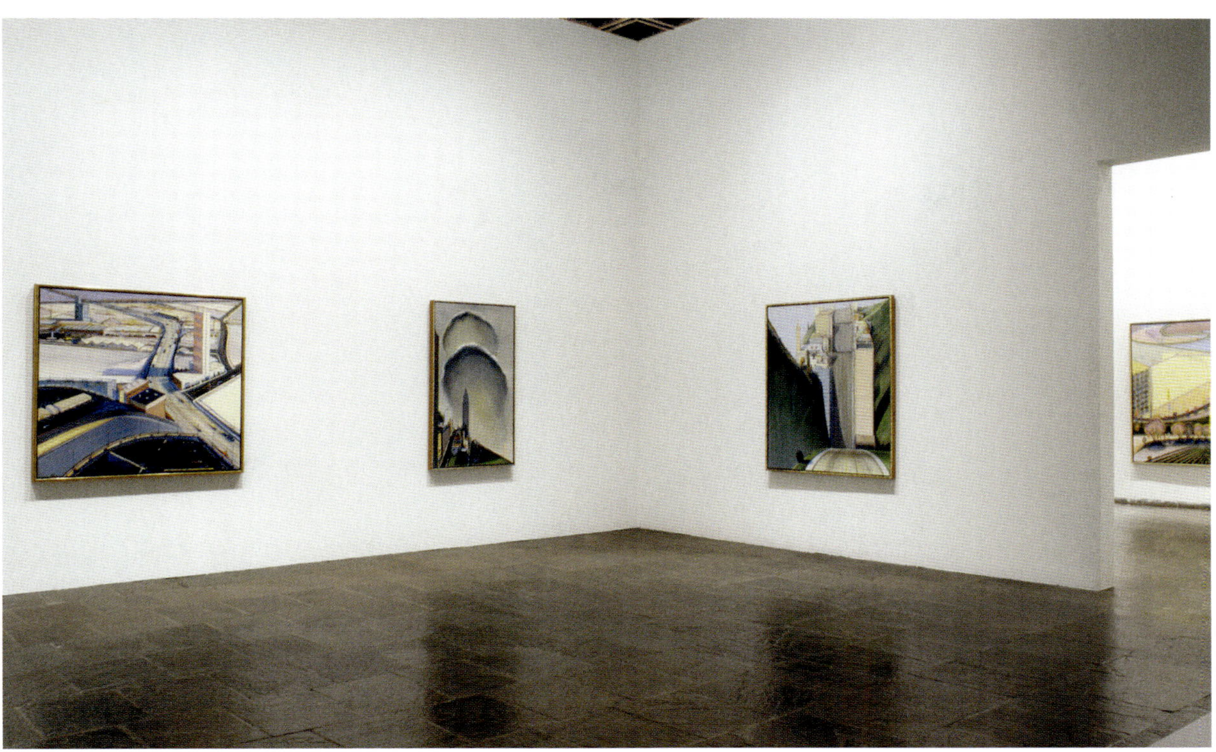

Installation view of *Wayne Thiebaud: A Paintings Retrospective*, Whitney Museum of American Art, New York, 2001

culmination of Thiebaud's cityscapes, the painting also marks a return to landscape: another change of subject was soon to come.

In 2001, San Francisco's de Young Museum included *Cloud City* in Thiebaud's latest retrospective. The painting hung alongside just two cityscapes painted after it; the exhibition made clear that the work marked the end of an era. By this time, Thiebaud had turned his attention to panoramic views of the rivers and byways of the Sacramento delta. Paintings like *Green River Lands* (1998) and *Reservoir and Orchard* (2001) are beautiful examples of his latest work (PP. 110 AND 111). While his subjects were different, their core concerns echo *Cloud City*. Again, Thiebaud was painting light, this time the dry crystalline light specific to the Central Valley. As always, he was more interested in a painting's construction than in what it depicted. The alchemical transformation of paint into icing, clouds, trees is the special painterly chemistry that sustained his practice for more than seventy years.

In May 1997, Thiebaud bought *Cloud City* at auction and brought his San Francisco portrait back home to his studio. This unusual action makes the artwork a special painting simply because Thiebaud admired it enough to want it back. He had more to learn from it. He wanted it back in studio rotation to see how it might affect his latest work, and indeed, *Green River Lands* and *Reservoir and Orchard* bear the impact of *Cloud City*. Look at the trees nestled along the water's edge in both paintings. The trees are backlit with a buildup of paint where the top curl folds back onto itself like a wave coming to shore; Thiebaud cajoled these trees of light from his painterly palette exactly as he coaxed his clouds into being. *Cloud City* was generative for Thiebaud. The painting is more than special, and more than treasure. It is a culmination and an opening to new horizons.



Note

1. Richard Wollheim, "An Interview with Wayne Thiebaud," in *Wayne Thiebaud: Cityscapes*. Campbell-Thiebaud Gallery, November 9–December 18, 1993, unpaginated.

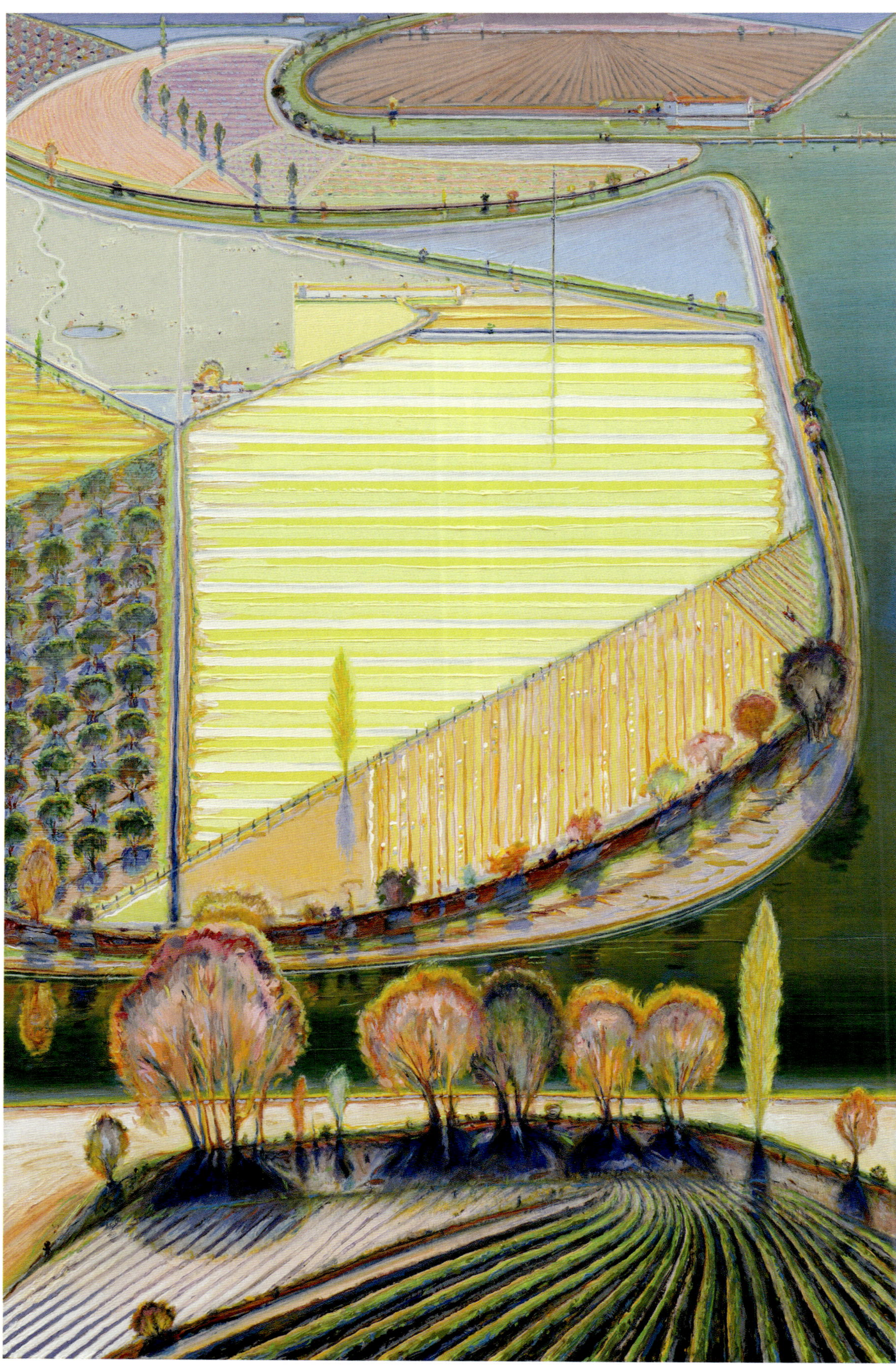

Wayne Thiebaud
**Green River Lands**, 1998
Oil on canvas
72 × 48 in.
Collection of Wayne Thiebaud Foundation

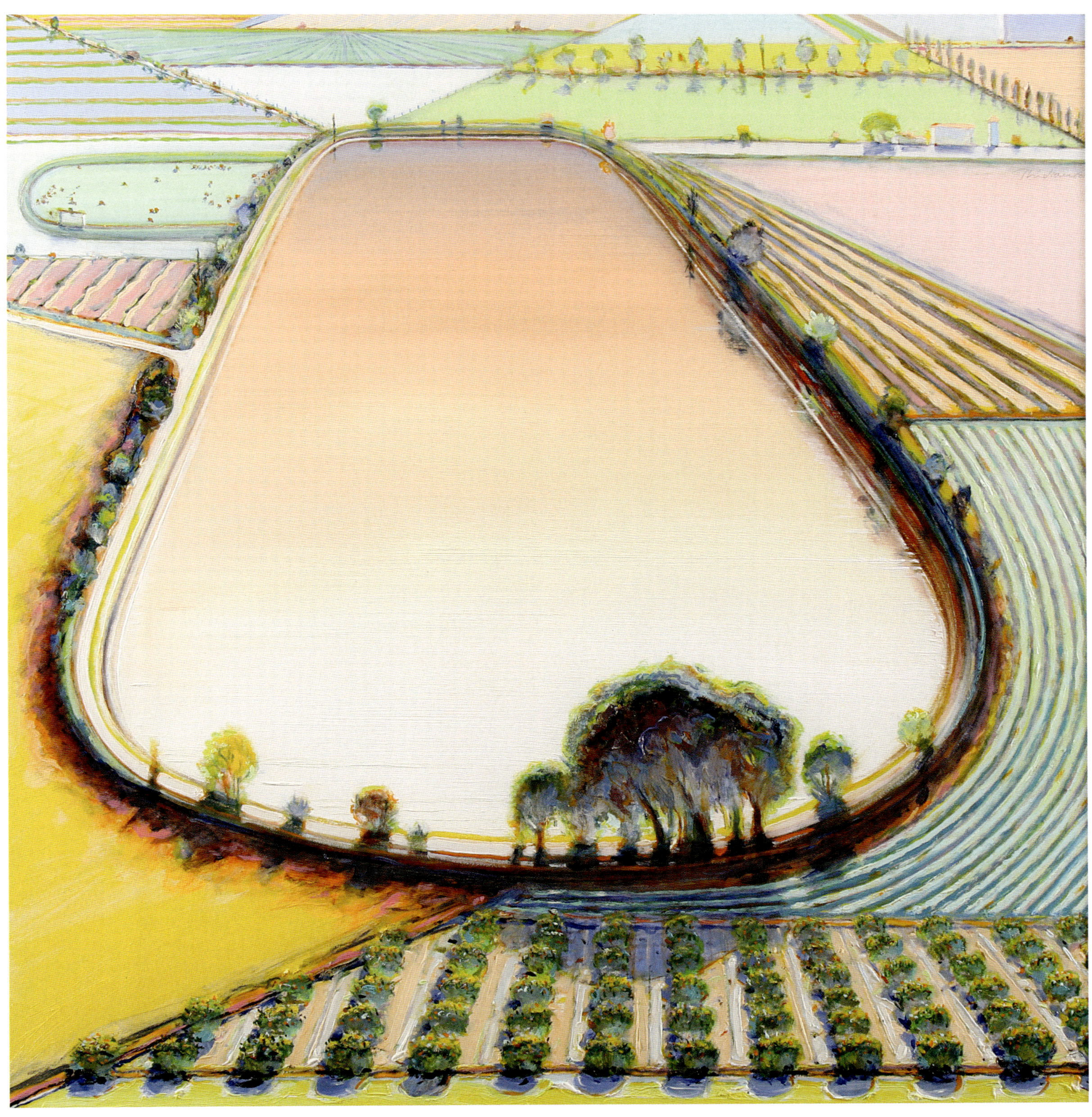

Wayne Thiebaud
**Reservoir and Orchard**, 2001
Oil on canvas
40 × 40 in.
Collection of Matt and Maria Bult

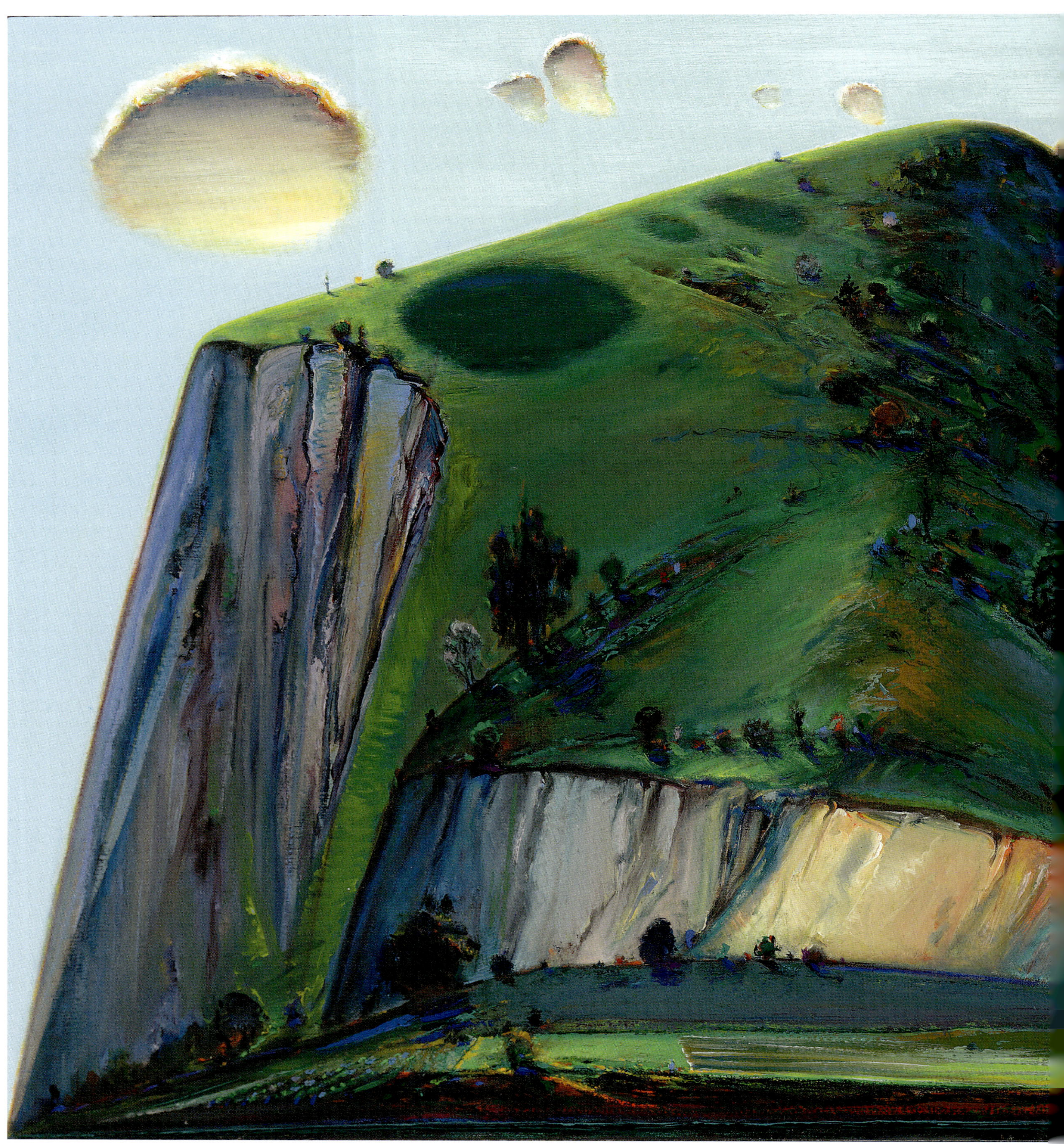

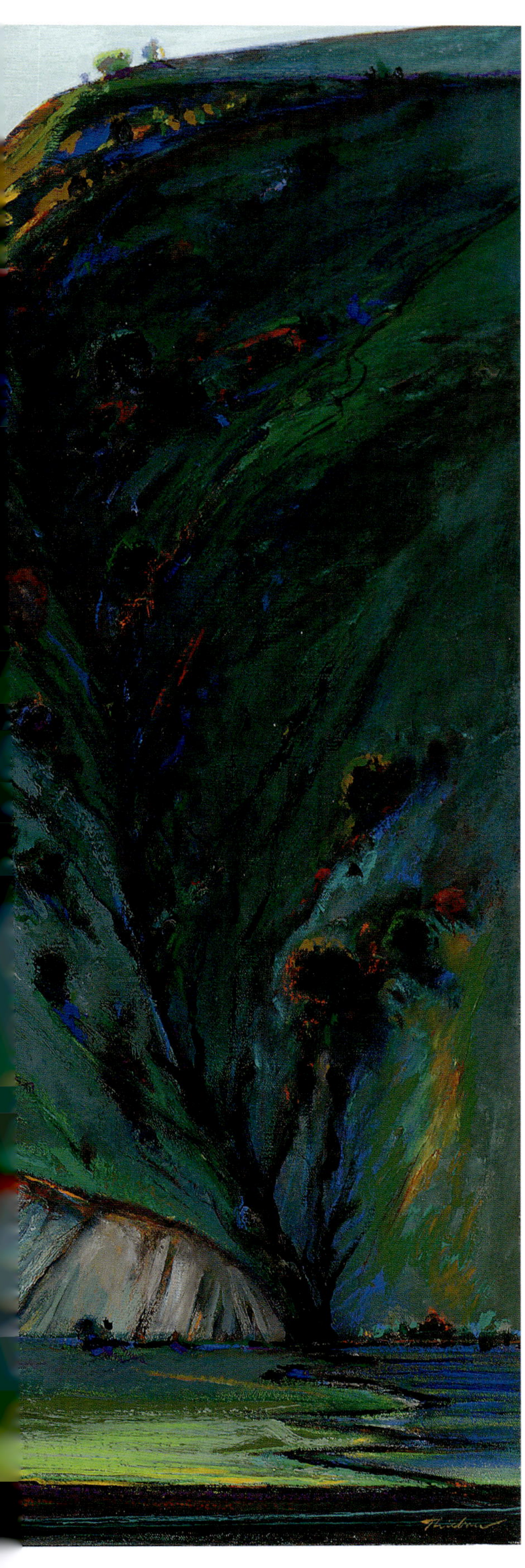



Wayne Thiebaud
**Napa Valley Ridge**, 1986–97
Oil on canvas
36 × 48 in.
Private Collection

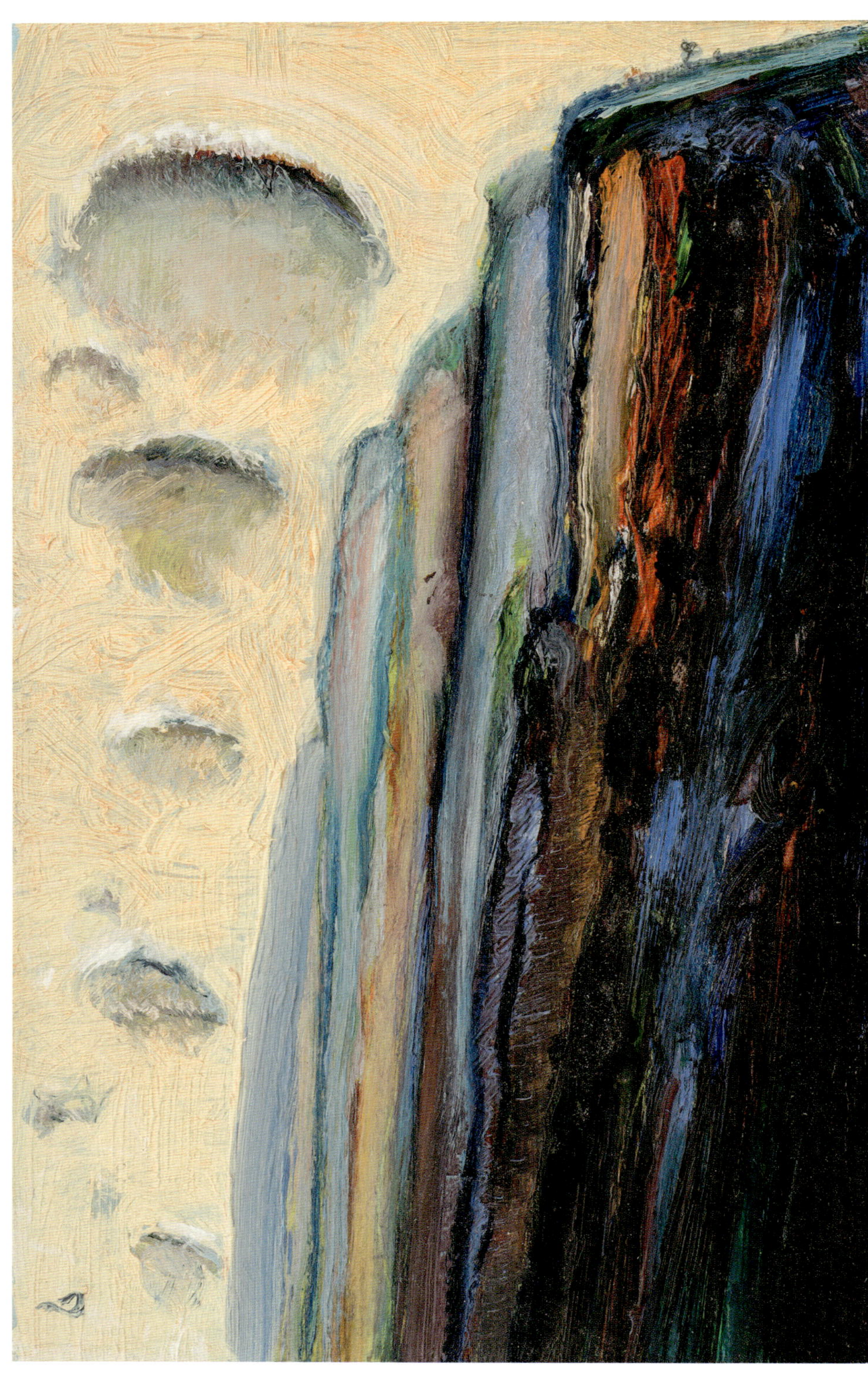

Wayne Thiebaud
**Dark Ridge and Clouds**, ca. 1990
Oil on board
7 ⅝ × 4 ⅞ in.
Private Collection

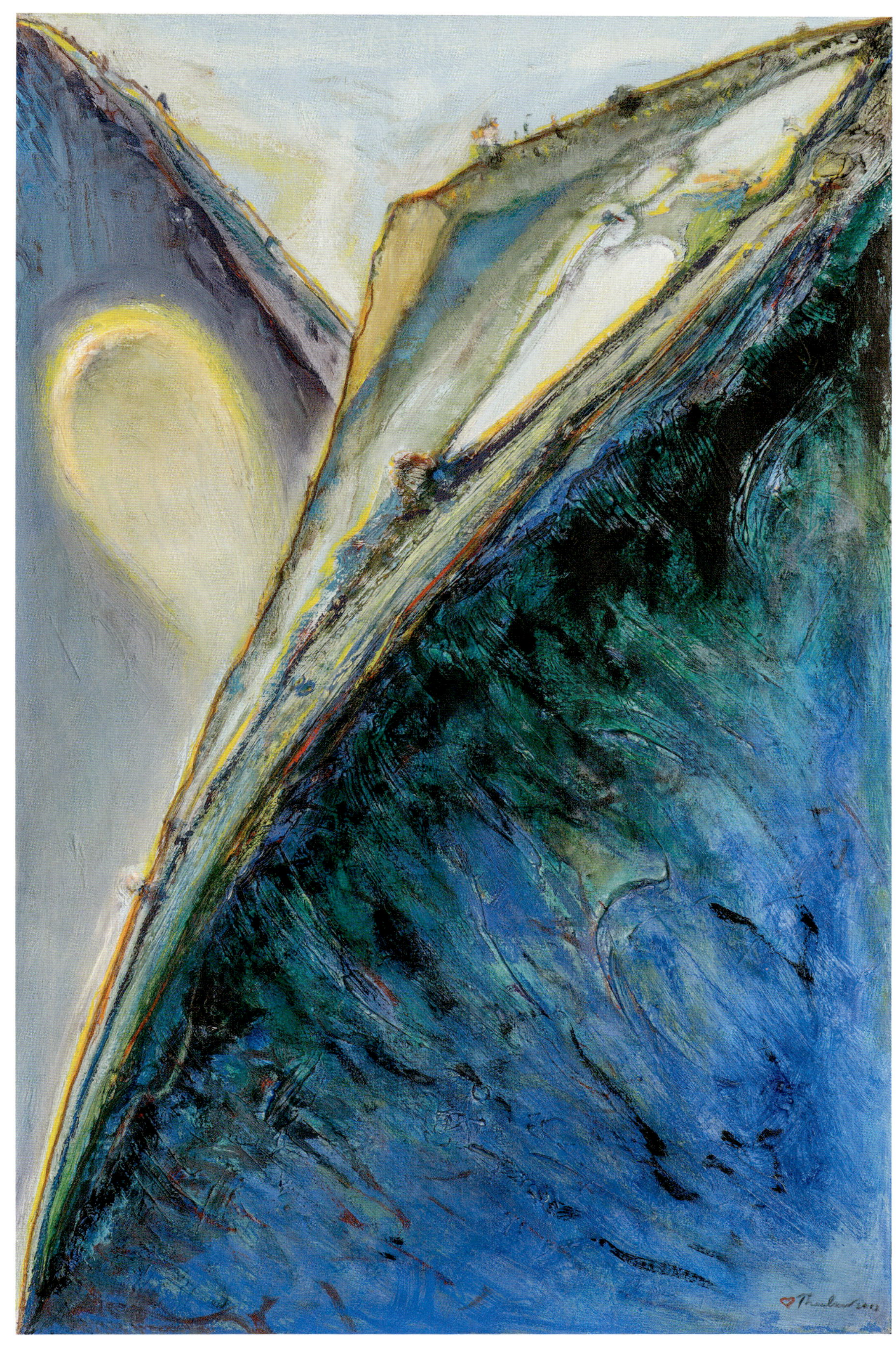

Wayne Thiebaud
**Blue Mountain Cloud**, 2013
Oil on canvas
35 ¾ × 24 in.
Private Collection

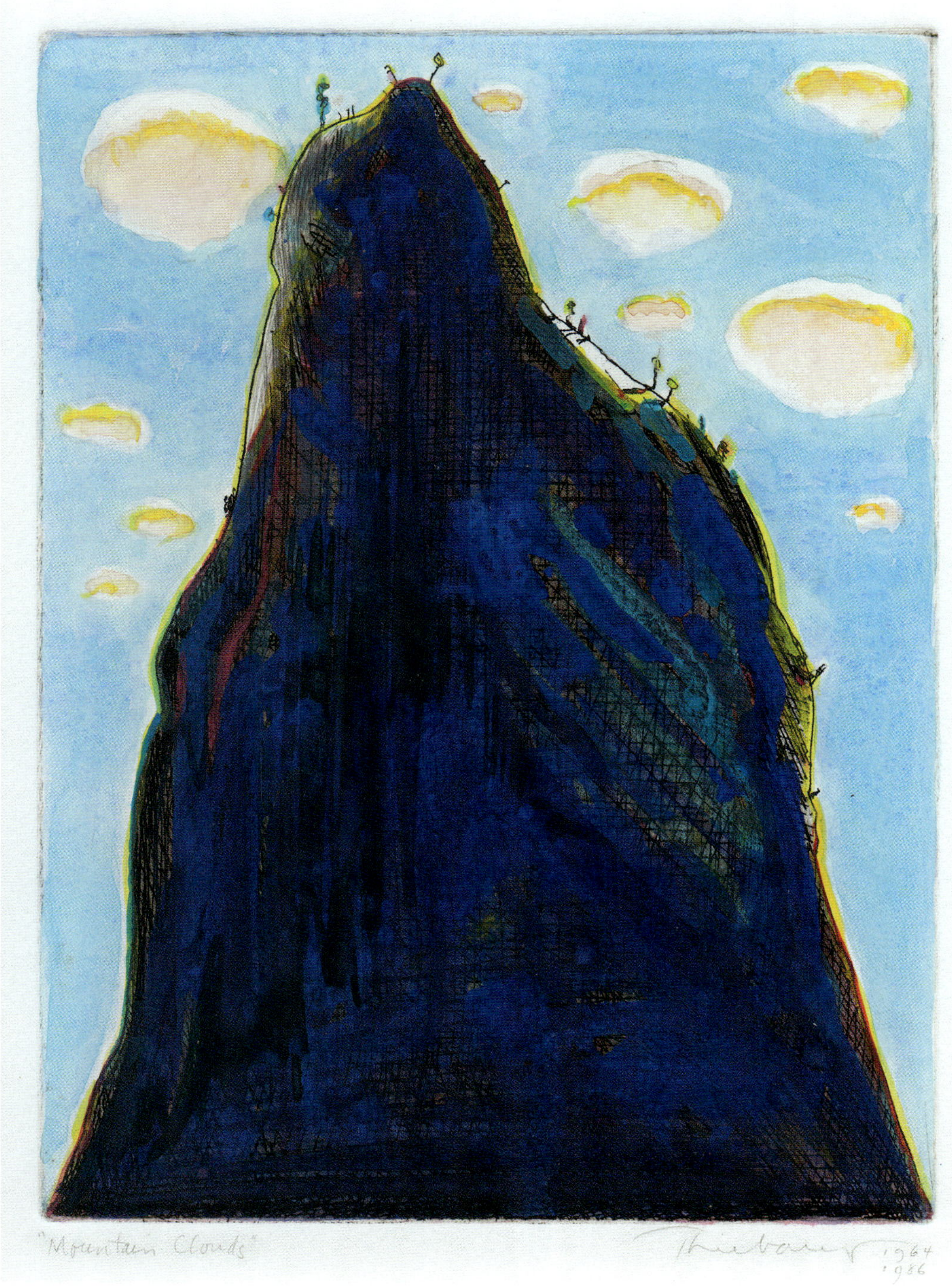


ABOVE
Wayne Thiebaud
**Mountain Clouds**, 1986
Watercolor over hardground etching and drypoint
7 × 5 ½ in.
Private Collection

OPPOSITE
**Palm Tree and Cloud**, 2012
Oil on board
12 ⅛ × 9 ⅞ in.
Courtesy of Wayne Thiebaud Foundation

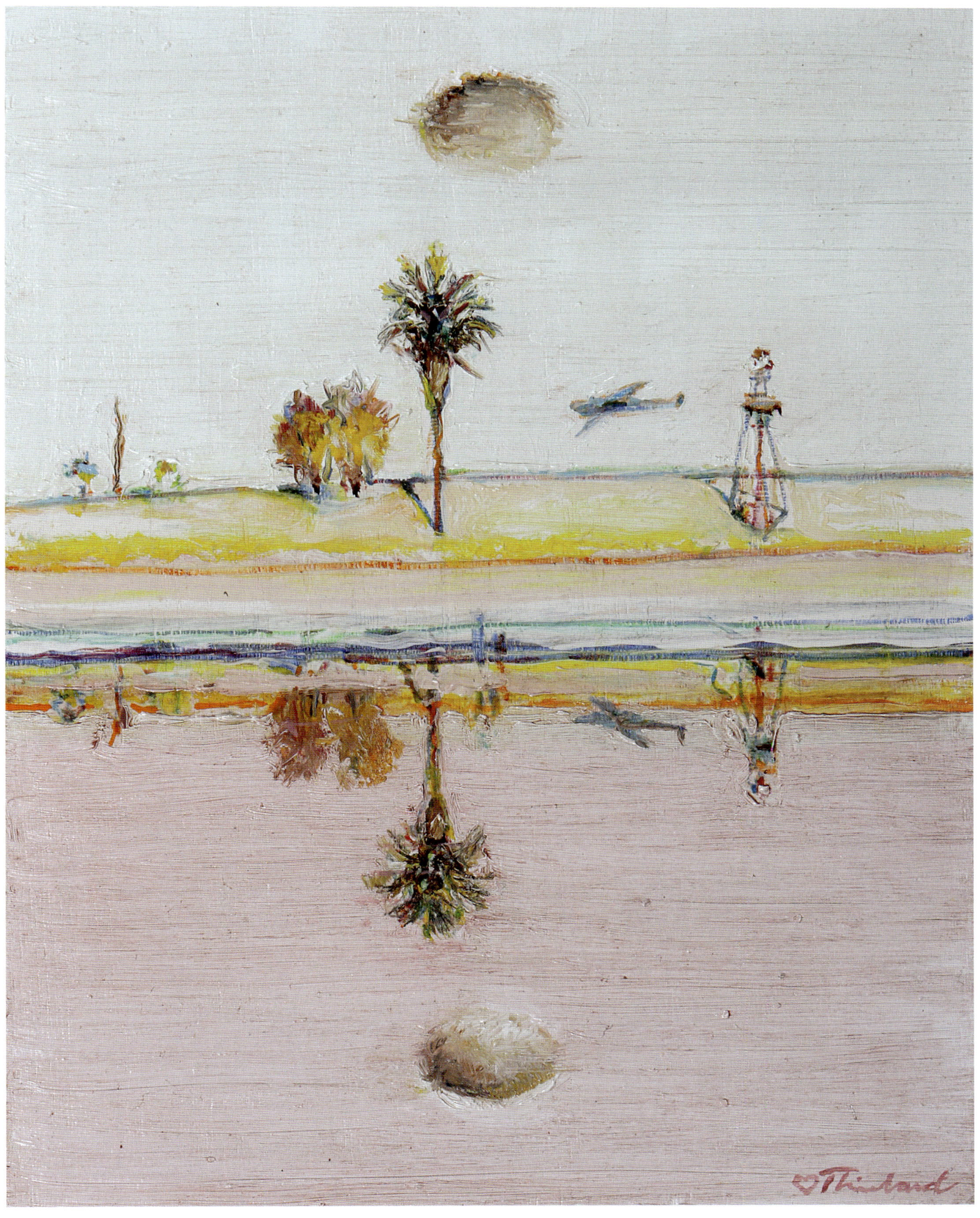

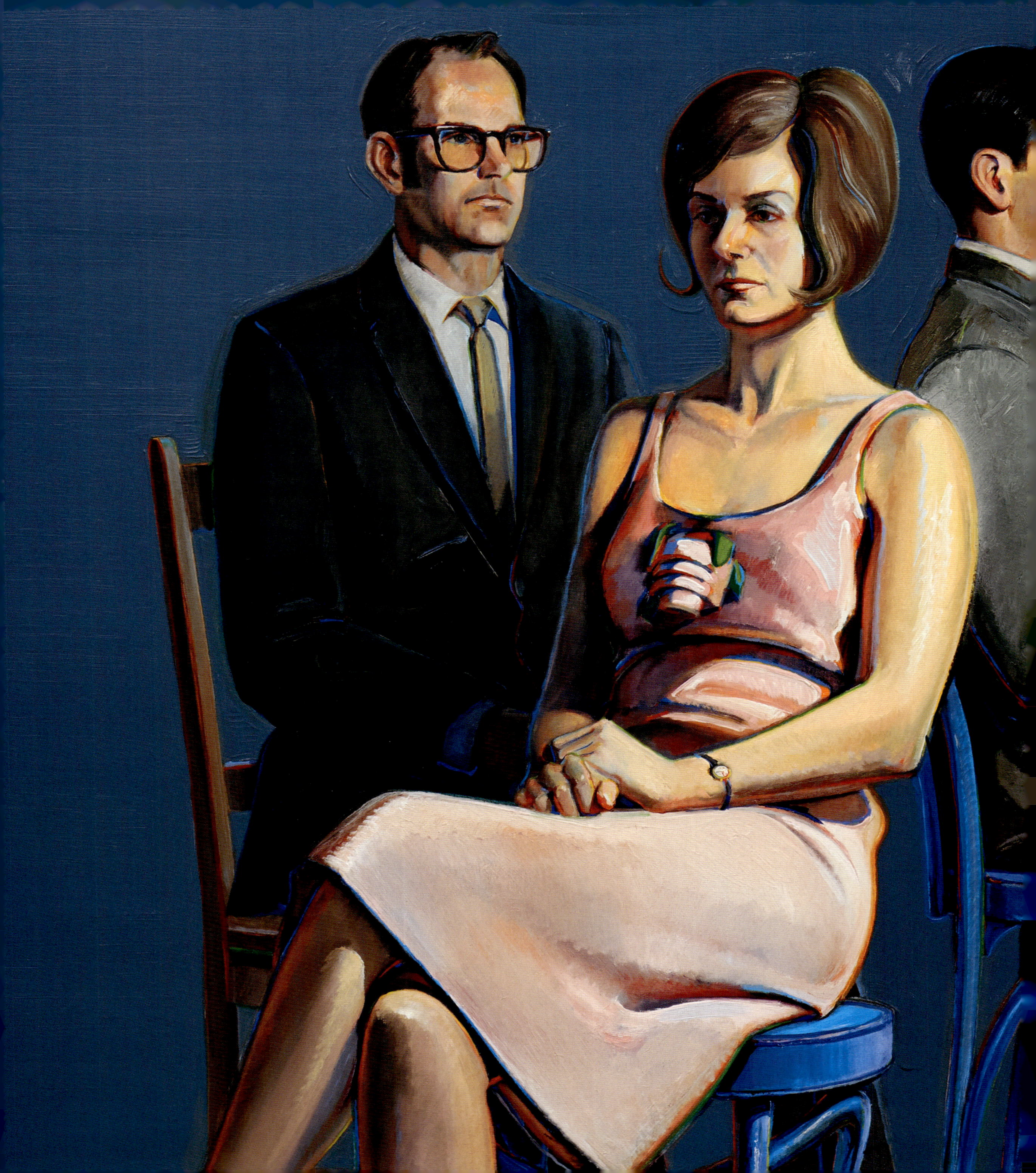

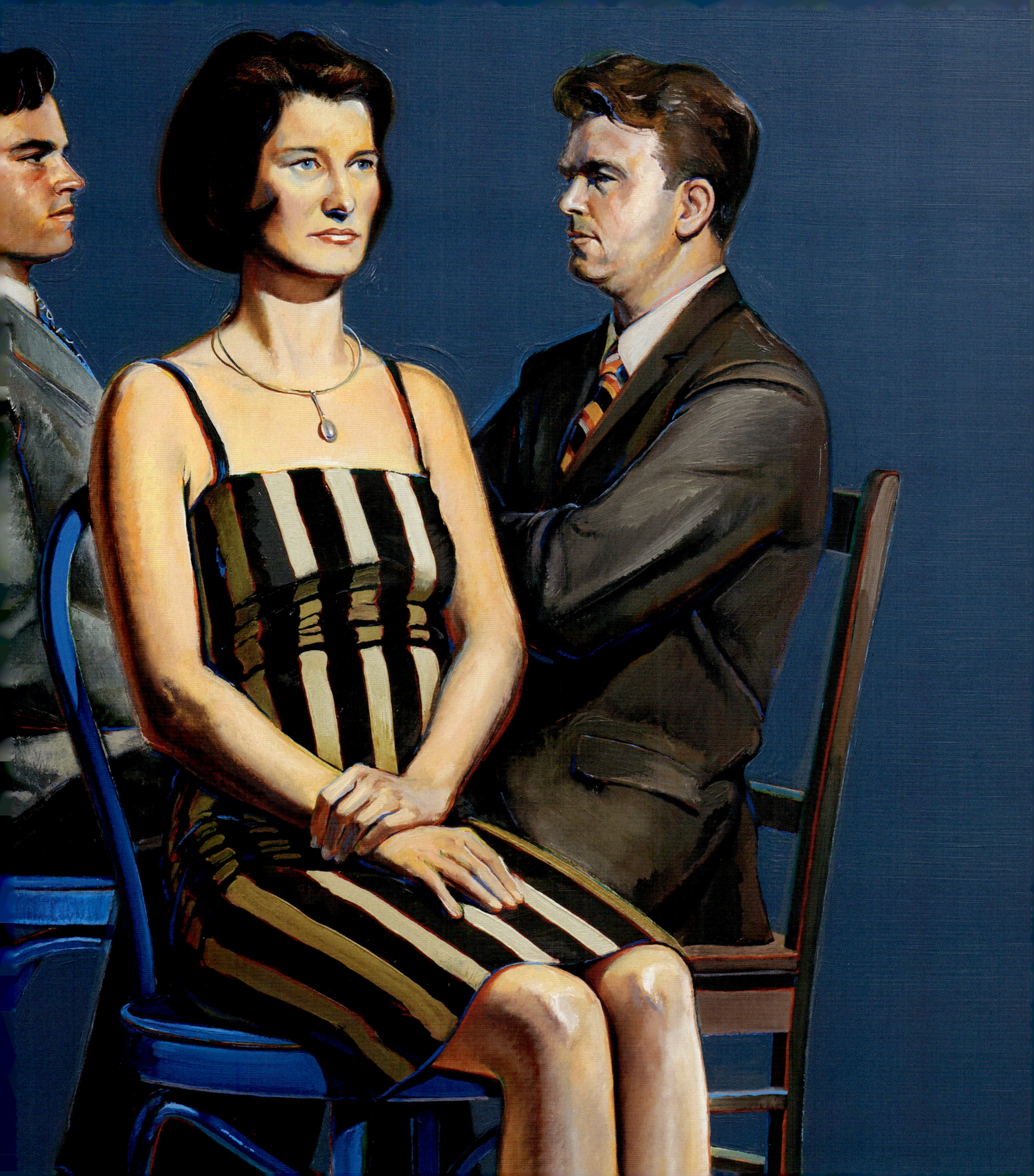

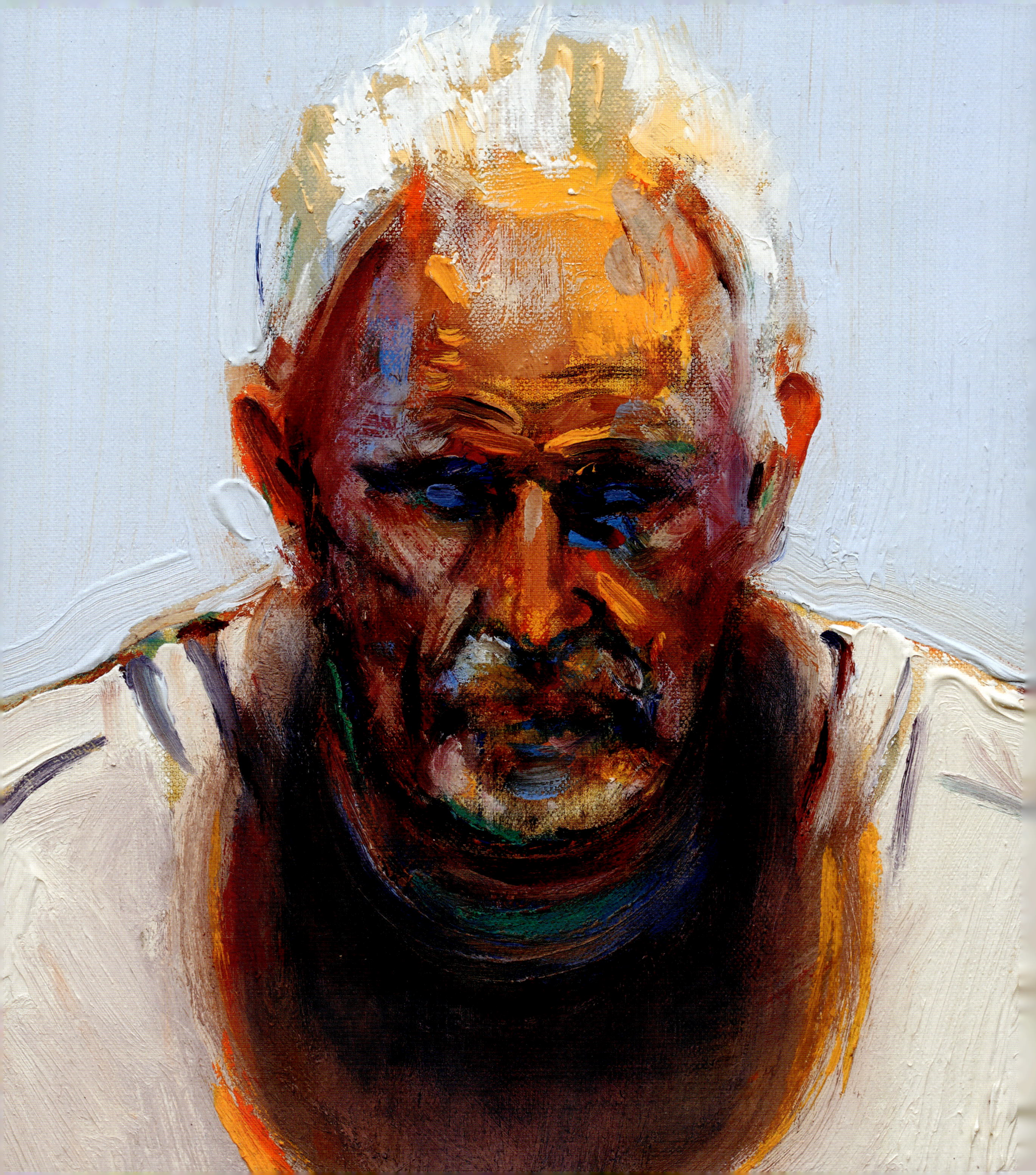

# "Anyone Can Be My Protagonist"

Julia Friedman

> "The truth is that every strong artist builds on his weaknesses: it is only weak artists who deny them."
> —Richard Wollheim, *Painting as an Art*, 1987

In early 2001, shortly after Wayne Thiebaud turned eighty, writer and essayist Adam Gopnik interviewed him at the historic Herbst Theatre in San Francisco.[1] Toward the end of their hour-long exchange, Gopnik asked whether Thiebaud had any regrets about what, if anything, he could have done better. The response was that he had "not worked with the figure enough." The figure, said Thiebaud, "is the devil," because to simply represent the figure within a given artistic convention, or style, is to dodge the challenge of giving the painting "some degree of real feeling, and transporting character." He concluded: "that's the thing that bedevils me. I keep trying, I even try now, making these disastrous attempts, but I keep on trying anyway." To be sure, Thiebaud's persistent return to figure paintings and drawings over the course of his long career is a proof of his tenacity and determination to re-create in the American vernacular the "real feeling" and "transporting character" found in the paintings of Velázquez, Degas, and Eakins. Many of his later "disastrous attempts" were witnessed firsthand by the British philosopher Richard Wollheim, who Thiebaud mentioned early in the Herbst Theatre interview. Wollheim was his friend and occasional colleague at UC Davis between 1989 and 1996. The two became acquainted sometime after Thiebaud's San Francisco Museum of Modern Art retrospective of 1985, which was also the year Wollheim moved to the Bay Area to join the faculty of UC Berkeley. This was just one among many mentions of the philosopher in Thiebaud's lectures and interviews. The frequency with which the painter revisited his conversations with Wollheim reflects the importance of their dialogue, which ended with Wollheim's passing in 2003 but continued to influence Thiebaud's painting until his own death in 2021.

There is little mystery in Wollheim's opinion of Thiebaud's work. It is detailed in a 1989 review for *Artforum*,[2] and a longer essay entitled "A Painter's Alchemy," which he wrote the same year for the British journal *Modern Painters*.[3] Wollheim argued that Thiebaud worked against the grain of postwar American figuration in that he did not subscribe to the sentimental vision of his compatriots, for whom everyday, empirical objects could achieve the status of poetry. Boldly forgoing irony, "the great alibi of contemporary art,"[4] Thiebaud rejected the facile and banal approach that puts painting and its subject matter on an equal footing. He was not interested in "the pursuit of appearances"[5] and did not use the illusion of replicating the real world on canvas as his justification for painting. Wollheim saw Thiebaud as "rescu[ing] painting from the charge of superfluity."[6] Far from turning the easel into a window through which the real world is represented in oil paint, Thiebaud understood that "the value of painting must lie in a visual experience to which it gives rise: an experience which at once derives from looking at the real world, and enhances the real world when we return to

Wayne Thiebaud, **Untitled (Gene Cooper)** (detail), 2019

it."[7] Painting does not have to compete with reality. Its goal is to become its own *visual species* by using "the traditional features of art"[8] such as lighting, composition, and color.

Long before he wrote about Thiebaud's alchemy, Wollheim had made his reputation as a philosopher (there is even a paradox named after him), and also contributed to the rarefied subfield of the philosophy of art. In 1984, he was invited to deliver the prestigious A. W. Mellon Lectures in the Fine Arts at the National Gallery of Art—an honor normally reserved for art historians. In 1987, these lectures were expanded, and published by Princeton University Press in a volume called *Painting as an Art*.[9] It is the third chapter, "The Spectator in the Picture," that Thiebaud repeatedly referenced in his talks and interviews, and which points to the reasons behind the formal and philosophical complexity of his figures. It stems from the viewer's preconception of how any given pictorial genre functions. This is especially true for figure paintings whose sitters are not nameless models, but friends and family members of the artist. Their names are known, their likenesses are familiar. Even when Thiebaud differentiates between "straight portraits" and figure paintings that do not amount to "direct encounters" with the sitter's appearance,[10] viewers are conditioned to look for an activated character, a vivid personality, a transmitter of emotion. Ever since Hegel's *Lectures on Aesthetics*, the critical emphasis has been on identity and the inner world (often the inner turmoil) of the sitter. German idealist philosophy, with its principle of inwardness, gave rise to the twentieth-century Expressionist portrait, dominant in the post-WWI works of Chaïm Soutine and, when Thiebaud began painting figures in the 1960s, in the works of Alice Neel and Lucian Freud.[11]

Thiebaud refused to conform to the conventions of portraiture, or even the rules governing pictorial genres in general, seeing all paintings—whether landscapes, still lifes, or figure paintings—as the locus of "'inherently' the same kind of problem."[12] That bred confusion in the viewers' (and the critics') perception of his figure paintings, which were often seen as lacking some essential quality that ought to be present in the depictions of human beings. Critics who attempted to identify what was missing have often remarked that Thiebaud's most puzzling paintings treat human figures in a similar manner to the foodstuffs and haberdashery of his still lifes. But men and women are not cupcakes and ties; they are expected to enact their humanity, or at least to adjust themselves to the viewer's projections of their presumed behaviors. And while there are similarities in modeling and lighting, perhaps the most intriguing parallel between Thiebaud's still lifes and his figure paintings is the "stilling" of the figures by representing them in the moment either immediately before or after an action. In a 1974 interview with Dan Tooker, Thiebaud explained his technique using the image of chronological "centering": "what I am interested in, really, is the figure that is about to do something, or has done something, or is doing nothing, and with that sort of centering device try to figure out what can be revealed."[13] Thus the balance of action is purposefully left out.

Wollheim describes the action left out of the painting as "representational content in excess of what [paintings] represent . . . what is given to us along with what the painting represents."[14] Such content "in excess" reveals itself through "an unrepresented spectator." This spectator, Wollheim tells us, is different from both the external spectator—the *spectator of the picture* (an actual person in the room that contains the painting) and from the internal spectator—the *spectator in the picture* (the person in the locale and historical period represented in the painting). The distinction between the external and internal spectators is important, because only the external spectator is aware of the painting's marked surface, which the internal spectator does not see. In addition to these two, Wollheim purports that some paintings also contain an *unrepresented* internal spectator who "must be so located in the represented space that he can see everything that the picture represents and he can see it as the picture represents it."[15] This is "the protagonist," who facilitates "centrally imagining" the event, since his point of view is at the center.[16] The protagonist does not have to be a specific person: "anyone can be my protagonist provided only that I know enough about that person to keep him, her, constant in my thoughts . . . It can be merely a person of some particular kind, the kind being more or less specific." Critically, it is the artist who endows the protagonist—the unrepresented spectator—with "a body of dispositions."[17] It follows that if the protagonist, as a surrogate of the painter, sustains the painter's action—stilling, in the case of Thiebaud—then the external spectator will be compelled to empathize with the emotional register of stillness.

The true content of the picture is now accessible to this external spectator who will not be limited to what the painting represents. From the vantage point of the painter, this model makes the unrepresented internal spectator (the protagonist) indispensable for delivering the content of the painting to the external spectator in its entirety, with clarity and cogency:

> First, the external spectator looks at the picture and sees what there is to be seen in it; then, adopting the internal spectator as his protagonist, he starts to imagine in that person's perspective the person or event that the picture represents; that is to say, he imagines from the inside the internal spectator seeing, thinking about, responding to, acting upon, what is before him; then the condition in which it leaves him modifies how he sees the picture. The external spectator identifies with the internal spectator, and it is through this identification that he gains fresh access to the picture's content.[18]

In other words, the internal spectator acts as a proxy for the external spectator—the spectator *in the* picture enables the spectator *of the* picture to gain access to what the painting contains but does not represent.

To illustrate his argument, Wollheim uses the example of Édouard Manet's figures, which are "turned in upon themselves by some powerful troubling thought; they are figures who are temporarily preoccupied, figures who have retained and cherish, who cosset, a secret, to which their thoughts have now reverted."[19] As in Thiebaud's interview with Tooker, in which he described his figures as either pre- or post-action, so Manet's mutable characters are in a temporary freeze-frame: "a moment later and the mood may dissipate, but until it does, they are absent from the world."[20] It is this proximity in the emotional registers between Manet's and Thiebaud's figures that makes Wollheim's knotty theory of the "unrepresented spectator" appealing. The philosopher's multitiered system, which necessitates multiple spectators to access a painting's content in its entirety, suggests a way to interpret some of Thiebaud's most enigmatic figure paintings. That is not to demystify them, which would be a fool's errand, but to underscore the fact that, just as with Manet, whose frontality or near-frontality in figure paintings was, according to Wollheim, one of his works' most provocative features, but was dismissed as "mere ineptitude,"[21] Thiebaud's stilling of his figures "opens up an undefined or irrational volume of space in which a perambulating internal spectator might insert himself."[22]

Thiebaud goes to great lengths to entice the external spectator into careful looking. As he stated in the interview with Bill Berkson, the "speculative arena is one of the intrigues of painting."[23] And as one scholar noted, his unadorned white backdrops have a specific purpose: their "clinical austerity creates a nonnarrative context that forces the artist, and the viewer, to concentrate on the figure."[24] Removing the anecdotal pushes figure paintings away from the realm of illustration, the explicit, where nothing remains unrepresented, into the realm of fine art, the implicit, where, as Wollheim argues, content may reside outside what paintings seem to represent.[25]

Take for instance Thiebaud's canonical *Girl with Ice Cream Cone* from 1963 (P. 124)—one of his

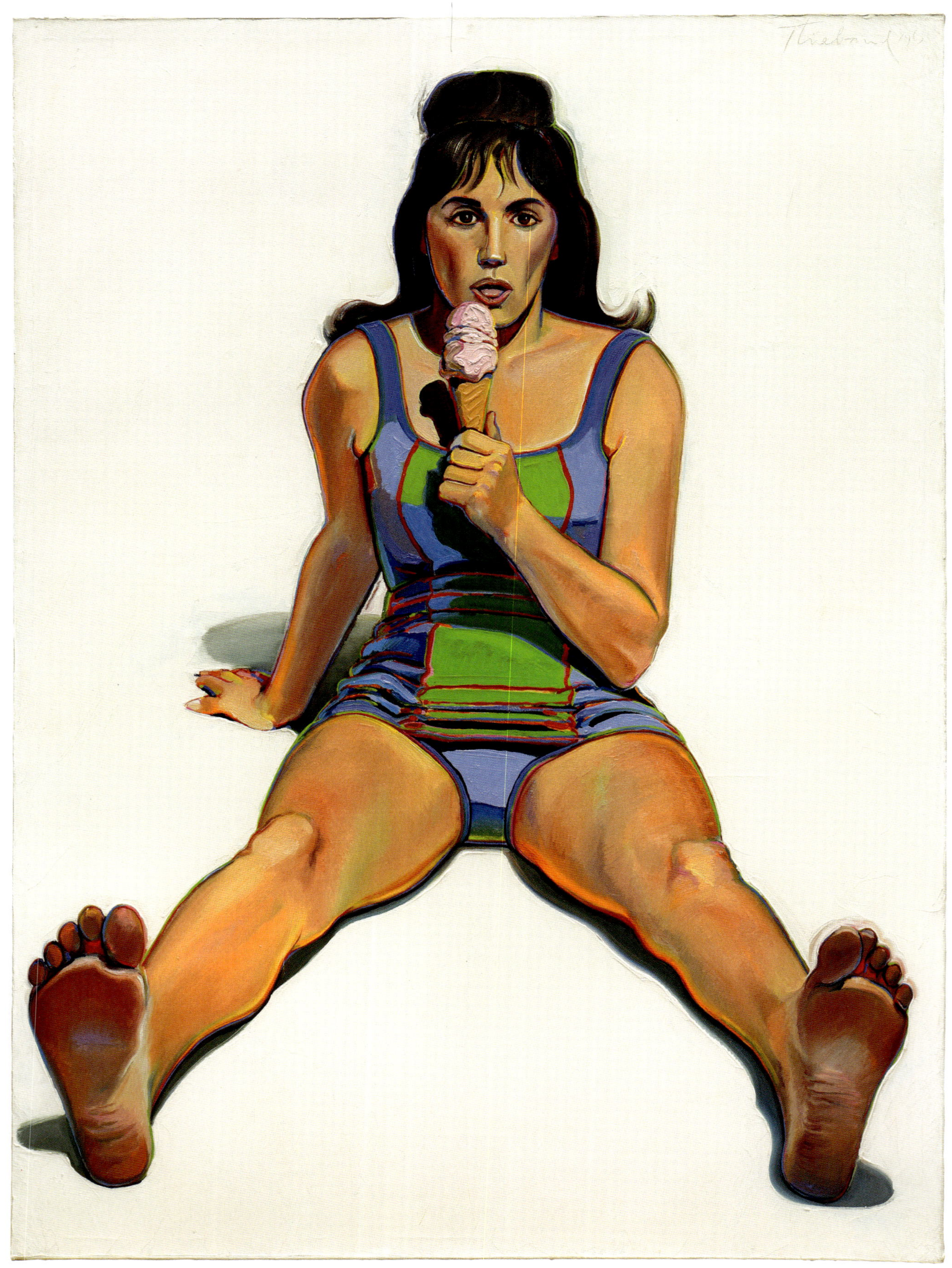

Wayne Thiebaud
**Girl with Ice Cream Cone**, 1963
Oil on canvas
48 ⅛ × 36 ¼ in.
Hirshhorn Museum and Sculpture Garden
Joseph H. Hirshhorn Bequest Fund,
Smithsonian Collections Acquisition
Program, and museum purchase, 1996

Wayne Thiebaud
**Untitled (Gene Cooper)**, 2019
Oil on canvas
18 × 18 in.
Collection of Wayne Thiebaud Foundation

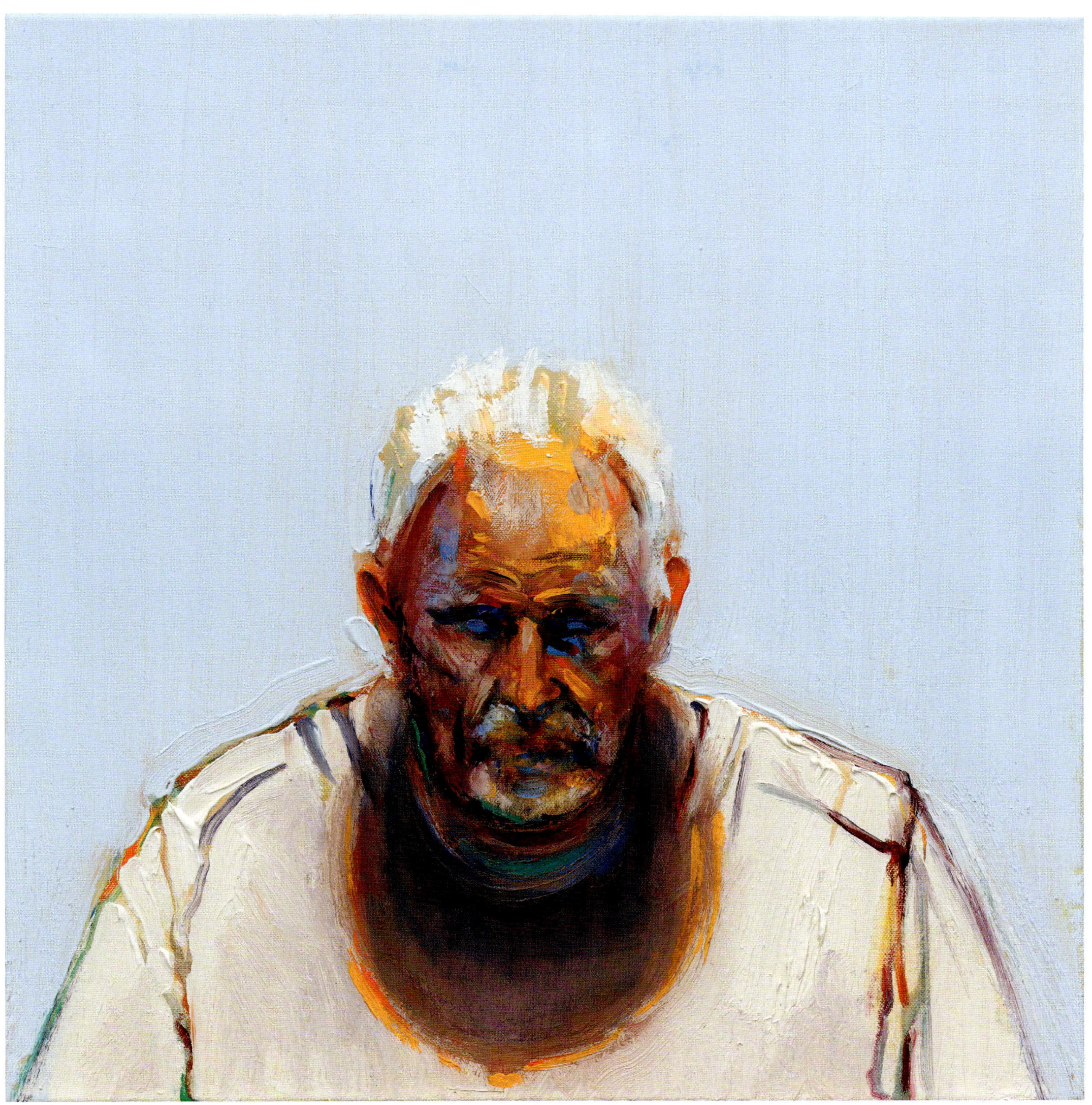

earliest figure paintings that followed his shift to the new style of brightly lit still lifes. The frontally posed model (Thiebaud's wife, Betty Jean), illuminated by a 32K photo floodlight,[26] is positioned in the middle of the canvas; she faces outward and is parallel to the picture plane. Wollheim referred to this placement as "the arbitrary viewpoint *par excellence*: head on."[27] Given the setting—the ice cream cone and the bathing suit imply she is oceanside or at least poolside—the model's lack of any emotion appropriate to enjoying a cold treat on a hot day, and her failure to attend to the cone she is holding up to her mouth, present a palpable threat of the ice cream dripping down the improbably neat folds of her garment. Yet she is oblivious to the physical facts. This should suggest to the external spectator that the humdrum narrative of the soon-to-be-melted ice cream is not the point here. The point is the suspended eroticism presented to the external spectator, through the suggestive pink of the cone with its phallic shadow, the model's parted lips, her legs akimbo, and the gradient darkening of her inner thighs. Her body is transfixed in the pictorial space. Caught in the austerity of the white background, the figure is pushed forward by the purple shadow she casts, and held back by the unrepresented internal spectator—the protagonist right in front of her. It is this protagonist who conveys to us, the external spectators, the suspended eroticism he is "seeing, thinking about, responding to, acting upon." Thiebaud employs the frontality in this painting in the manner of Manet.



Something similar, albeit in reverse, happens in *Untitled (Gene Cooper)* from 2019 (P. 127), a portrait of art historian Gene Cooper, Thiebaud's longtime friend. Cooper has been the subject of a half-dozen paintings over the past four decades, ranging from conventional portraits to generalized depictions and caricature. *Untitled* contains a centrally positioned *en face* bust, illuminated from the top, and depicted against Thiebaud's trademark grayish-white background. Because of his forward-tilted head, his light-colored clothing, and the position of the floodlight, Cooper appears to be weighed down by an X-ray lead apron covering his chest. The figure is stilled in its pictorial space in the same way as the girl with the ice cream, only here the sitter exudes experience, certainty, solidity. He is an actor; she is acted upon. He leans forward, into the space occupied by the external spectator, not backward as she does. The undifferentiated ground remains behind him, permanently arrested by his broad figure dominating the foreground. This is in stark contrast to the voidlike space that envelops the girl with the ice cream. Instead of suspended eroticism, the protagonist of *Untitled* projects the gravitas of old age, inviting the external spectator to contemplate the natural order of things.

At times, the proximity between Manet's and Thiebaud's treatment of figures is uncanny. Wollheim's characterization of the French painter's 1868–69 masterpiece *The Balcony* (P. 129) could be applied verbatim to several of Thiebaud's figure paintings: "We see a group of people who are in close propinquity—in *Le Balcon*, crowded together as if they were inside some transparent capsule—but who, for all their physical closeness, fail to make contact." If it were not for the mention of "*Le Balcon*," this could easily refer to Thiebaud's 1963 *Eating Figures (Quick Snack)* (P. 130), in which a woman and a man—he used Betty Jean and his dealer Allan Stone as models—perch on adjacent diner stools, their sides pressed together to the point of making them look like conjoined twins, yet oblivious of each other's presence. It might also describe his iconic 1965 canvas *Five Sitting Figures* (PP. 132–33), where three men and two women confined to an invisible closed circle serve as a perfect illustration of Wollheim's account of Manet's *Balcony*: "contact between them has been broken. Something has impinged upon them with the effect that, for the duration of the picture, for that special time, they are locked up in their own private thoughts."[28]

We might wonder why the philosopher's discussion of Manet's "suspended encounters" and "transient moment[s] of intense, shared isolation" seem to chime so harmoniously with Thiebaud's ballroom paintings from the early

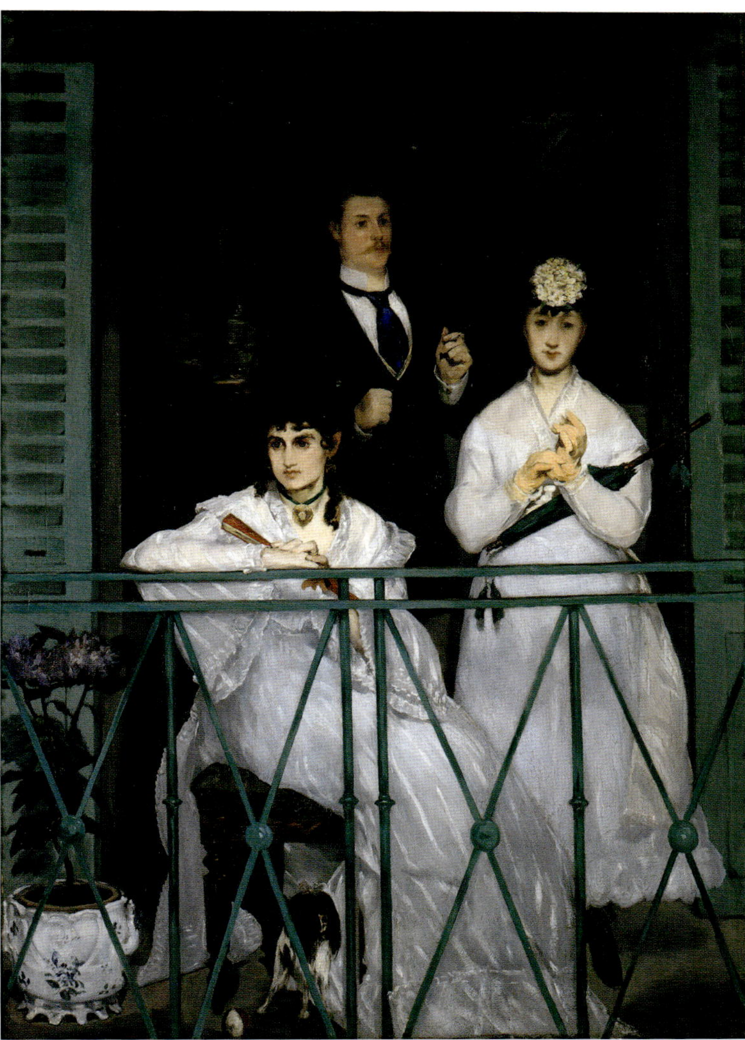

Édouard Manet
**The Balcony**, 1868–69
Oil on canvas
67 × 50 in.
Musée d'Orsay, Paris

1990s. Why Wollheim's statement about how "we anticipate the vehemence with which, once their heads clear, the two protagonists will re-enter the moment,"[29] which was actually written about Manet's 1879 *In the Winter Garden*, so clearly evokes Thiebaud's *Eating Figures*? Or we might question why his characterization of Manet's group paintings as manifestations of "momentary withdrawal, of abstraction, of secretiveness, along with a strong register of physical presence, by the particular way in which he captures the fleeting relations—the non-relations [. . .] between the members of the group" so perfectly describes Thiebaud's *Five Sitting Figures*, whose "transient mood" also "was established by the oblique gaze, the averted look, the failure of one pair of eyes to look into another—with the implicit sense that all this could change from one moment to the next, so that, as concentration returned, communication would be re-established."[30]

Perhaps the answer to all these questions rests in Wollheim's and Thiebaud's shared fascination with the ambiguity of painting—the only art form that could be perceived simultaneously as a marked surface and as a realistic illusion of life. Wollheim thought that Manet was able to retain the balance between these two modalities, ensuring what he called the "twofoldness" of his paintings by emphasizing the *matière*, "the empathic thematization of the brushstroke." Neither imagination nor perception could be allowed to dominate: "Manet seeks to activate the aspect of twofoldness that imagination occludes: that is, awareness of the marked surface." Whenever the external spectator is in danger of losing sight of the marked surface, it is the painter's task to use the resources of his medium to regain balance. Wollheim offers the example of the evolution of Manet's portrait of Théodore Duret, whose recollections of his sittings confirm that Manet added embellishments to the portrait (impasto brushwork, stronger colors) after the fact. He did so "to recall the external spectator to twofoldness, from which he had been induced to depart" because the portrait was too much of an illusion of real life, which made the external spectator lose track of the *matière*. In the case of Manet, "embellishment is deployed so that imagined entry into the picture-space is cut short and the spectator is returned to ordinary seeing-in."[31]

I believe that Thiebaud did something similar in the recent reworking of the 2003–8 canvas *The Speaker* (P. 134). Wollheim, who died in 2003, the year the painting was started, did not pose for it, and although Thiebaud drew the scholar on multiple occasions, *The Speaker* is a generalized representation, not a portrait. It is painted from imagination. In 2019, Thiebaud adjusted some colors and added writing to the blackboard in the background, thus effectively bringing it forward, all the while intensifying the impasto brushwork. These changes shifted the image from looking like an illustration of "a type" (a lecturer), in the vein of Norman

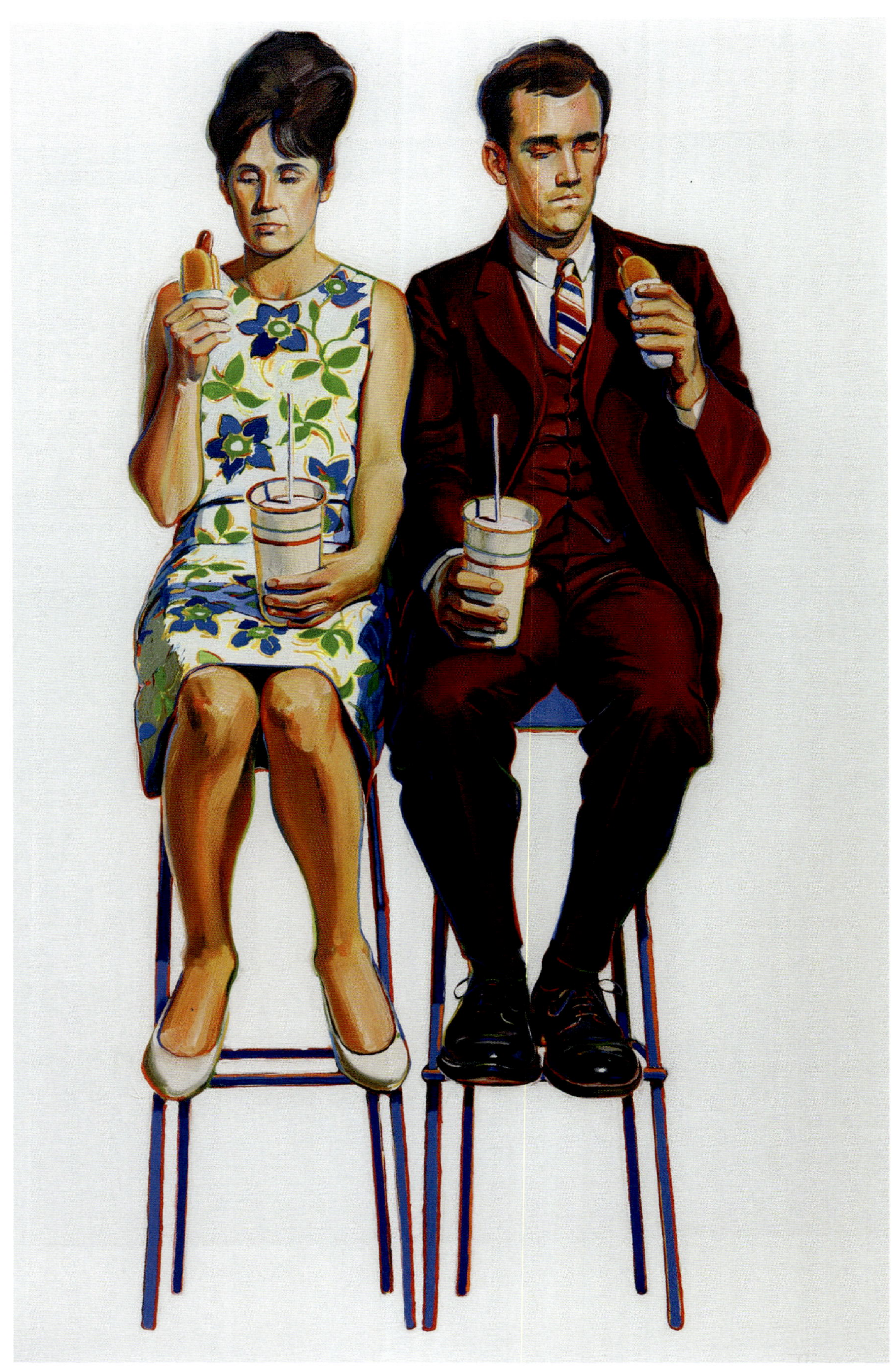

Wayne Thiebaud
**Eating Figures (Quick Snack)**, 1963
Oil on canvas
71 ½ × 47 ½ in.
Private Collection

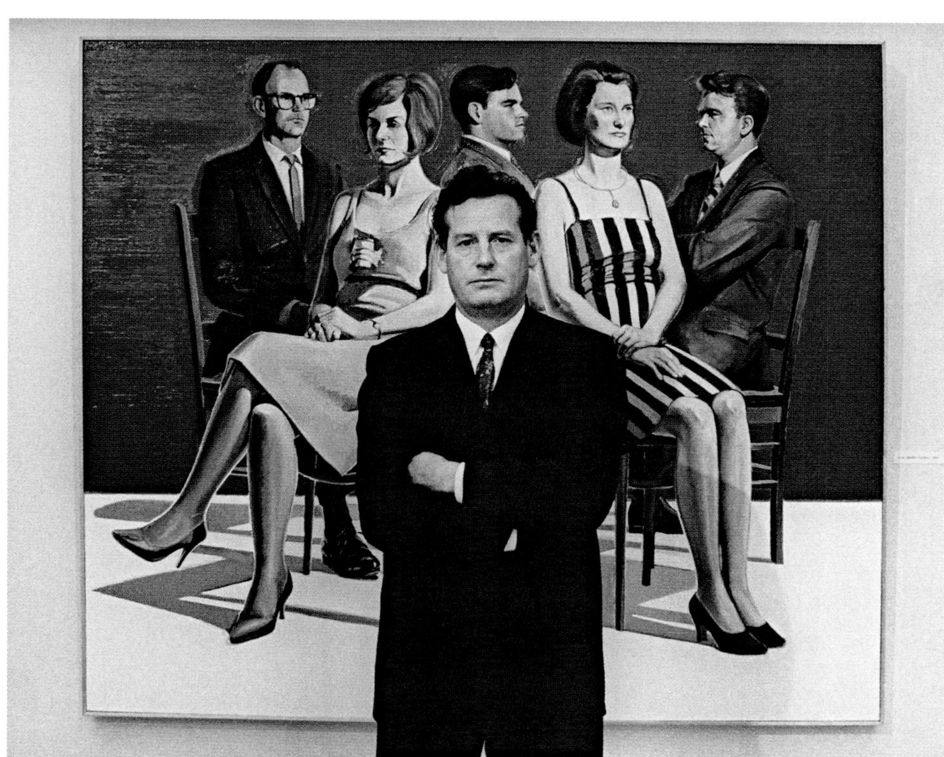

Wayne Thiebaud in front of **Five Sitting Figures**, 1965
© The Estate of Leo Holub

Rockwell, to making the external spectator irrevocably aware of the marked surface. The reworking was the way to highlight the *matière*, by juxtaposing the impasto of the figure with the smooth anonymity of the lectern, which is a prop, both literally and formally—a broad, uninterrupted geometrical block that contains and constrains the human figure. This is precisely the kind of adjustment from the explicit to the implicit that Wollheim describes Manet performing, as the painter added the embellishments via color and impasto, to realign the imagination and perception of Duret's portrait into perfect twofoldness.

Of course, the question of balance between the marked surface and the image in the painting has been the holy grail of painting since the Renaissance, and several Old Masters have been credited with obtaining it. Both Thiebaud and Manet had Velázquez in their sights as they pursued their own twofoldness. Wollheim cites Manet's reference to Velázquez's 1635 *Pablo de Valladolid* portrait at the Prado Museum as "perhaps the most astonishing piece of painting ever done." Thiebaud had always been aware that the quest for "the combination of round figures and a flat surface" began centuries ago, and that his attempts to solve this visual riddle are part of a historical continuum.[32] He told Adam Gopnik, only half-jokingly, that painting the figure was "practically impossible to do . . . [you] go to the Prado and see Velázquez, and then you are ready to shoot yourself." As Wollheim put it in his 1998 Thiebaud essay: "[a painter] becomes part of the tradition that he invokes."[33] Manet's paintings "were undertaken in direct competition with the Old Masters" and he "[saw] his task as finding an up-to-date equivalent for what his predecessors had done."[34] Thiebaud continued Manet's project, by translating Velázquez into the twentieth-century American vernacular.

Translating, however, does not mean simplifying. Thiebaud's all-American protagonist is considerably more complex than a crude template of West Coast Pop. Echoing the painter's real-life interests and associations, his protagonist is an amalgam of various subcultures: California leisure athletes, workers' union advocates, readers of Sartre, and spectators of Beckett's plays. The protagonist who acts as the external viewer's proxy in *Five Sitting Figures* possesses a knowledge of existentialist philosophy and of absurdism. In the mid-1970s, Gene Cooper contextualized this painting in an article on Thiebaud's engagement with the theatre in general, and with the Theatre of the Absurd in particular.[35] Cooper argued that the Theatre of the Absurd, with its realization that if "cut off from his religious, metaphysical, and transcendental roots, man is lost; all his actions become senseless, absurd, useless"[36] perfectly aligned with Thiebaud's approach to life, society, and art. He also saw a close kinship between the painter "representing his figures as stilled beings, inserted into a vacuous space" and the Absurdists relying on minimal means to generate maximal content.[37] Both shun falsely obligatory but superfluous action in favor of genuinely existential experiences.

In Thiebaud's case, it was the experience of looking at paintings. Without an overt, easily identified action to perform, the figures in *Five Sitting Figures* just "are,"[38] and it is up to the

Wayne Thiebaud
**Five Sitting Figures**, 1965
Oil on canvas
60 × 72 in.
Collection of Wayne Thiebaud Foundation

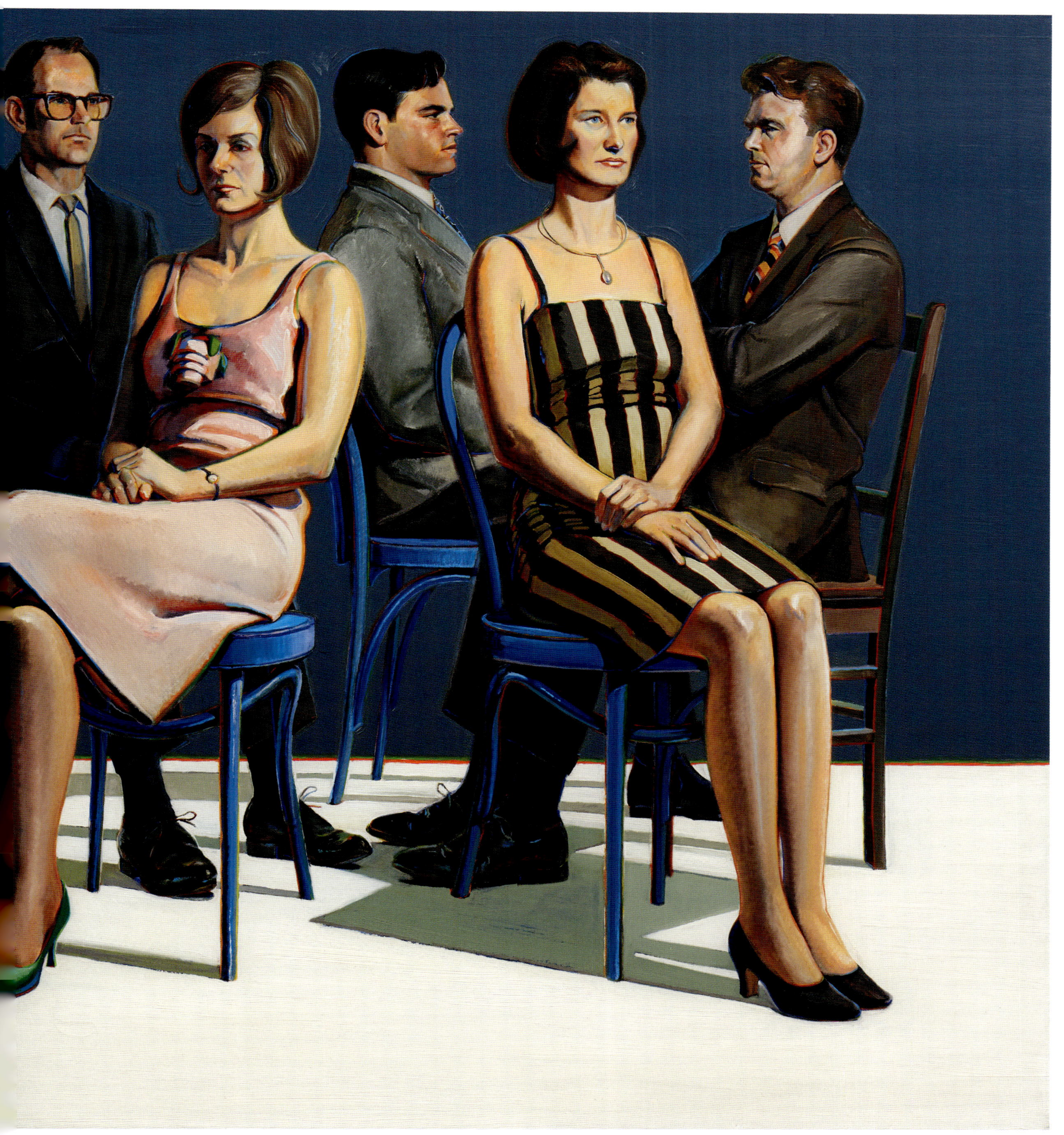

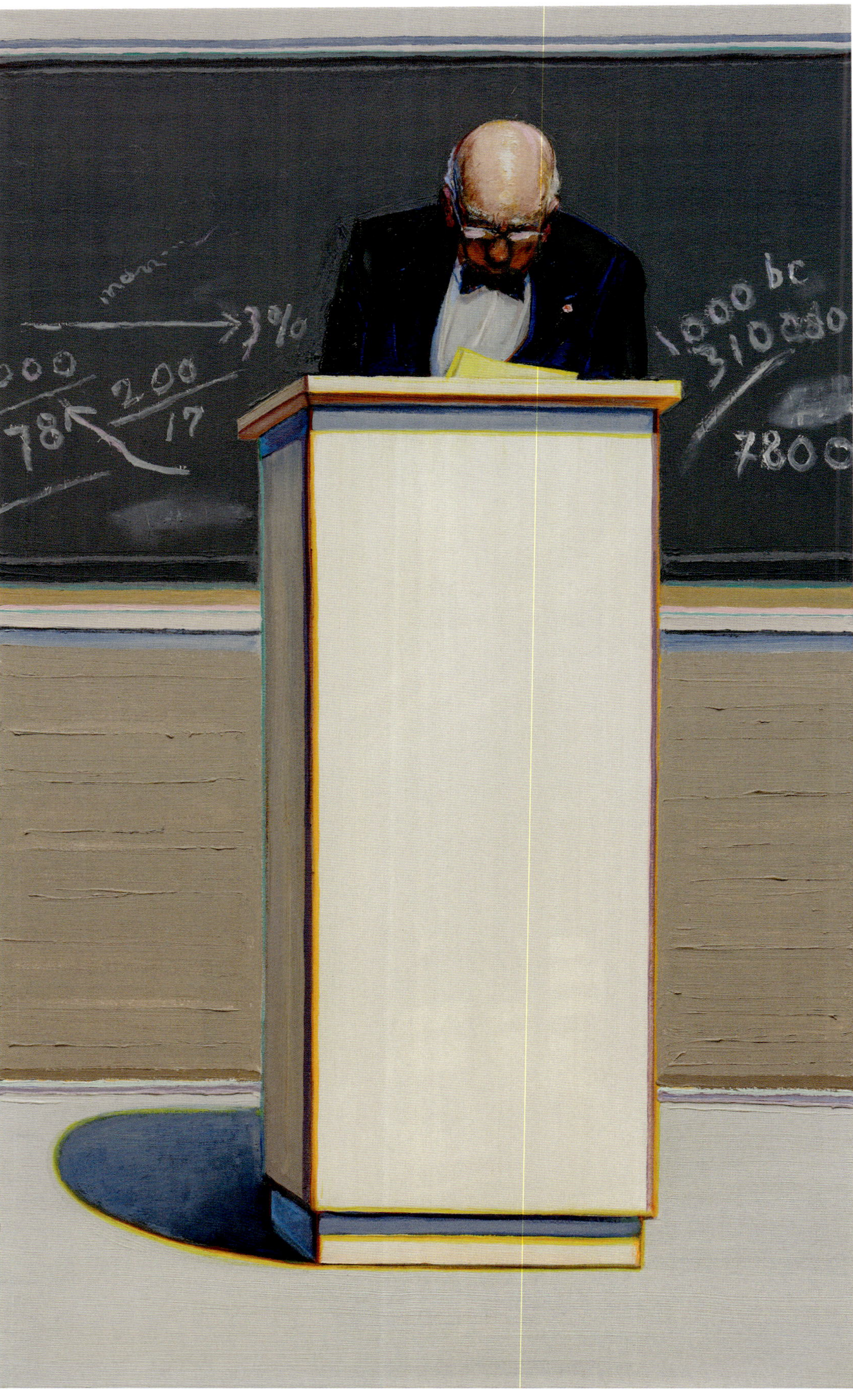




Wayne Thiebaud
**The Speaker**, 2003–8
Oil on canvas
48 × 30 in.
Collection of Wayne Thiebaud Foundation

external viewer "to feel the painting, or see the painting, or if the painting is going to mean anything—it has to come through you as well as through the painter."[39] The painter becomes the lingering protagonist in his own imagination, which he passes on to the external spectator.[40] By "stilling" the figures, by letting them just be, without engaging in any action or *purposefulness*, Thiebaud compelled his external spectators to take their time and *look* at his paintings. The same was true for his philosopher friend. Those who knew Richard Wollheim often commented on the unusual length of time he dedicated to looking at a single painting. So, while Thiebaud and Wollheim accepted that "anyone can be a protagonist," close looking was nonnegotiable.

Notes

1. On January 17. Originally broadcast on KQED for their City Arts & Lectures program. Introduced by Linda Hunt.
2. Richard Wollheim, "Wayne Thiebaud: Green River Lands, 1998." *Artforum* 38, no. 2 (October 1999): 134–35.
3. Richard Wollheim, "A Painter's Alchemy," *Modern Painters* 11, no. 2 (Summer 1998): 20–24.
4. Wollheim, 1998, 20.
5. Wollheim, 1998, 22.
6. Wollheim, 1998, 22.
7. Wollheim, 1998, 22.
8. Wollheim, 1998, 23.
9. Richard Wollheim, *Painting as an Art*. The A. W. Mellon Lectures in the Fine Arts, 1984. (Princeton: Princeton University Press, 1987). At some point Thiebaud attempted to substitute E. H. Gombrich's *Art and Illusion* (also based on the A. W. Mellon Lectures and published by Princeton UP) with Wollheim's *Painting as an Art* but students rebelled because they found the latter text too challenging. As Wollheim's Berkeley colleague Svetlana Alpers put it in his obituary: "the critical writing in *Painting as an Art* is exceedingly complex—in part because it is used to tease out elements of a general system." (*Artforum*, May 2004).
10. Bill Berkson, "Thiebaud on the Figure," in *Wayne Thiebaud. Figurative Works 1959–1994* (Wiegand Gallery. College of Notre Dame, 1994), n.p.
11. Norbert Schneider, *The Art of the Portrait: Masterpieces of European Portrait Painting 1420–1670* (Los Angeles: Taschen, 1999), 15.
12. Wollheim, 1998, 22.
13. Dan Tooker, "Wayne Thiebaud," *Art international* (November 1974): 22–25, 33. Cited in Tsujimoto, 105.
14. Wollheim, 1987, 101.
15. Wollheim, 1987, 102.
16. This is the case because, as Wollheim explains, "visual imagery . . . is inherently perspectival," and "it is only if it is imagined as occupied that, in imagining the event, I imagine from the inside someone seeing it, hence that I centrally imagine that event." Wollheim, 1987, 103.
17. Wollheim, 1987, 104.
18. Wollheim, 1987, 129.
19. Wollheim, 1987, 141.
20. Wollheim, 1987, 141.
21. Wollheim, 1987, 161.
22. Wollheim, 1987, 162.
23. Berkson, "Thiebaud on the Figure," n.p.
24. Karen Tsujimoto, "Figure Paintings," in *Wayne Thiebaud*. San Francisco Museum of Modern Art (Seattle & London: University of Washington Press, 1985), 103.
25. It is important to keep in mind that while Wollheim's multiple-spectator model might be useful in appreciating certain figure paintings, it is not a unified theory for interpreting all representational work. As Wollheim pointed out: ". . . *some* paintings contain a spectator in the picture. Some do: some don't. More precisely, some do, most don't." (1987, 103)
26. Wayne Thiebaud, "Personal Notes on Painting," in *Figures* (Palo Alto: Stanford Art Museum, Stanford University, 1965). Introduction by Gerald M. Ackerman, statement by the artist.
27. Wollheim, 1987, 161.
28. Wollheim, 1987, 149.
29. Wollheim, 1987, 155–56.
30. Wollheim, 1987, 157.
31. Wollheim, 1987, 166.
32. Thiebaud, "Personal Notes on Painting."
33. Wollheim, 1998, 22.
34. Wollheim, 1987, 142–43.
35. Gene Cooper, "Thiebaud, Theatre and Extremism," in *Wayne Thiebaud* (Phoenix: Phoenix Art Museum, 1976), 11–30.
36. Here, Cooper quotes Eugene Ionesco, 28.
37. In his interview with Bill Berkson, Thiebaud confirms that his minimal approach is part of a larger strategy.
38. In the exhibition catalogue for his 1985 retrospective at the San Francisco Museum of Modern Art, curator Karen Tsujimoto recognized Thiebaud's grounding in both mid-twentieth-century discourse, and in the Old Masters' treatment of the figure. Her astute argument accounts for the painter's continuous emphasis on his formal investigations, his skepticism of artistic conventions, his purposeful divestment of the personal and the anecdotal, his eschewing of narrative content, his ability to "evoke a sense of disquietude," and his propensity for painting the figure that "just is." Thiebaud's figure paintings freeze the moment, transfixing their sitters the way Edward Hopper froze his solitary subjects. Tsujimoto compares the viewer of Thiebaud's figures to a voyeur, who furtively catches them "in an instant of quiet expectancy." Tsujimoto, 1985, 106.
39. "Wayne Thiebaud with Hearne Pardee," *The Brooklyn Rail*, 2019. https://brooklynrail.org/2019/03/art/WAYNE-THIEBAUD-with-Hearne-Pardee.
40. "[W]hen I centrally imagine an event, the person whom I imagine from the inside must be me, or that I must be the protagonist in my imaginings." Wollheim, 1987, 103.

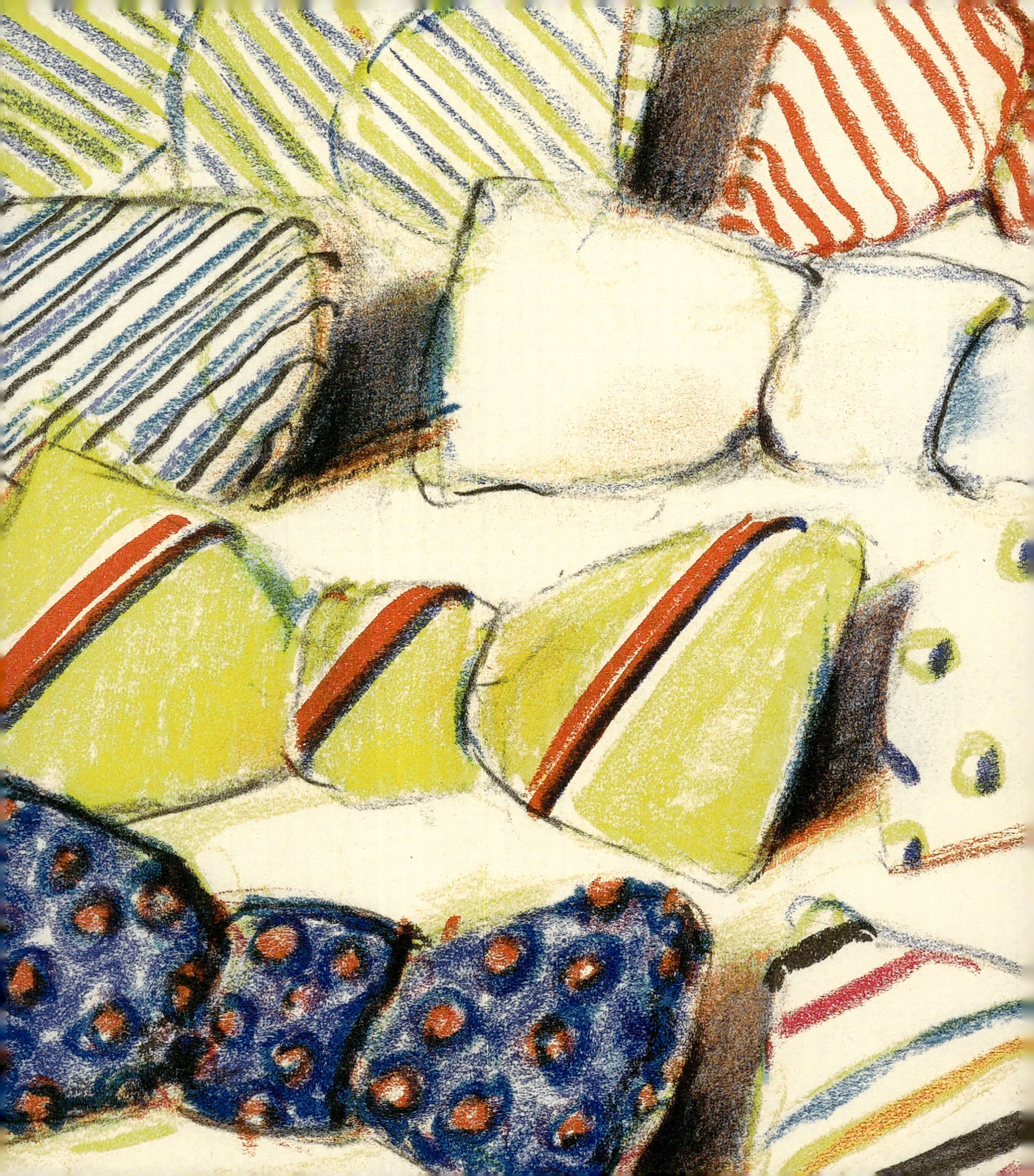

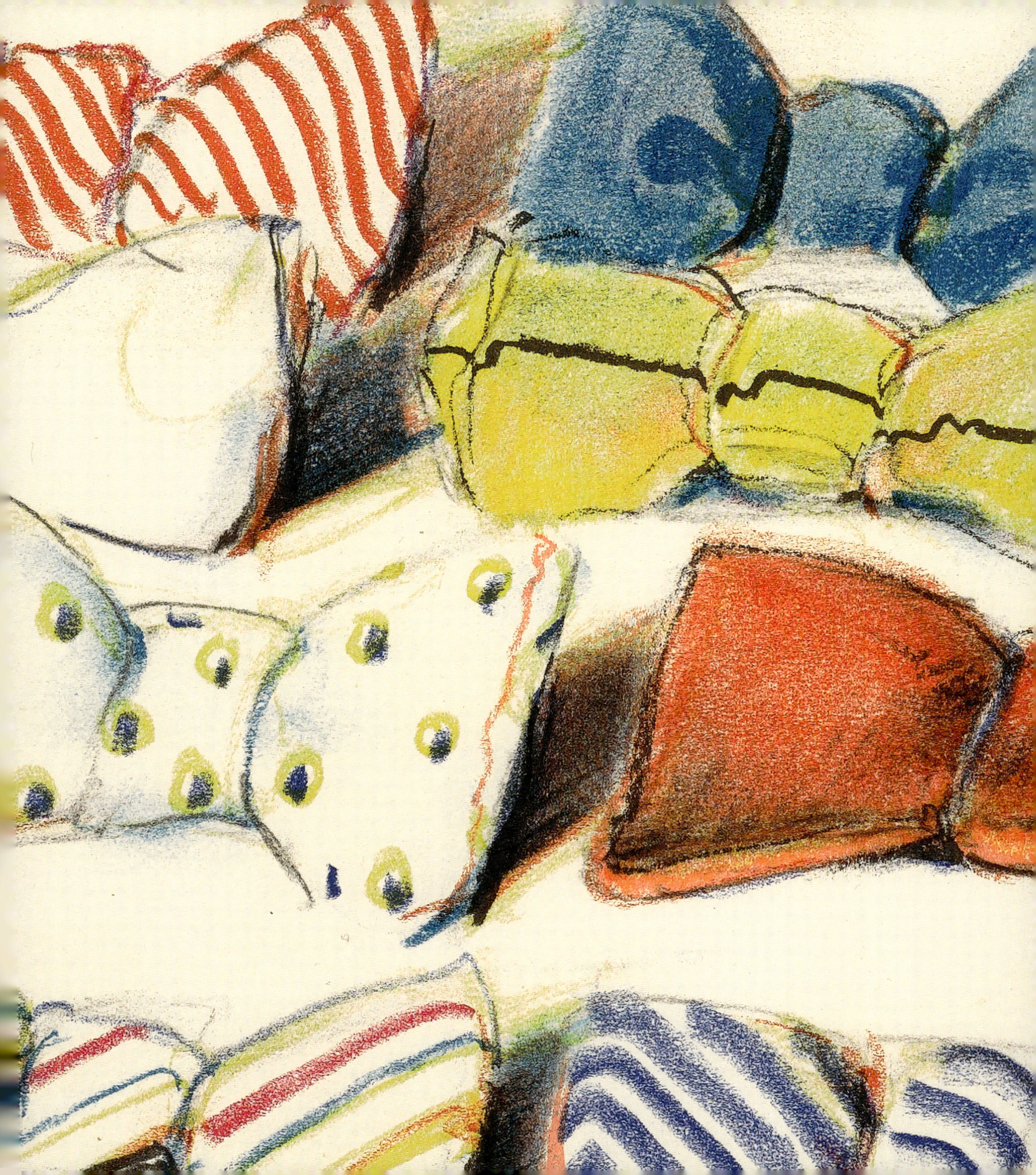

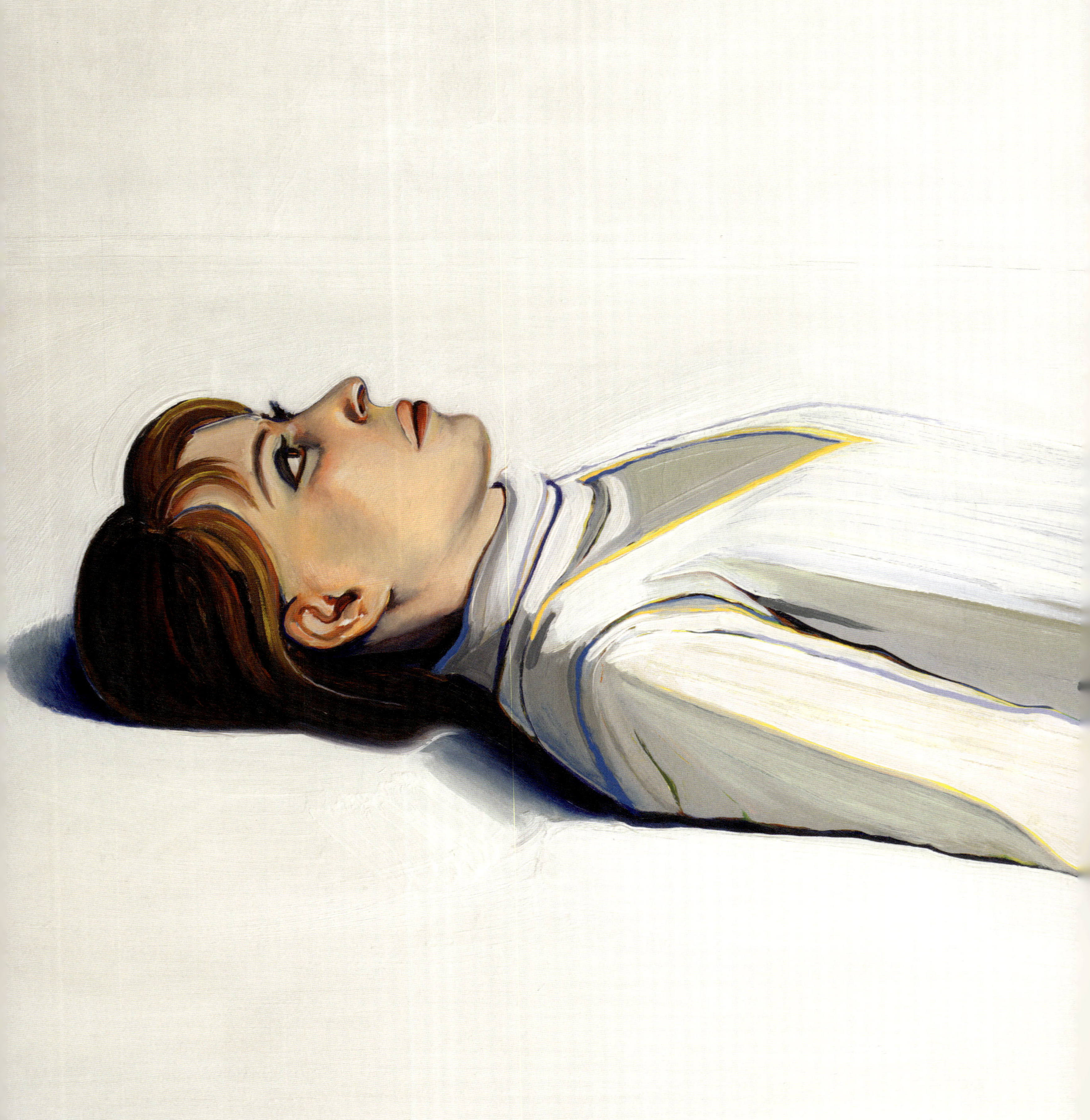

# Punch Lines: Anguish and Humor in Wayne Thiebaud's Lifework

Derrick R. Cartwright

> "I have only rarely painted steaks, but I have painted soup."
> — Wayne Thiebaud[1]

In an otherwise prescient review of the exhibition *New Painting of Common Objects* (P. 141), John Coplans miscast Wayne Thiebaud as a timid Pop wannabe. "He lacks the guts and total commitment of the rest of the others in this group," the critic claimed. Coplans went on to argue that "the anguish of the situation is not well enough reflected" in Thiebaud's contributions.[2] A row of hot dogs (P. 140), half a meringue pie, and another slice of dessert *à la mode* represented him in that early museum display. Today, those subjects seem perfectly typical of the artist from the vantage of more than sixty years' hindsight. We might ask "why anguish?," "what situation exactly?," and "how lacking?" Let's wait a bit to respond more fully to those questions. The context that produced them matters, however. In the fall of 1962, it is worth observing that, for some (including Coplans), the artist stood visibly apart from the others that Walter Hopps selected for his show at the Pasadena Art Museum: Andy Warhol, Roy Lichtenstein, Jim Dine, Ed Ruscha, Joe Goode, Philip Hefferton, and Robert O'Dowd. In meaningful ways, Thiebaud merits being considered separately from these peers but, I would argue, not in the ways so coarsely outlined in Coplans's *Artforum* review.

At forty-two, Thiebaud was slightly older than the rest of this group, Lichtenstein being his nearest contemporary among the *New Painting* artists. He was already being slotted into the emerging stereotype of the blissfully angst-free Northern California painter and soon enjoyed success in other major museums throughout the region (P. 141). Finally, Coplans viewed his identity as the lone academic artist in the group as a decisive proof of difference from the others. Goode worked at Chouinard Art Institute but was excused by Coplans for only "doing odd jobs" at this time, in contrast to Thiebaud, who had taught professionally for the better part of a decade before being appointed to the rank of an assistant professor in UC Davis's art department in 1960. Taken together, these attributes were proof that his approach missed the targeted "crisis" and "loneliness" that distinguished the other Pop works clustered in New York and Southern California. We can say with confidence, now, those traits were never Thiebaud's primary concerns, although they bubble up from time to time throughout his prodigious lifework.

It is not an aim of this essay to quarrel about Coplans's poor ranking of Thiebaud among the likes of Warhol, Lichtenstein, and Ruscha. However, not all critics of that time believed the painter was so blithely unaware of

Wayne Thiebaud, **Supine Woman** (detail), 1963

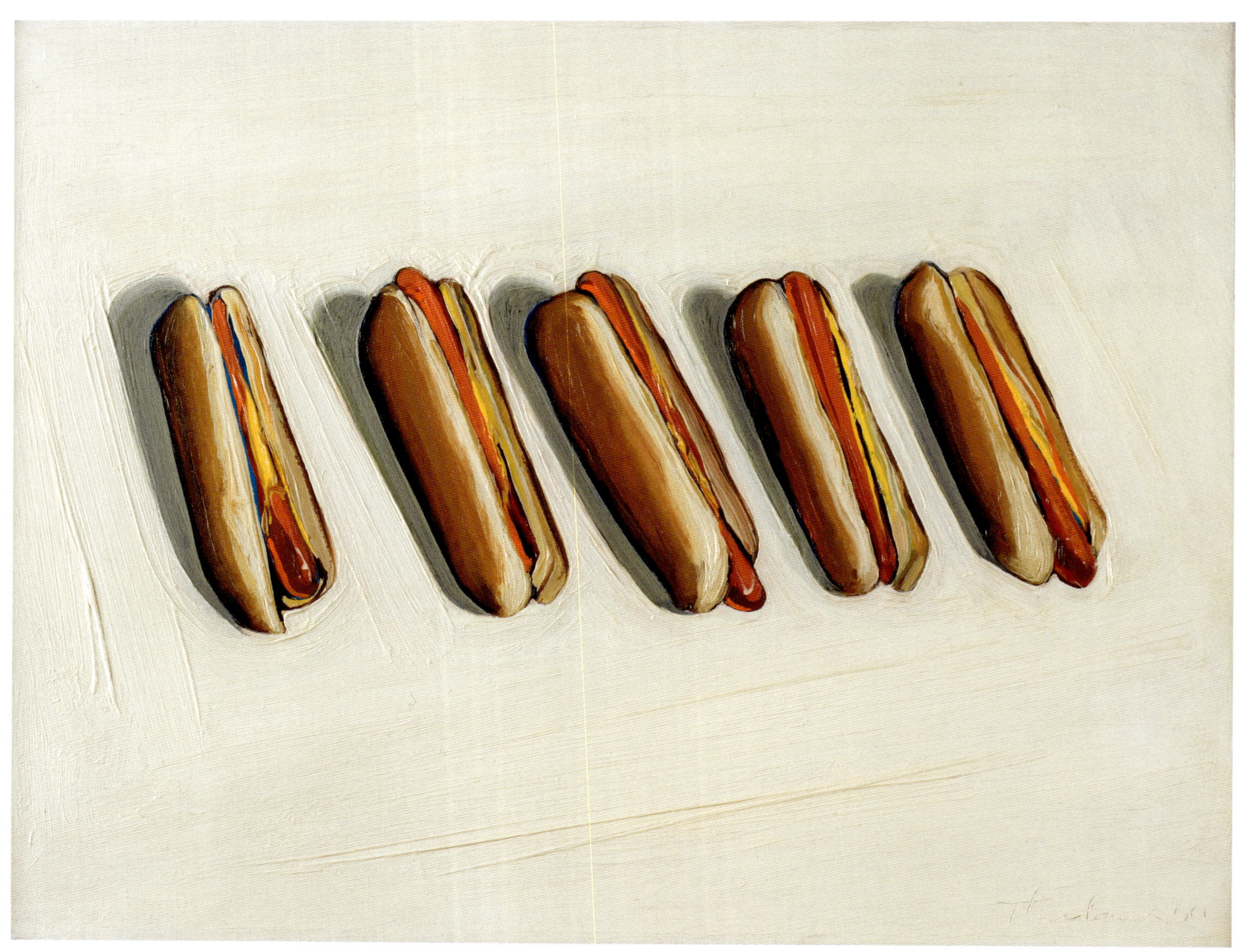

Wayne Thiebaud
**Five Hot Dogs**, 1961
Oil on canvas
18 × 24 in.
Private Collection

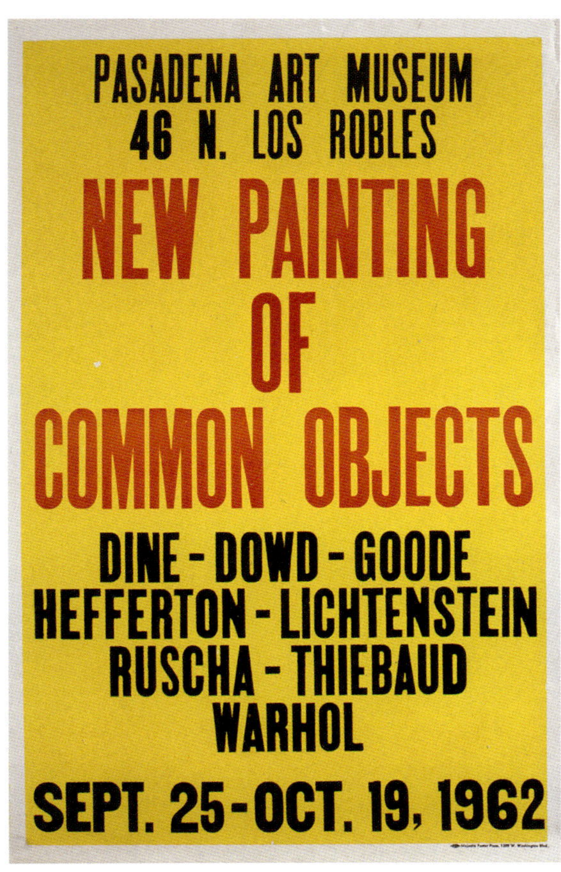


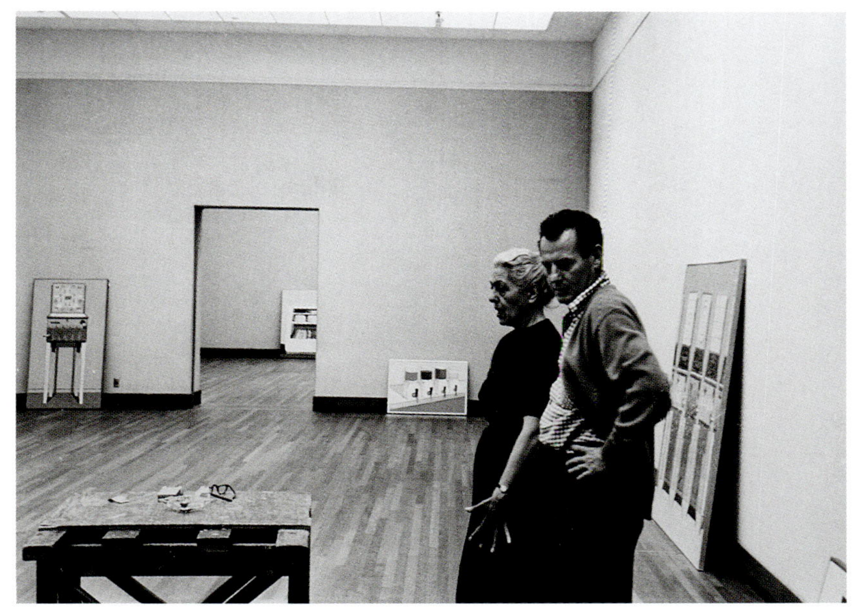



the surrounding cultural milieu.[3] For his own part, the artist himself never fully accepted the Pop sobriquet that was soon to be applied to this same clan of artists and which served to join him, episodically, to their efforts.[4] It still seems worth noting that identifying Thiebaud as "clever and flippant, rather than deeply perceptive" is unfair, at bottom, and misses the painter's fine regard for the canonical aims of realism, which might often include registering some anguish. While Pop art busily critiqued and turned a skeptical eye toward consumer culture, Thiebaud could appear slightly less detached, but he always remained alert to the complex, seductive appeal of mass culture. If Coplans was predisposed to discount the mid-career, academically ensconced California artist, it bears recalling that this British-born critic helped found *Artforum* magazine on the West Coast in the year that this review appeared. In the early sixties, within the context of a West Coast project like *New Painting of Common Objects*, Thiebaud's superficially guileless gestures toward both the history of art and presentist appetites offered a puzzling mix for still-evolving positions among artists and critics alike.[5] Not unlike Thiebaud, Coplans was himself happily performing multiple roles, having recently taught at UC Berkeley and Chouinard, all the while exhibiting his own artwork.[6]

Only a short time later, this critic had the opportunity to rethink his initial, negative assessments of the West Coast artist. As the guest curator for a solo exhibition of Thiebaud's recent work at the Pasadena Art Museum in 1968, Coplans was kinder (P. 142). Edginess and social commentary were never truly missing from the painter's essential aesthetic outlook, it turned out. What changed? The critical discourse around Pop's presumed superiority over the merely banal had progressed in the interim, without question. Thiebaud's favored iconography, not so much. Although never one to bother with correcting the art world snubs directed toward him, the painter took time on subsequent occasions to clarify his position regarding his choice of everyday subject matter. Consider the ideas expressed in a later

LEFT
Ed Ruscha
**New Painting of Common Objects**, 1962
Letterpress
40 × 26 ⅛ in.
Museum of Modern Art, New York
© Ed Ruscha

RIGHT
Wayne Thiebaud installing *An Exhibition of Paintings by Wayne Thiebaud* with curator Ninfa Valvo at the M. H. de Young Memorial Museum, July 1962
Collection of Wayne Thiebaud Foundation

interview that reflected upon the place of "common objects" in his oeuvre:

> We have a tendency to overlook the gumball machine (P. 143), perhaps because of its commonness. But there are also funny reasons—we turn away from such things in a way as if we were playing down our senses . . . In many gumball machines there are other things to note—one may have one's fortune told, one can comb one's hair in a mirror, there is no end to the way one can get involved in a simple thing like a gumball machine; so, calling it a commonplace object is really a bit simplistic, I think. We tend toward a sort of over-simplistic preoccupation, it is helpful, but when you think about a gumball machine, it is both a most elementary mechanism and a gadget for stimulating the grandest sort of associations and references. Thus, one can see how difficult it is to sift out the reasons why one gets interested in a particular object—why one paints people—why one is interested in pies.[7]



Coin-operated machinery, tempting sweets, and other ready-to-consume foods (PP. 144 AND 145), isolated bodies, and vertiginous landscapes became the mainstays of Thiebaud's output for the next fifty years, *pace* their commonplace appearances. Their worthiness as subject matter was part of an abiding concern—the "funny reasons"—that surrounds the spaces and circumstances of everyday life. Another way of saying this: Thiebaud was nothing if not "perceptive" when making choices. In his many interviews, the artist repeatedly made clear that these common subjects implicate us, in the same way that Édouard Manet's *A Bar at the Folies-Bergère* (1882) implicates the spectator in its dancehall-of-mirrors abyss (P. 147). These works reflect the artist, and us, in deliberate ways, maybe not always with obvious anguish, but also not without some pervasive sense of loneliness and disaffection. In what follows, I want to retrace these mixed origins, both in the artist's early career and as part of the modern realist tradition in which Thiebaud excelled, energized, and ultimately excepted himself. All the while, I want to chase the terms that Coplans employs and overtly values: being gutsy, showing commitment, communicating anguish. These are likely at play within Thiebaud's practice from the start, too, albeit masked by a comic sensibility, one rooted in the artist's own modesty, as well as his astute awareness of formidable art historical precedents. Throughout, it is the artist's own ideas that help navigate our evolving sense of urgent realism.

Even a quick scan of the scholarship devoted to Thiebaud reveals abundant references to his art historical heroes and models, not to say "influences." A learned artist, he knew his sources and celebrated them without ever limiting himself to their simple emulation. Like so many committed lifelong pupils of art, he made copies based on his realist forerunners including, for example, vignettes based on Honoré Daumier.[8] He also talked about these sources. Few artists possess the degree of critical and art historical fluency that Thiebaud brought to his practice, a familiarity that extended from the Renaissance up to his own moment, embracing Paolo Veronese and Giorgio Morandi alike.[9] Indeed, from the beginning of his career, Thiebaud considered

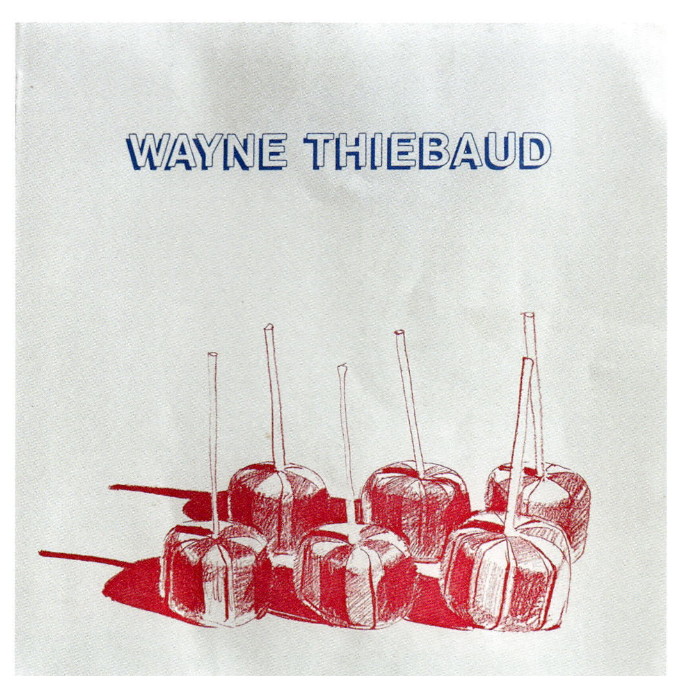


John Coplans, *Wayne Thiebaud* exhibition catalogue (Pasadena Art Museum, 1968) Collection of author

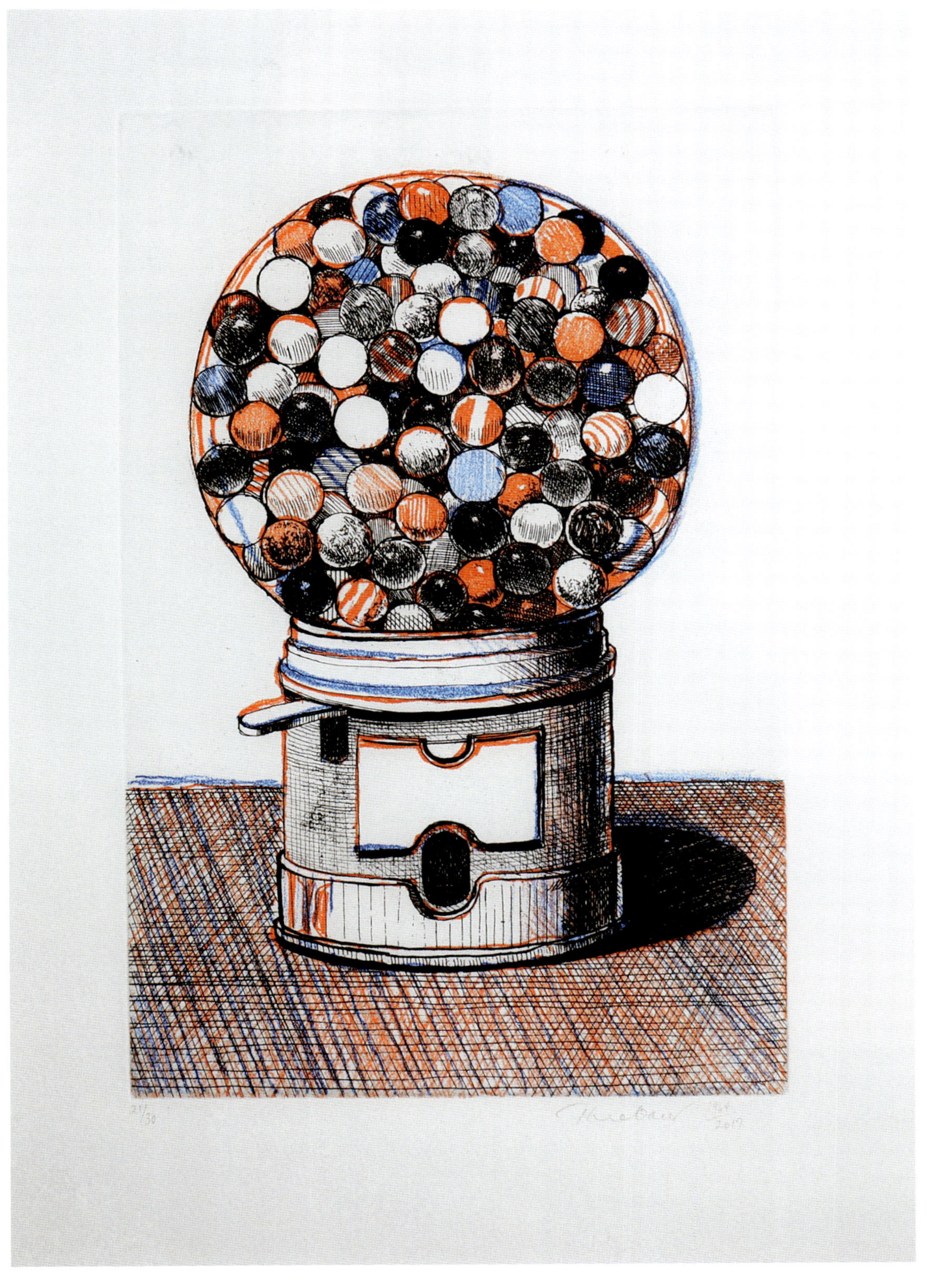



Wayne Thiebaud
**Gumball Machine**, 1964–2017
Color etching
17 ⅞ × 13 in.
University of San Diego Print Collection

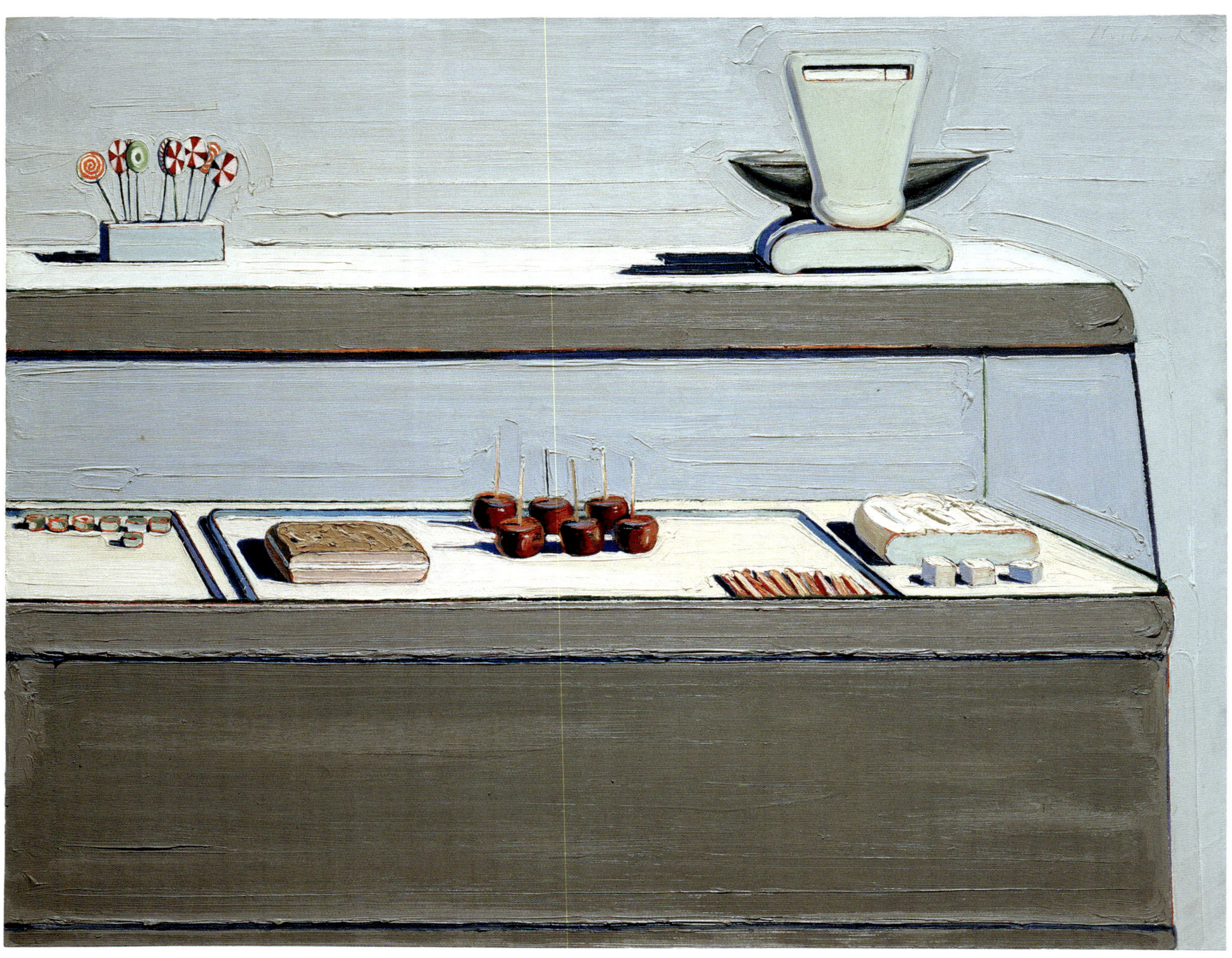

Wayne Thiebaud
**Candy Counter**, 1962
Oil on canvas
55 ⅛ × 72 in.
Anderson Collection at Stanford University
Gift of Harry W. and Mary Margaret
Anderson, and Mary Patricia Anderson Pence
2014.1.006

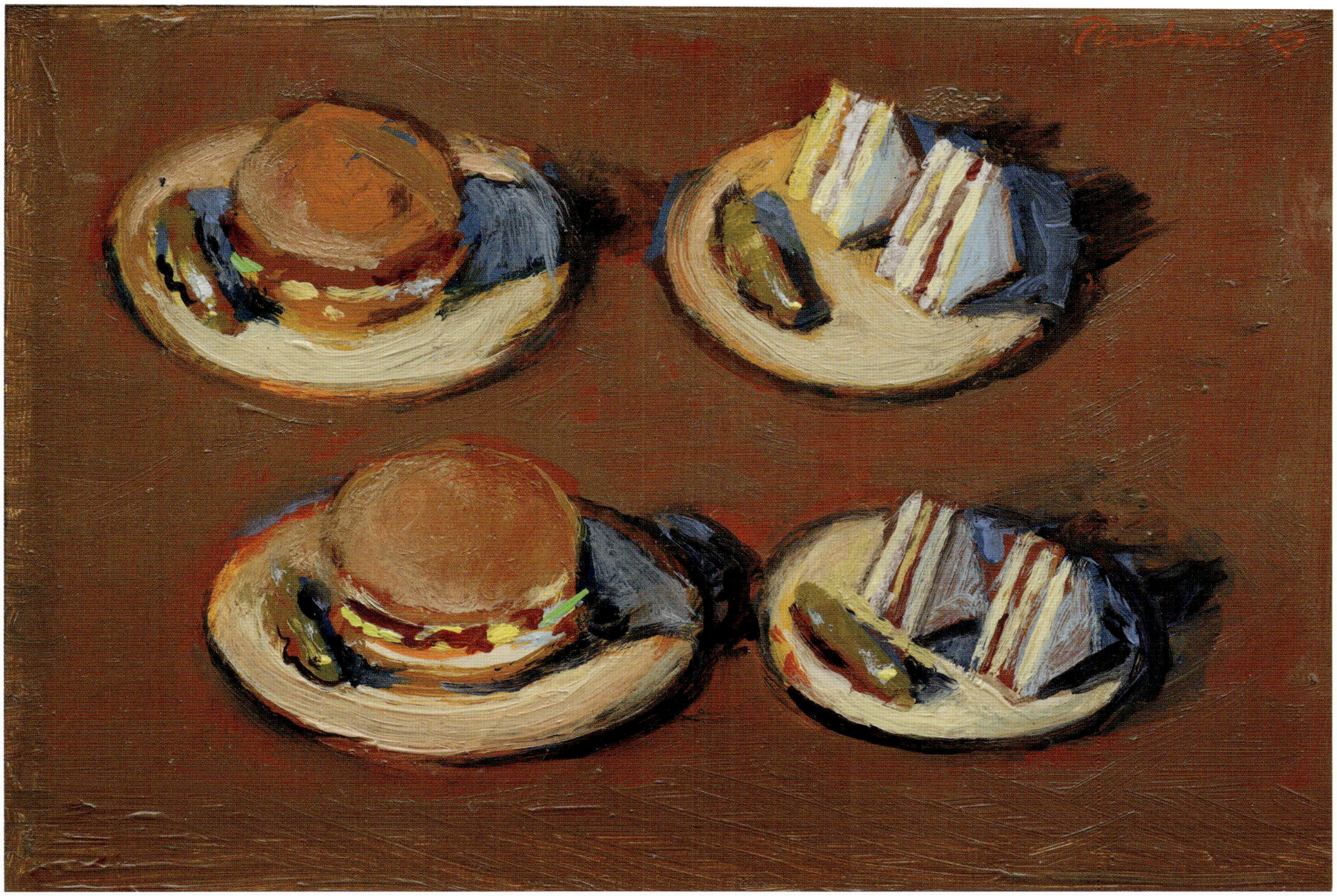

Wayne Thiebaud
**Four Sandwiches**, ca. 2003
Oil on illustration board
4 ¾ × 7 13/16 in.
Private Collection

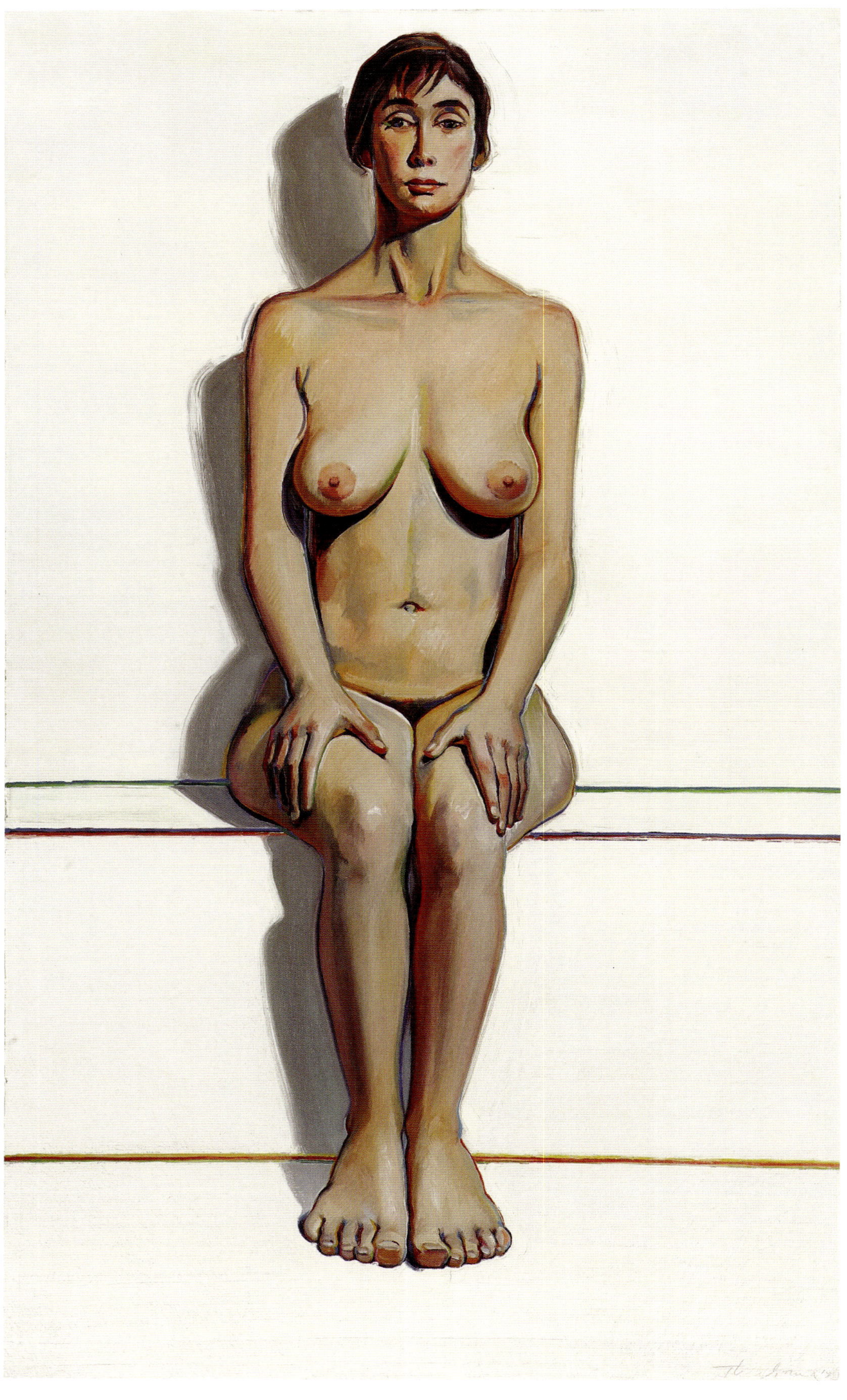

Wayne Thiebaud
**Nude**, 1963
Oil on canvas
60 ⅛ × 36 ¼ in.
Private Collection

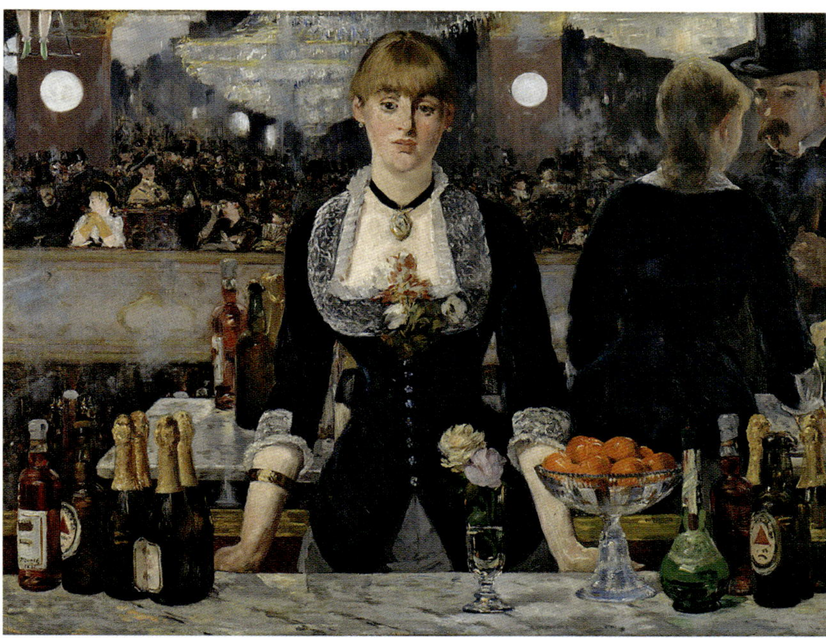

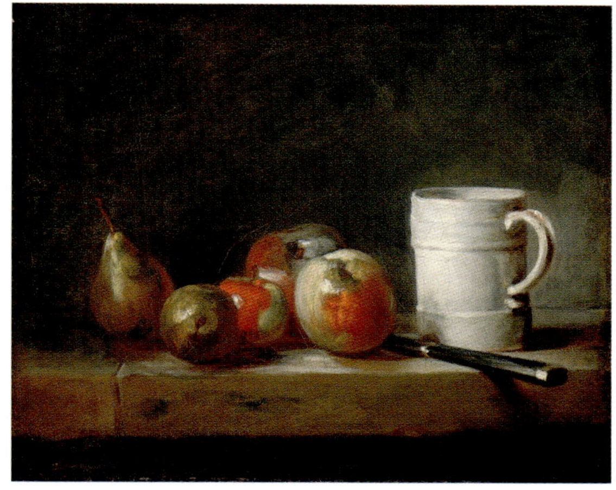

LEFT
Édouard Manet
**A Bar at the Folies-Bergère**, 1882
Oil on canvas
38 × 51 in.
The Courtauld Institute of Art, London
(Samuel Courtauld Trust)
P.1934.SC.234

RIGHT
Jean Siméon Chardin
**Still Life with a White Mug**, ca. 1764
Oil on canvas
13 ¹⁄₁₆ × 16 ¼ in.
Courtesy National Gallery of Art,
Washington, DC
Gift of the W. Averell Harriman Foundation
in memory of Maria N. Harriman

the offerings of the automat in terms of their historical relationship to the pies baked in open air ovens that appear in the peasant revels of Pieter Bruegel the Elder. Similarly, the humble objects depicted with lavish care in an eighteenth-century still life by Jean Siméon Chardin (ABOVE RIGHT) were a source of wonderment and deep admiration, qualities that informed his own spare plates of sardines (P. 148), teetering rows of cupcakes, or stands of ice cream cones (P. 149). Jacques-Louis David's *À Marat* (1793) provided Thiebaud with a striking inspiration for *Woman in Tub* (1965), which captivated viewers at both his Stanford University and Allan Stone Gallery exhibitions in 1965, the year in which it was painted (PP. 150 AND 151). "One of the problems was to in some way devise a painting of a person in a bathtub that did not look too much like the David painting," the artist later reflected.[10] While not expressing anguish, per se, the artist's framing of his belated position as a "problem" is worth remarking. Others have observed these persistent affiliations and explored them more thoroughly than I will attempt here.[11] For now, let's suggest again that these self-conscious echoes resound with a sense of concern for the present situation. It was a representational issue potentially visible to astute spectators of the time, although not everyone took the time to observe it as such. David's portrait of a revolutionary martyr presages Thiebaud's tragic bather while not overdetermining it. In the same way that his earlier painting of an *Electric Chair* (1957) summons a cultural outrage that was later shared by Warhol, *Woman in Tub* offers renewable commentary on the weariness, the roughness, the ennui, of modern life.



Among French artists, none, perhaps, was more enduringly meaningful to Thiebaud than Manet. Although Thiebaud's career nearly doubled the length of Manet's, both stand out as long-term, insightful observers of a public sphere in abrupt and discomforting transition. They, too, shared interests in working across a variety of media—oil painting, pastels, monotypes, and etchings were familiar to both men. Working a century apart, the two artists observed urban landscapes and peopled interiors alike with a shared circumspection. Recall that Manet's and Thiebaud's sitters are uniformly bourgeois in dress, except only when clownishly costumed or unclothed, and as such they seem equally eager to press on the limits of their respective moments' mainstream standards. Similar to his admiration of Morandi's merger of hard material and abstract

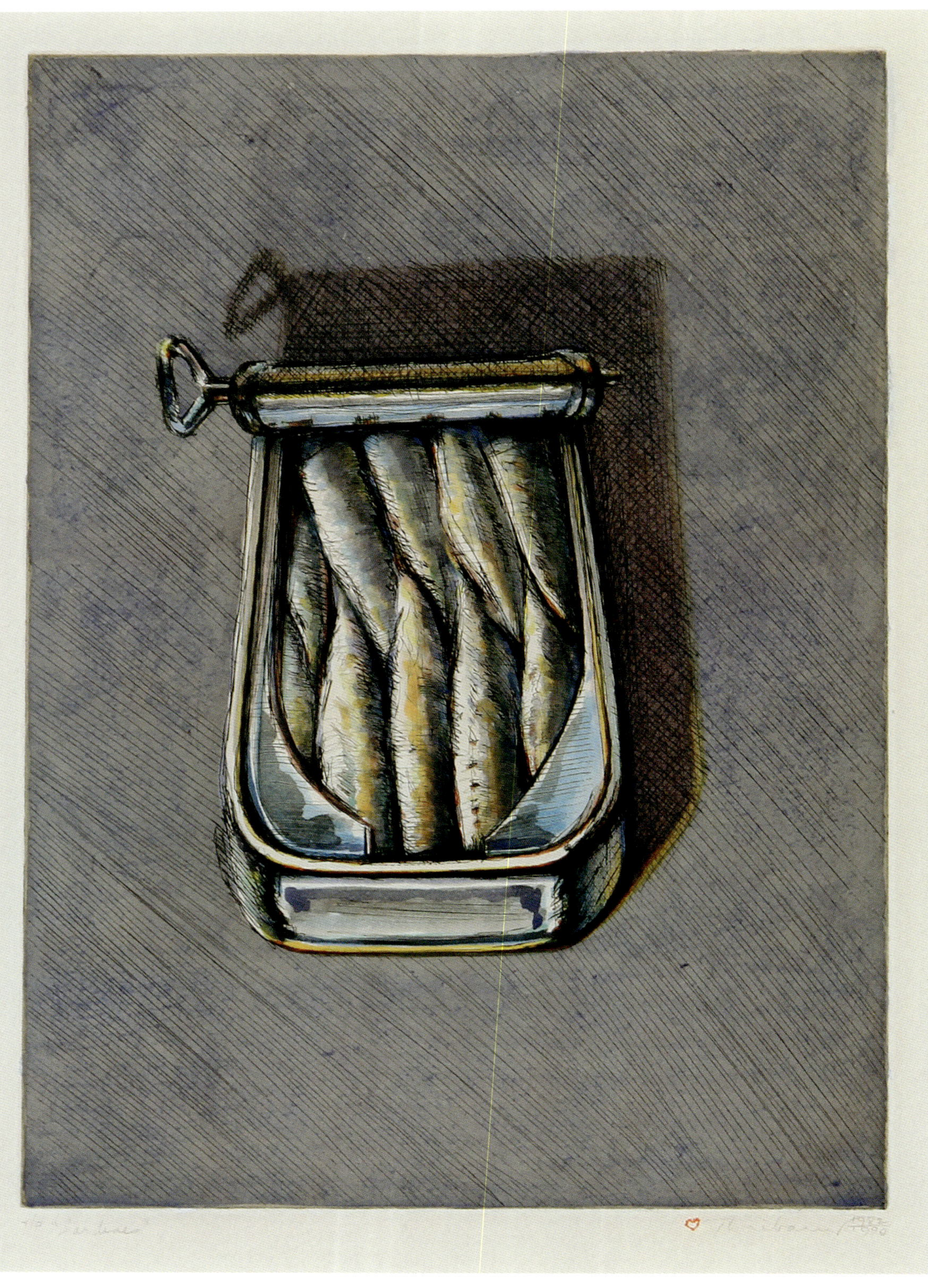

Wayne Thiebaud
**Sardines**, 1982/1990
Watercolor over hardground etching
16 $\frac{9}{16}$ x 12 $\frac{7}{8}$ in.
Private Collection

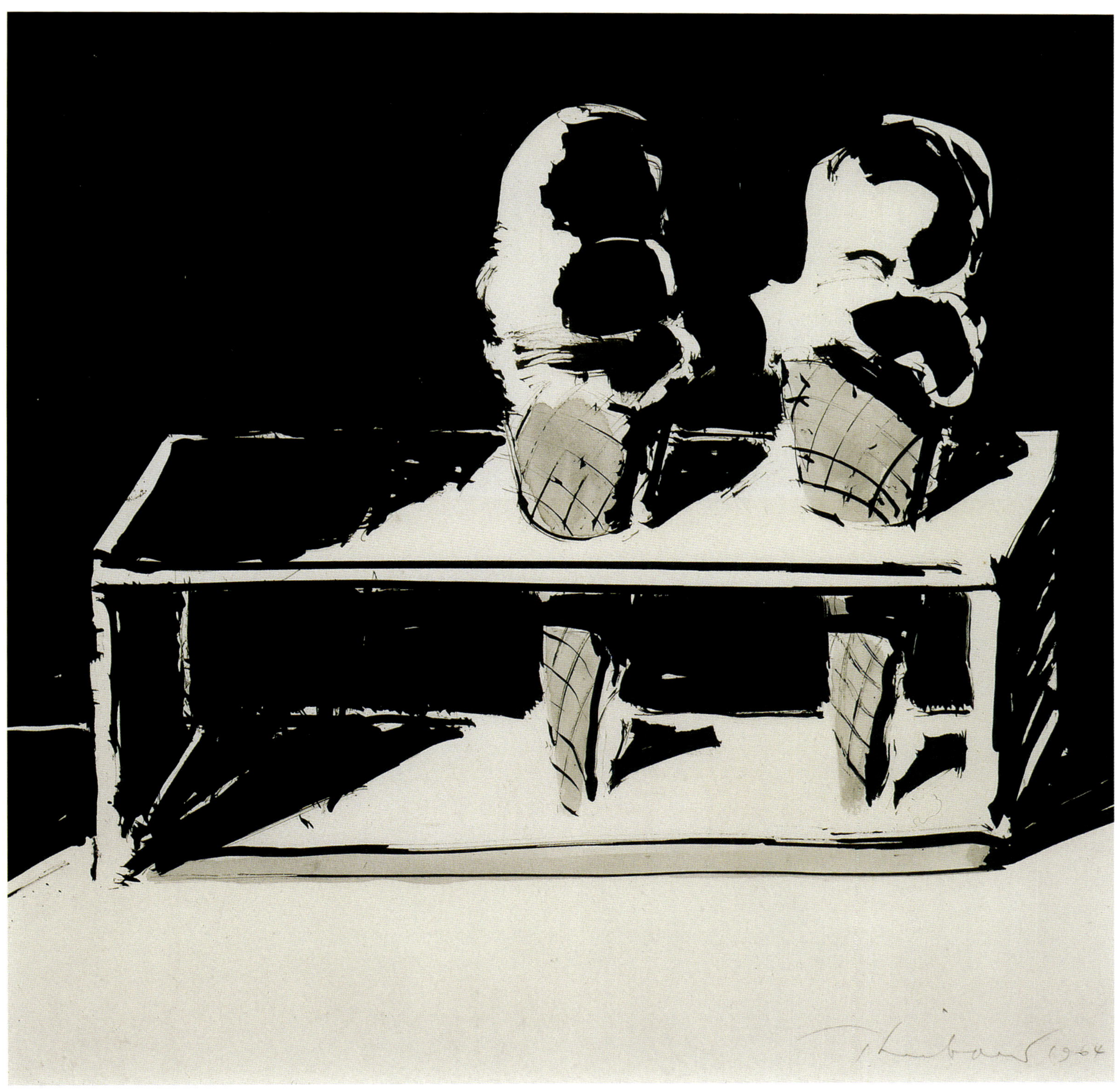




Wayne Thiebaud
**Ice Cream Cones**, 1964
Ink and wash on paper
11 × 11 ½ in.
Private Collection

ideals, Thiebaud's large reverence for Manet begs viewers to consider their shared, canny ability to bring modern life, along with many of its attendant cultural contradictions, into lastingly sharp if disgruntled focus.

A delicate pencil drawing of a nude (P. 152) by Thiebaud from the 1970s, for instance, recalls the extreme foreshortening of the body in Manet's *The Dead Toreador* (ca. 1864) (P. 153). At the same time, the careful study mirrors the frank insolence of his notorious *Olympia* (1863). A painting like *Supine Woman* (1963) (PP. 154–55) goes still further in its direct acknowledgment of Manet as a highly significant art-historical precedent. Like Manet, the twentieth-century painter employs a blunt touch that, while somewhat heavier in impasto than his precursor's, bears close consideration. The dark outline of the human form that drew such harsh rebukes from conservative critics in the 1860s became a standard practice in Thiebaud's repertoire a full century later. Similarly, the smooth strokes of paint that make up a plate of asparagus by Manet are cousins to the lush application of pure color that makes an early grocery-shelf painting like *Half Salmon* (1961) such a success. The fluid application of color enables Thiebaud to construct a bowl of cherries—a subject he turned to on multiple occasions—in ways that trace back to Manet's *Street Singer* (ca. 1862) where the well-known model Victorine Meurent consumes cherries from a paper sack nestled precariously by her elbow. The way in which the French realist celebrates the fruit and the concomitant invitation to consume are sources of lasting admiration, forces that persist well into the twentieth century, penetrating Thiebaud's repertoire.

Let's pause to reflect on the most durable source of realist wonderment for Thiebaud: Manet's *A Bar at the Folies-Bergère*. As art historians have never grown tired of pointing out, the inscrutable look on the face of Manet's server hovers someplace between boredom and exasperation. Placed as she is at the apex of the pyramidal composition, this young person's expression cannot help but seem at merciless odds with her jubilant surroundings. The French painter implores us to consider the bartender's hapless condition and, in so doing, invites us to consider that we—like the hatted bourgeois drinker reflected in the large mirrored glass behind her—are ourselves a source of her general dismay.[12] In a series of works created over a long stretch of time, Thiebaud pays homage to this forlorn commercial situation. Starting in the 1960s, the artist experimented with expressionless, vulnerable figures placed in direct confrontation with their viewers, celebrating their indifference. Typically, these compositions featured women housed in ticket-vending booths, or locked into fortune-teller kiosks, or behind glass display counters, conditions which highlight their constriction and reinforce these pictures' relationship to Manet's scene at the *café concert*.[13] The culmination of this concern can be seen in a series of works that stage these encounters in terms that still more closely reflect Manet's memorable strategy. These works, all of which feature women wearing fine clothing and positioned so that their actions are limited, suggest that *A Bar at the Folies-Bergère* was a familiar situation, one not witnessed without a sense of anguish, that intrigued Thiebaud.

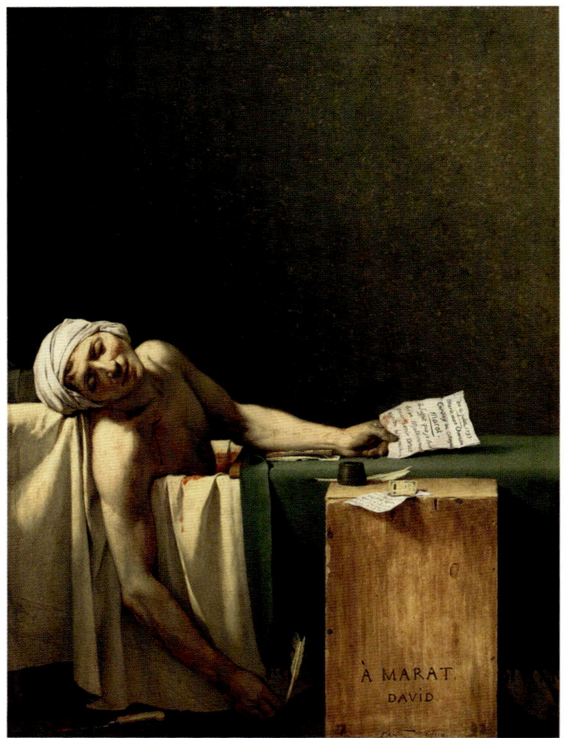


Jacques-Louis David
**À Marat**, 1793
Oil on canvas
64 × 50 in.
Musées royaux des Beaux-Arts de Belgique, Brussels

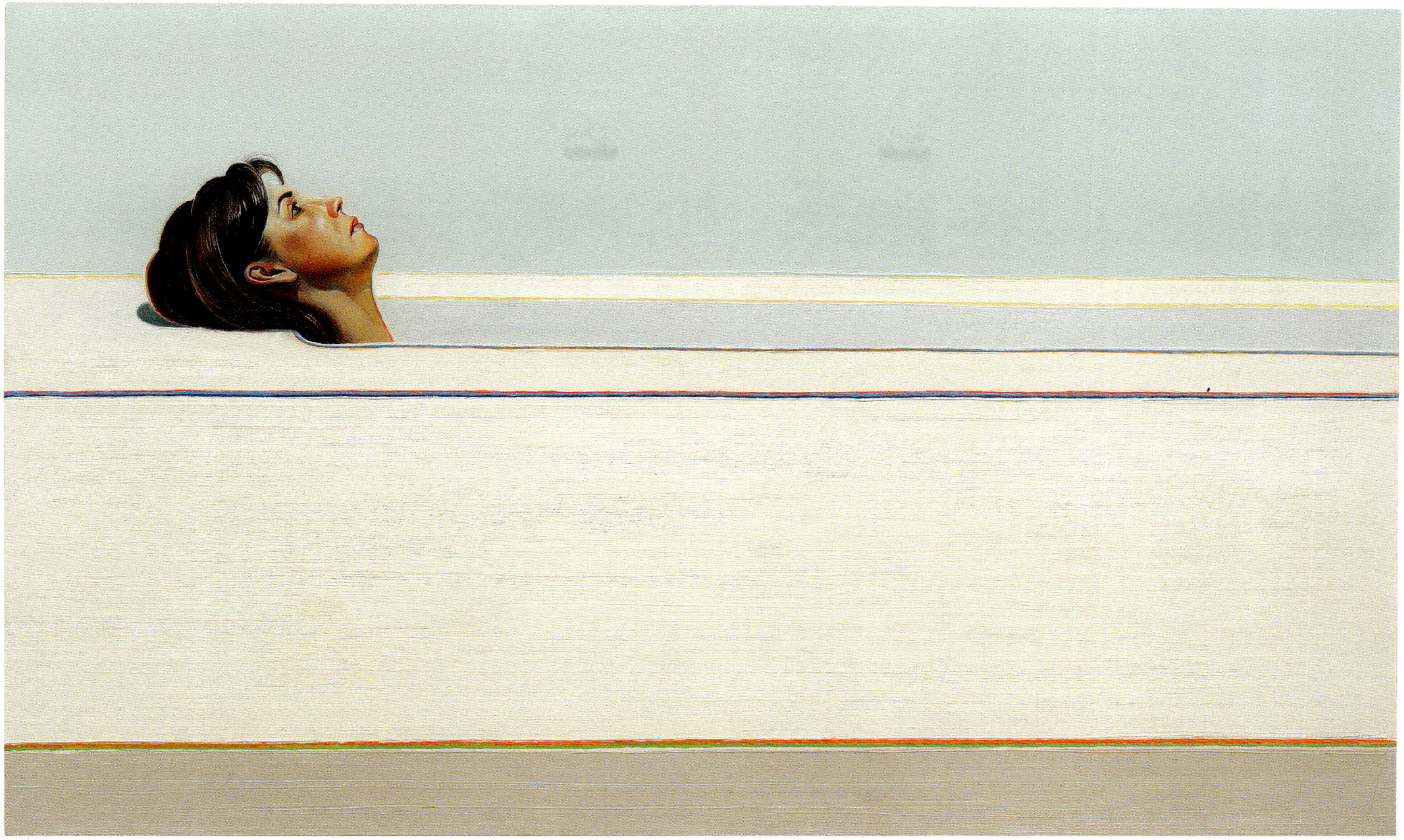

Wayne Thiebaud
**Woman in Tub**, 1965
Oil on canvas
36 × 60 in.
Private Collection

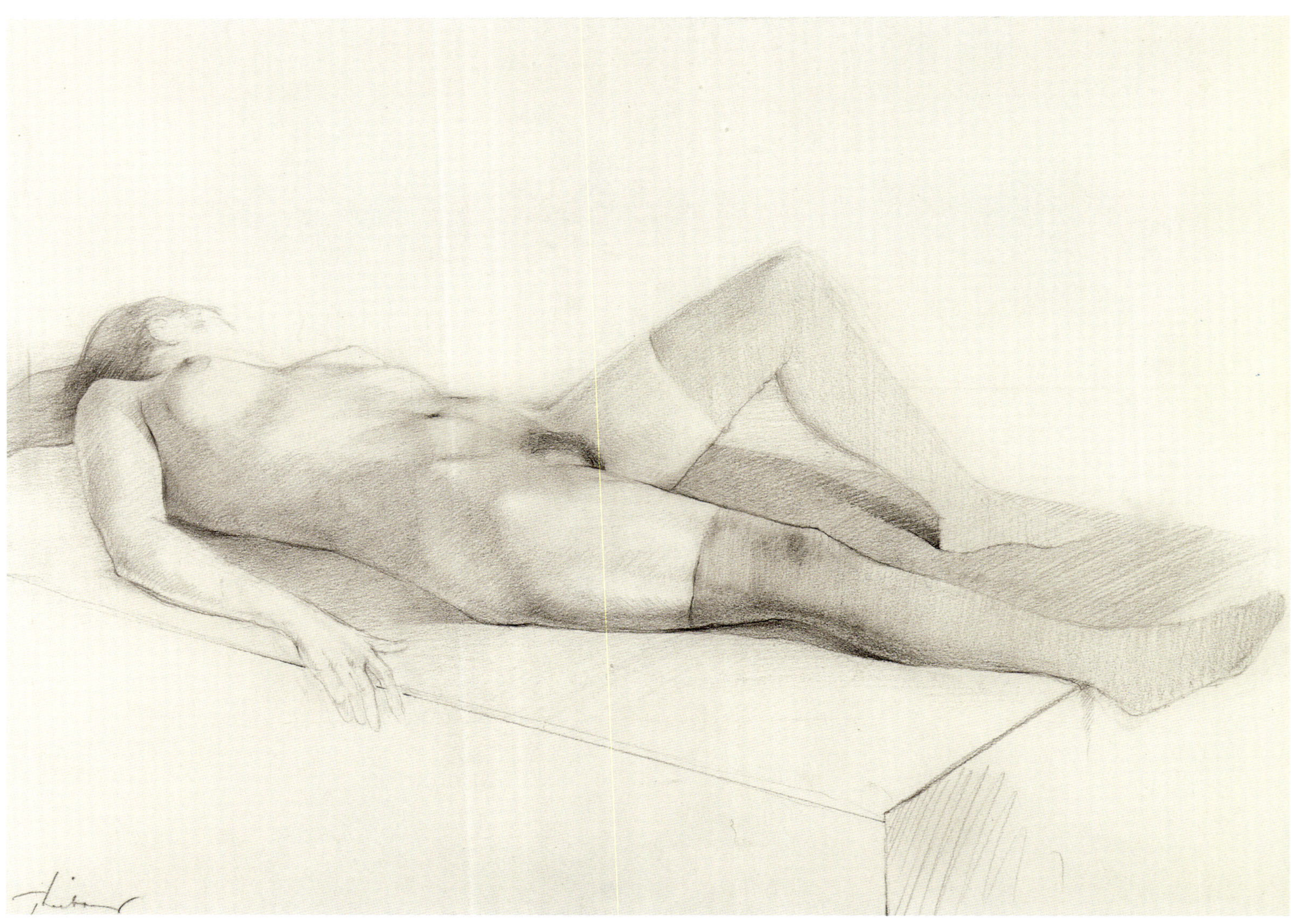



Wayne Thiebaud
**Untitled (Reclining Nude with Stockings)**, 1975
Graphite on paper
15 × 19 ⅞ in.
Private Collection

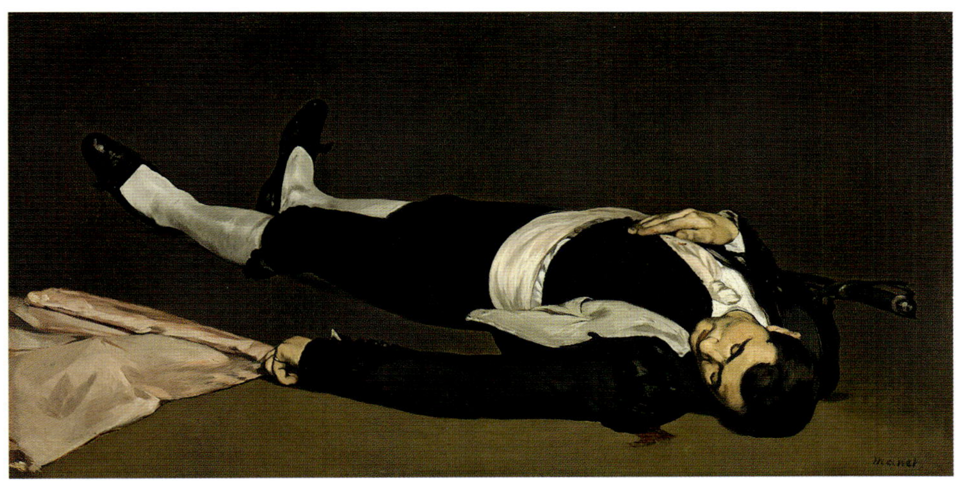

Édouard Manet
**The Dead Toreador**, ca. 1864
Oil on canvas
29 ⅞ × 60 ⅜ in.
National Gallery of Art, Washington, DC
Widener Collection, 1942.9.40

On occasion, the California artist expressed self-doubt about the extent of his gifts as a figurative painter. Never was he more aligned with Manet than when depicting the body—nude or clothed—with an unsparing regard borrowed from French realist models (P. 146).

A late etching by the artist helps clinch the point (P. 156). The small work compresses its female subject, shown in a dark dress with plunging neckline, her hair gathered loosely around a bare neck. *Counter Woman*'s (2015) expressionless face and rigid pose invite obvious comparisons to Manet's anonymous server. The products she vends—lipsticks, perfumes, and handbags—are *accoutrements* of haute bourgeois leisure, only slightly in variance with the inviting bottles of champagne and Bass Ale that populate the Impressionist canvas. These products constitute complex signs, critiques of the commercial transactions taking place in the sparkling, new social spaces of Paris in the late 1800s as well as the stuff of everyday life in the late twentieth century. In both artists' work, the bar/department store counter is revealed as a barrier, a patrolled border that the California artist habitually doubles by enlivening it with bright color. Colorful lines separate, highlight, and draw attention to the space between the spectator and these enticing but ultimately unreachable commodities. The philosopher Richard Wollheim once referred to this particular technique as "'halation,' or the distribution around the contour of an object of small dots of highly saturated color."[14] Their appreciation is intrinsic, according to Wollheim, to this artist's lasting achievement and contribution to modern painting.

These vibrant strokes, punch lines, point us back to foundational moments in Thiebaud's career, the time when he discovered his talents as an illustrator and cartoonist. In an interview with the ninety-five-year-old artist that I conducted in 2015 (SEE P. 169), Thiebaud shared his deep and early admiration for George Herriman's illustrative genius in creating the *Krazy Kat* comic strips (P. 157, TOP).[15] Published between 1913 and 1944, Herriman's long-running series of unpredictable mini-narratives graced American newspapers with their "own universe of the page."[16] The graphic impact of these panels and the irreverent attitude they took toward conventional ideas about narrative, perspective, composition, and horizon—the very framing of what's possible in an image—are worth connecting to Thiebaud's lifework. *Krazy Kat*, like Degas's photographically inspired haphazard cropping, offered the artist a model for taking humorous, if sometimes startling, risks with pictorial space. Thiebaud's first successes as an artist came in cartooning while still in high school and, later on, in the army.[17] Those early cartoon efforts, notably the *Ferbus* series (P. 157, BOTTOM) that he drew for the Rexall Drug Company during the late 1940s, show him reveling in the comic cell's expressive potential. Text balloons reading "Sploosh!" and "Look!" in those strips link Thiebaud's interests to those of Lichtenstein and the other Pop artists, although in ways that Coplans hardly fathomed a little over a decade later.[18] They signaled the artist's interest in serializing his subject matter, increasing its humorous edge. Importantly, Thiebaud never felt a need to apologize for his early career experience in cartooning, stage design, and magazine illustration. All of those forms valued the concentration of imagery into given environments and put a premium on his own imaginative creations. Indeed, he was prolific

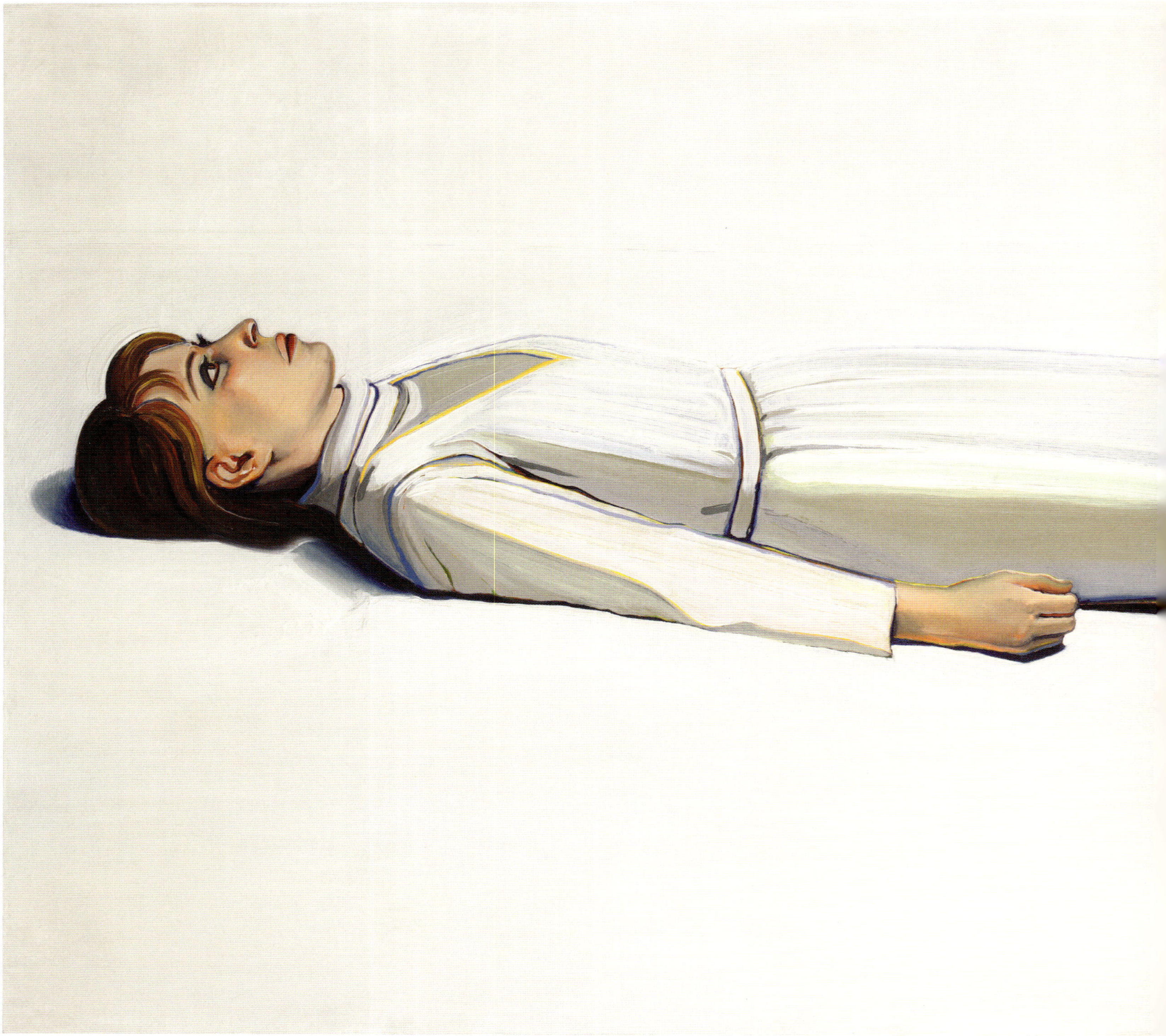

Wayne Thiebaud
**Supine Woman**, 1963
Oil on canvas
36 × 72 in.
Crystal Bridges Museum of American Art, Bentonville, Arkansas
2009.17

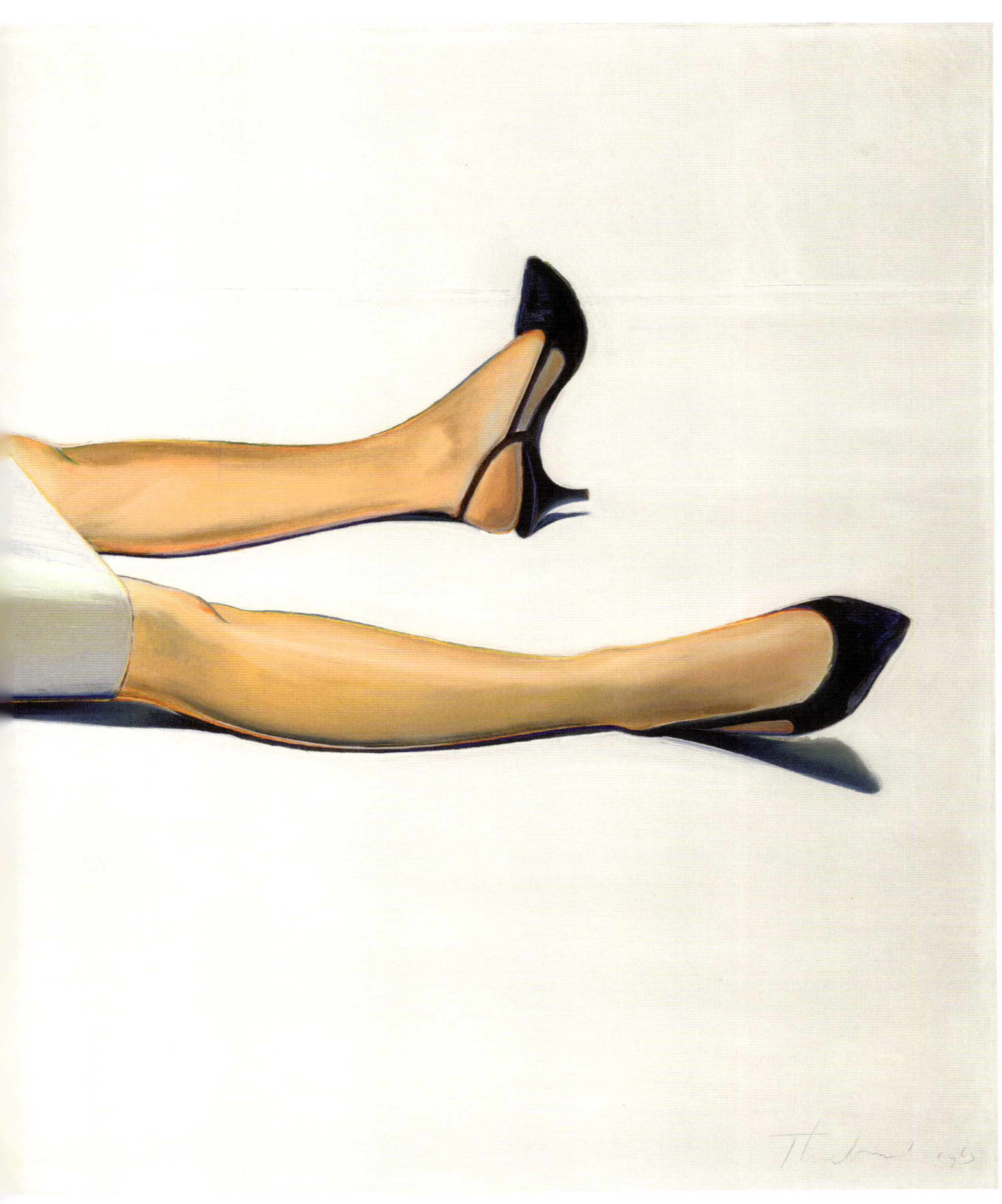

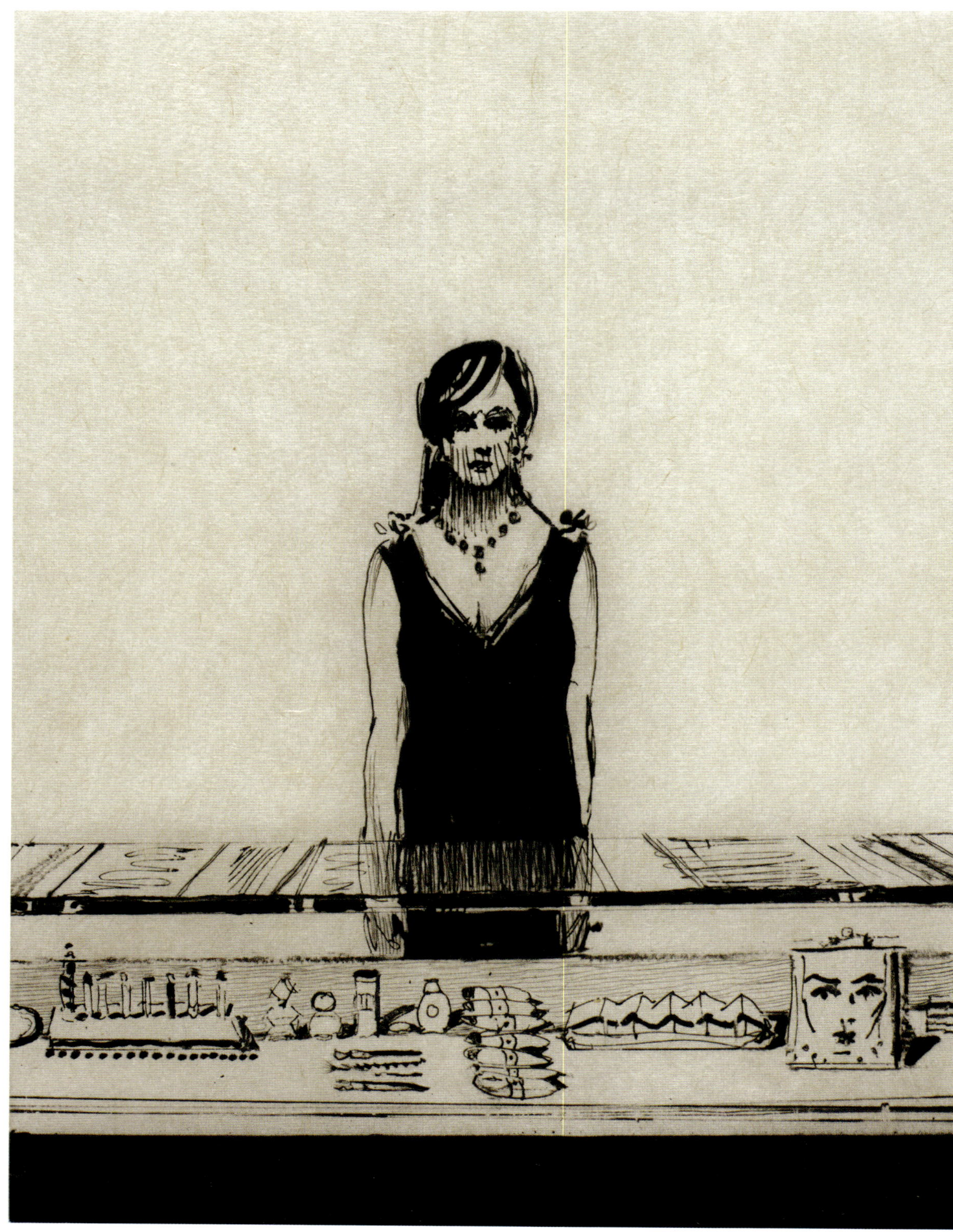

Wayne Thiebaud
**Counter Woman**, 2015
Direct gravure with drypoint on gampi chine collé
10 × 7 ½ in.
Edition of 25
Published by Crown Point Press, San Francisco

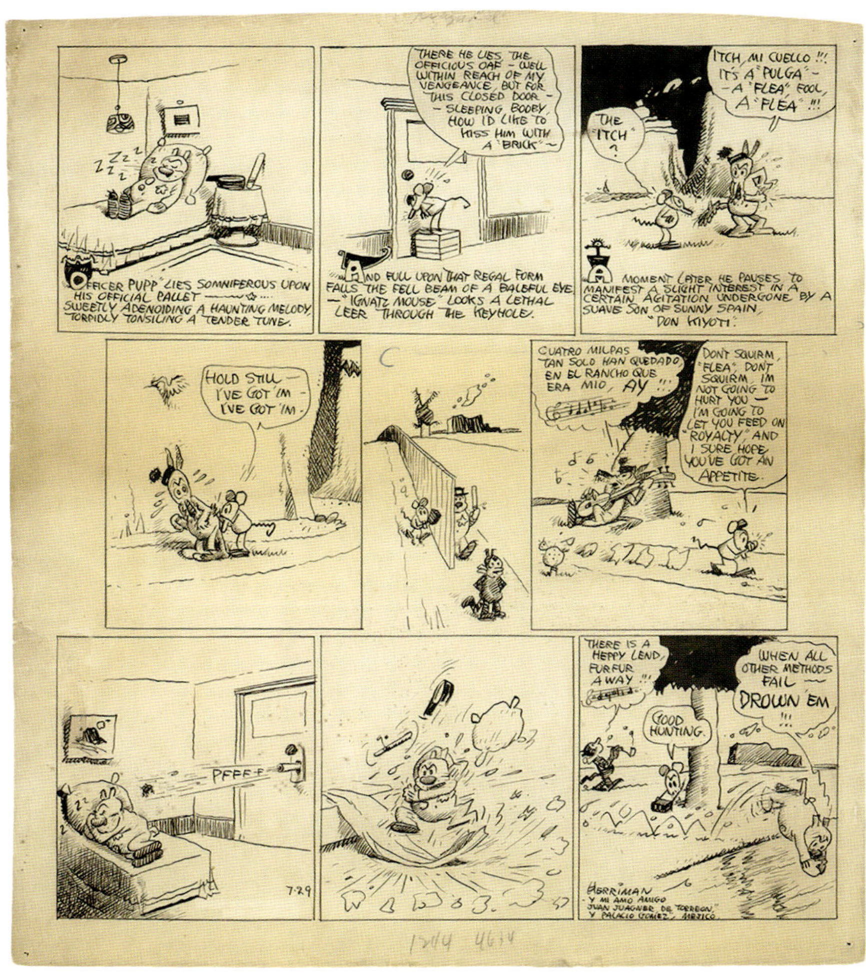




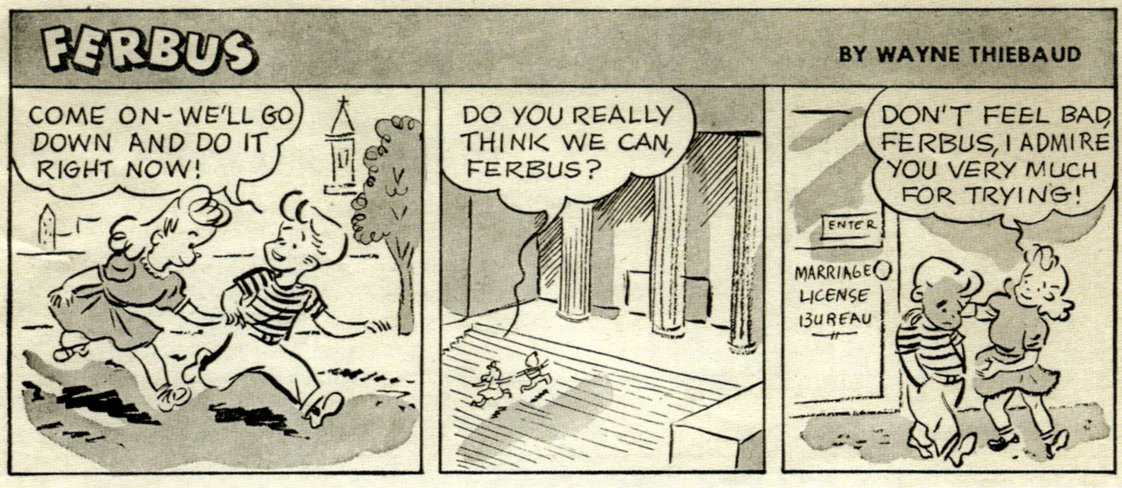


ABOVE
George Herriman
**Krazy Kat: Officer Pupp Lies Smoking . . .**, ca. 1928
India ink and graphite
20 × 18 in.
Library of Congress, Washington, DC

RIGHT
Wayne Thiebaud
**Ferbus** comic strip published in *Rexall Magazine*
November 1948
Courtesy of Wayne Thiebaud Foundation and The Morgan Library

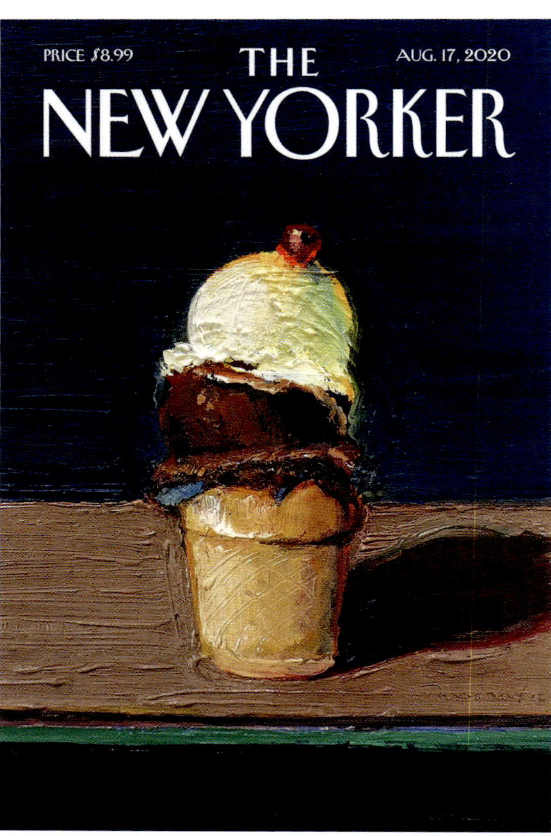

at commissioned work, producing jazz album covers and dozens of illustrations for *The New Yorker*, *Sports Illustrated*, and other mass-market periodicals throughout his long career, the last one of these, *Double Scoop*, appearing in 2020, a little over a year before the artist's passing at age 101 (ABOVE LEFT).

It is worth taking into account the artist's long-standing commitments to illustrative practice because doing so helps strengthen an appreciation of descriptive line throughout his broader oeuvre. Drawn elements, whether they take the form of energetic spurts in his early print efforts, crisp delineations of landscapes, or colored contours in his mature paintings, all underscore the degree to which careful draftsmanship and an unexpected insistence on linearity were, at once, unifying concepts and critical strategies within this artist's long career. One way to begin to grasp what is shared between a delicate drawing like *Landscape* (1965) (P. 161), with its Wyeth-like attention to place and atmosphere, and an ambitious, if ambiguous, painting like *Cloud City* (SEE ESSAY BY RACHEL TEAGLE, P. 103), which tilts toward abstraction, is to ponder the distinct ways in which the artist constructs perspectival systems. Both of these works share a plunging sense of spatial recession, more gently managed with the pencil and almost cartoonishly exaggerated in the oil painting. In each work Thiebaud insists that we take into account certain Renaissance toolkits, but also suggests that we be willing to set them aside when convenient, or when more interesting to do so. Details of both works are instructive: a sinuous, taut line guides the eye from foreground to the middle of the rural landscape while a halo of short blue brushstrokes surrounds the building forms just above the artist's signature on the urban hillside (ABOVE RIGHT). Thiebaud orchestrated his landscape compositions—*glissando* or *staccato*—according to carefully chosen mood and situation. "'Tempo' is a very Thiebaudian word," as Adam Gopnik astutely observed, ". . . by it, he means the implied rhythm . . . 'the brush dance' of the picture."[19] We witness this rhythm in both works.

LEFT
**Double Scoop**, 2020, cover for *The New Yorker*, August 10, 2020
Collection of author

RIGHT
Wayne Thiebaud, **Cloud City** (detail), 1993

Before turning to a conclusion to this outline of self-conscious continuities and disruptions, it seems worthwhile to return to the California situation in which Coplans's review of *New Painting of Common Objects* initially pigeonholed the artist. Even in the early 1960s, California was known for its carefree coastline and busy freeways; Thiebaud counted these domains as his own, and they were among his enduring favorites. Beaches provided the occasion for Thiebaud to return to his youthful homes in Long Beach and, later, in Laguna, and through these particular locales he returned also to the sometimes-agitated brushwork of his first forays into image-making. In works like *Beach Boys* (1959), the artist makes reference to John Singer Sargent's views of bathers in coastal Brittany or Joaquín Sorolla's figures on the *playas* of Valencia, all the while offering the slyest possible nod to the emergent youth culture of Southern California. Similarly, the series of *Freeway Curve*s on which Thiebaud worked from the mid-1970s until the end of his career takes a ubiquitous, grim fact of West Coast existence and turns it into the opportunity for pictorial invention.[20] A monoprint of this type mixes high speed and evanescence as experienced through the front windshield of a speeding car (P. 162). The resulting tension between frustration and aesthetic appreciation that courses through this imagery borders on hilarity, and might actually have been a source of confusion for Coplans and other viewers of these early works. It did not last as a valid critique of these efforts, however.

Angst and anguish end up being closely keyed terms for measuring Thiebaud's aesthetic and life goals. A close friend, Fred Dalkey, recognized "a dark side to his work," and Gopnik has noted the sadness that pervades Thiebaud's carefully ordered rows of uneaten, untouched sweets.[21] In an interview with Kenneth Baker, the painter responded blithely to doubts about his ability to combine carefree subject matter with career success. "Am I driven by angst?" he wondered not without irony. "No, it is just that I am just one of those lucky people who had a terrific childhood, was spoiled by my parents. For me, working is a joy." He went on immediately, however, to complicate assumptions about what his practice shared with other "tortured artists": "It's full of agony, of course, and you worry about what you're doing in terms of its quality of achievement, but the wonderful thing about being a painter is having that privilege of being in contact with a great tradition. And over time you come to see both the works in that tradition and the world differently."[22]

In an illuminating study of how Thiebaud's investigation of landscapes relates to themes of anguish and concern over the environment, Margaretta Lovell has pointed out the tension that exists between the professed joy that the artist finds in his work and his concern for what it meant to be living in an "Eden" that was interrupted by the "dissonant undercurrent in that buoyant narrative of joyful life and work."[23] Explorations of the American landscape, like critical takes on consumer desire, are prone to being unsettled by doubt and in this sense are inherently ironic. Thiebaud's inquiry is no exception to this rule, only his might be tempered by a sense of self-deprecation. As a proof of this, I want to turn at long last to those terms by which some critics misjudged Thiebaud harshly in 1962. Perceived as "lacking anguish" and failing to respond adequately to a "sense of crisis," a pale of perceived indifference separated him from the more arch sensibilities of Warhol, Lichtenstein, Oldenburg, and "the rest of the others" who were part of Hopps's selection in Pasadena.

This can't be right for any number of reasons. Without entering into a debate about what counts as detachment, or the relative degrees of possibility within Pop's deadpan aesthetic, it needs to be countered how deeply intentional Thiebaud's reflection upon commonplace reality was at the time, and remained so throughout his lifetime. Indeed, this might count as his topmost concern. As he memorably quipped, "I (too!) have painted soup." Still, in the early 1960s, Thiebaud's attraction to vending machines, bakery displays, rows of automobiles extending to the horizon, and otherwise isolated figures could be mistaken for a failure to treat as urgent any number of "crises" of the time, but doing so in the end has to be judged as unwarranted.

There is no evidence in his work, or words, to suggest he lacked "guts" or "commitment" when it came to implicating himself, and by extension us, in the complex allure demanded by everyday consumption. That he identified closely with this seduction, and also its disappointments, was explicit in his work from the very start. We might take lessons from Thiebaud on this front.

The artist once defended the place of humor in understanding contemporary representations, including his own: "I think . . . there's room for a sense of humor in the art world, which is not very apparent, usually. We're sort of scared of humor, in a way; it just doesn't seem serious or something."[24] When admitting he rarely painted steaks, but took due interest in soup, one feels him winking mischievously at Warhol. A final observation may help clinch this point where Thiebaud's humor intersects with larger, more broadly cultural concerns. Among the commonplace subjects that he returned to multiple times in his career, men's neckwear counts as a uniquely self-referential choice (P. 163). Pictures of ties, whether hanging from stands, arranged in neat rows, or displayed in shop windows, or even writhing in a messy pile, are rendered as emblems of a missing self, adornments of indulgence seeking bodies to enliven through their color. Sartorially, it needs to be pointed out, the artist himself occasionally favored a bow tie or brightly striped necktie. The ties in these paintings, drawings, and prints might be understood as comic rebuses, coded monikers for their maker, therefore.[25] In this way they perform like the clowns that Thiebaud painted on numerous occasions (and etched once), often seen taking a bow. As Julia Friedman has observed, the clown is a recurrent motif in Thiebaud's lifework, especially his late work.[26] Throughout, the comic figure shows up as something distinct from his otherwise crisp, figurative realism. It is tempting, therefore, to conclude the clown functions at some level as a stand-in for the artist himself (P. 164). The proliferation of these comic doubles suggests that the artist understood well the connections between the desire for common subjects and his own unique position as a maker within a ceaselessly expanding, ever-desiring consumer society. Not unlike the delicately incised heart that the artist appended to his signature in select favorite works, *tie bows/ Thiebauds* declare the artist's fierce identity, revealing something highly personal but ultimately subject to humble, regular exchange. Like so many other common objects in his impressively vast repertoire, these bow ties are commodities that are available to the urgency of the moment. These self-depictions suggest that Thiebaud approached whatever crisis was ahead of him with a certain measured ambivalence, choosing to represent himself as he was in life, the finest balance of generous heart, incisive observation, and self-deprecating humor.

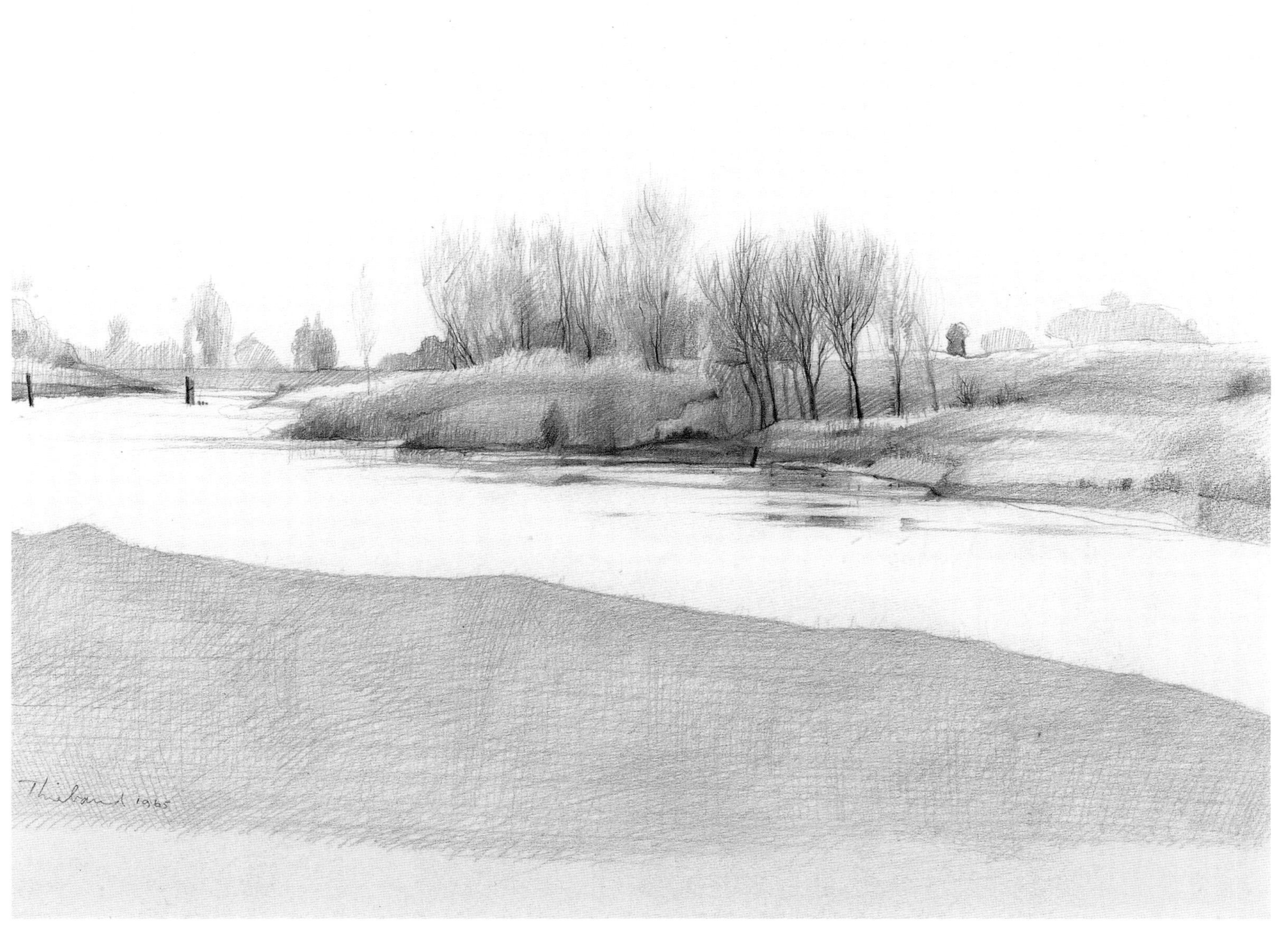



Wayne Thiebaud
**Landscape**, 1965
Graphite on paper
9 ½ × 12 ¾ in.
Private Collection

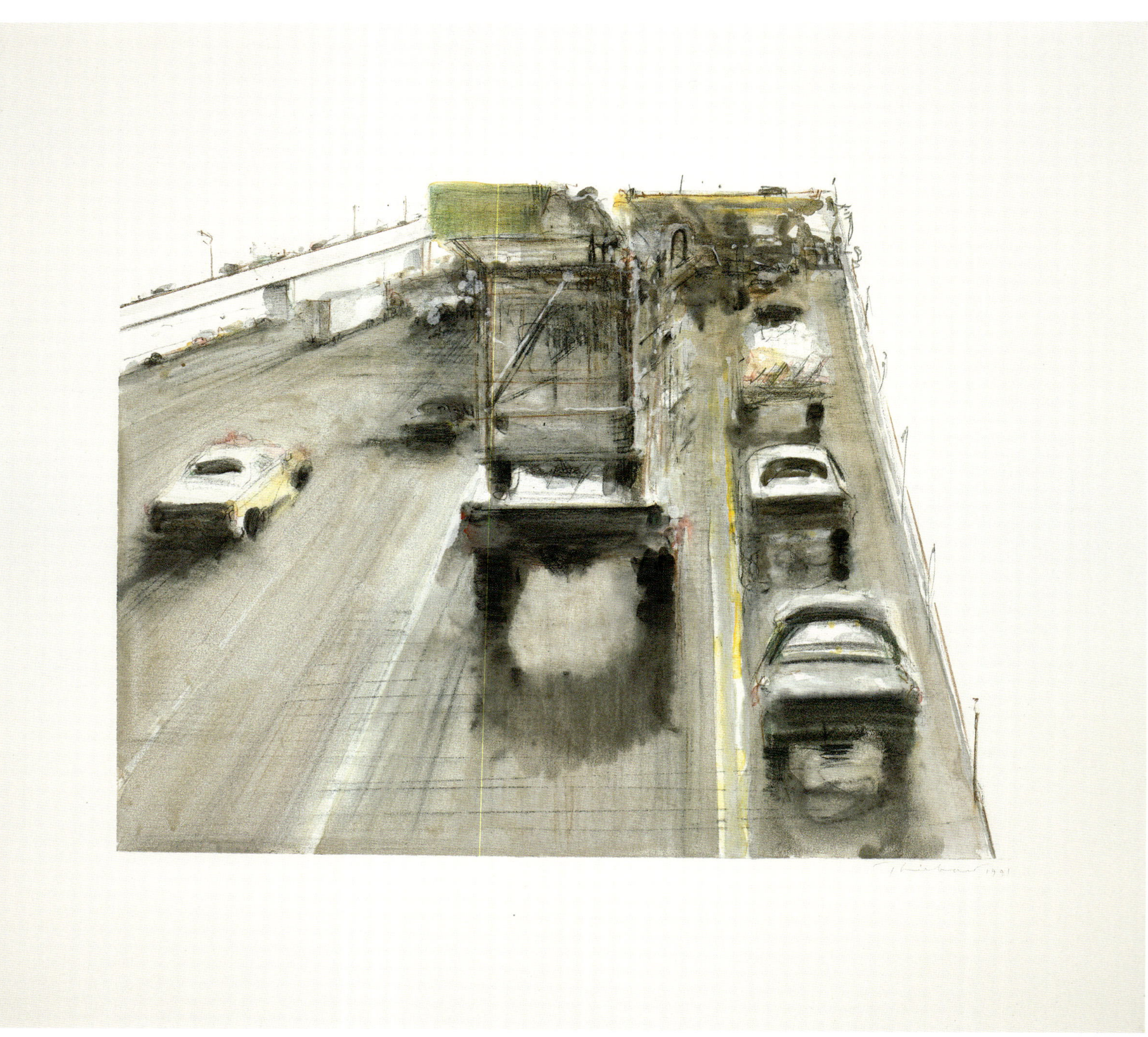

Wayne Thiebaud
**Untitled (Cars and Trucks)**, 1991
Monotype
28 ⅞ × 33 ¾ in.
Private Collection

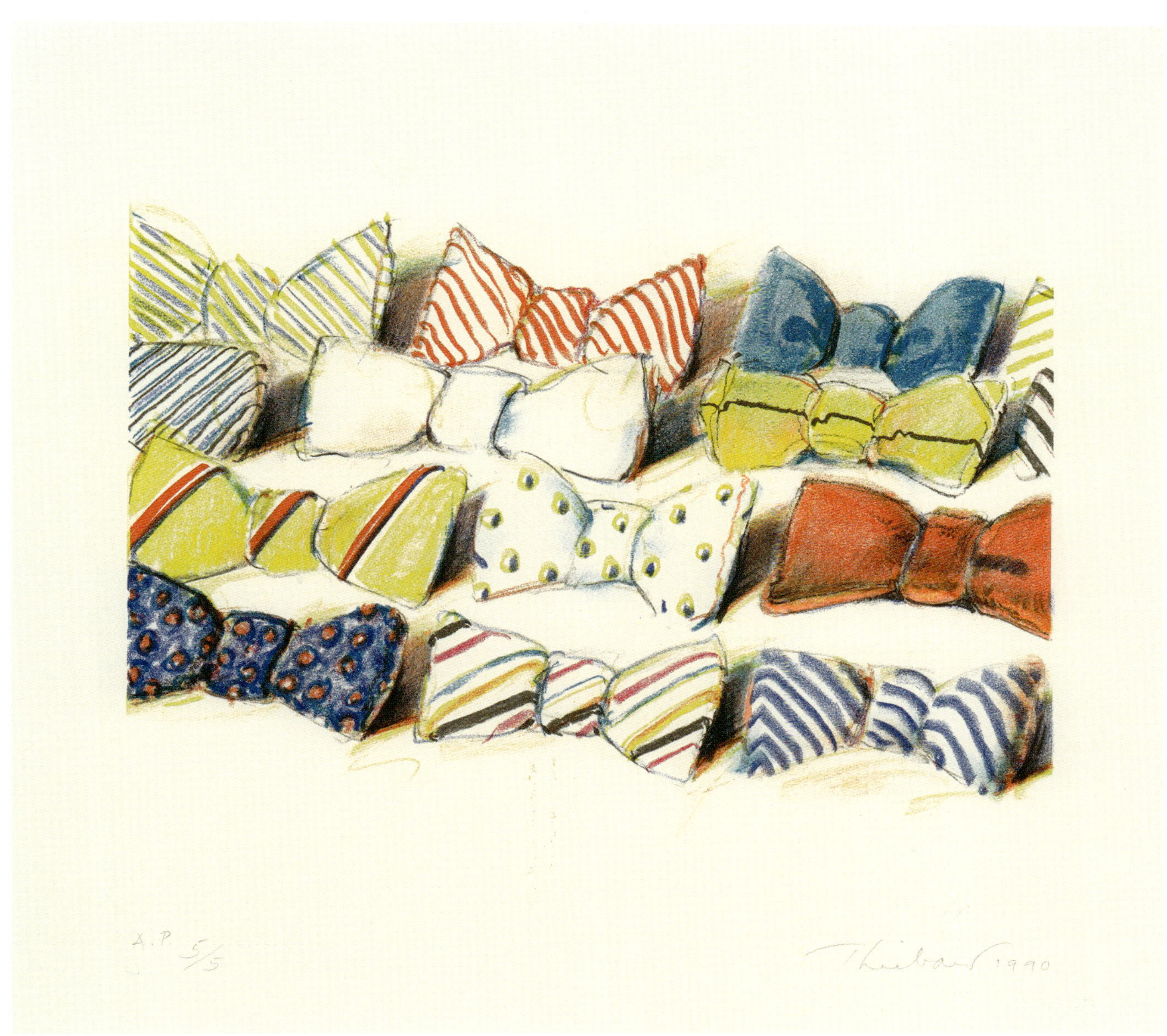



Wayne Thiebaud
**Bow Ties**, 1990
Color lithograph on wove paper
11 × 13 ¾ in.
National Gallery of Art, Washington, DC
Corcoran Collection
Gift of the Women's Committee of the Corcoran Gallery of Art

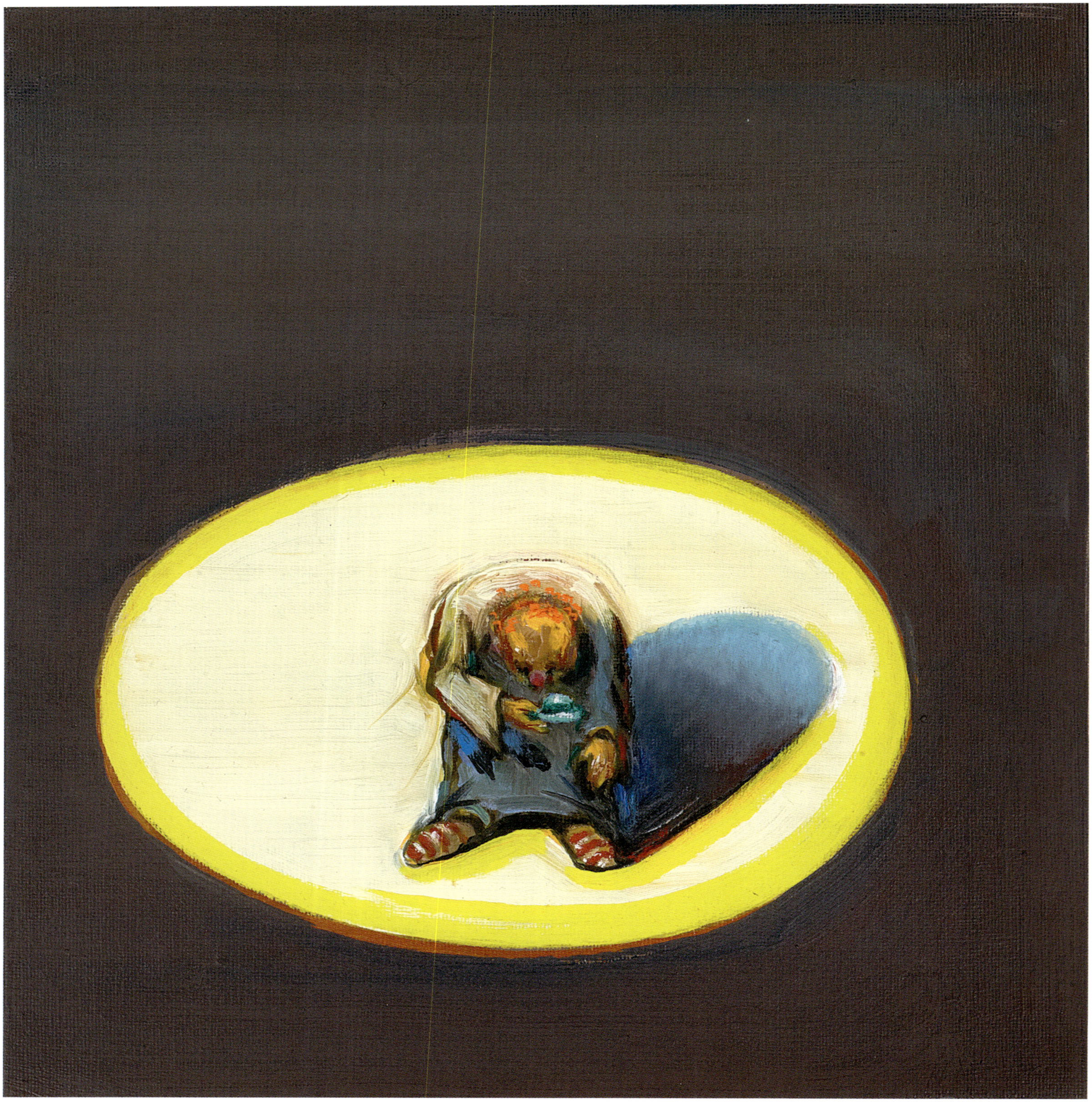

Wayne Thiebaud
**Bowing Clown**, 2016
Oil on canvas
12 × 12 in.
Private Collection

Notes

1. From "Wayne Thiebaud: An Interview," in John Coplans, *Wayne Thiebaud* (Pasadena: Pasadena Art Museum, 1968), 23.
2. John Coplans, "The New Paintings of Common Objects," *Artforum* 1 (November 1962): 26–29.
3. Insightful commentators like Donald Judd left open the idea that Thiebaud's work might be interpreted as satire in these very years. See Judd's review, "In the Galleries: Wayne Thiebaud," *Arts Magazine* (September 1962): 48–49.
4. Cathleen McGuigan, "Wayne Thiebaud Is Not a Pop Artist," *Smithsonian Magazine* (February 2011): 66–73. Retrieved, Jan. 2024 from https://www.smithsonianmag.com/arts-culture/wayne-thiebaud-is-not-a-pop-artist-57060.
5. For a nuanced take on these period differences, see Rachel Teagle, "Presence and Absence: Wayne Thiebaud and the Future of Painting," in *Wayne Thiebaud: 1958–1968* (Berkeley and Los Angeles: University of California Press and the Jan Shrem and Maria Manetti Shrem Museum of Art, 2018), esp. 27–29.
6. For these dates, see the "Complete Chronology," in *A Body: John Coplans* (New York: Powerhouse Books, 2002) available as a PDF through the John Coplans Trust: http://www.johncoplanstrust.org/selected-bibliography.
7. Quoted in A. LeGrace, G. Benson, David H. R. Shearer, and Wayne Thiebaud, "Documents: An Interview with Wayne Thiebaud," *Leonardo* 2 (January 1969): 66.
8. For Thiebaud's pencil sketch after Daumier's *Two Men, Half Length, Looking to the Left* (ca. 1860), see Isabelle Dervaux, et al., *Wayne Thiebaud: Draftsman* (New York: The Morgan Library and Thames & Hudson, 2018), 30–31, 89, and Gene Cooper's essay in this volume.
9. See, for example, Alessia Masi, "An Interview with Wayne Thiebaud," in *Wayne Thiebaud at Museo Morandi* (Mantova: Corraini Edizioni, 2011), 28–57.
10. Quoted in Rachel Teagle, et al., *Wayne Thiebaud, 1958–1968* (Berkeley and Los Angeles: University of California Press and the Jan Shrem and Maria Manetti Shrem Museum of Art, 2018), 134.
11. See John Yau, "Wayne Thiebaud's Incongruities," in *Wayne Thiebaud* (New York: Rizzoli, 2015), 26–33.
12. The most compelling interpretation of Manet's enigmatic composition remains T. J. Clark's. See his *Painting of Modern Life: Paris in the Art of Manet and His Followers* (Princeton: Princeton University Press, 1984), esp. 205–58.
13. It is not practical to pursue a full inventory of these works here. Briefly, however, I am thinking of works such as *Woman and Cosmetics* (1963), *Booth Girl* (1964), *Girl with Mirror* (1965), or even *Betty Jean Thiebaud and Book* (1965–69), all of which perpetuate attitudes ranging from mild indifference to disdain in their sitters' position. Perhaps the most striking comparison, however, is to be made with *Telephone Girl* (1970–85), where the sitter's look of pained boredom and contempt closely mirrors the unsettling regard of Manet's barmaid.
14. Richard Wollheim, "Wayne Thiebaud, Green River Lands, 1998," *Artforum* 38 (October 1999): 135.
15. See Derrick R. Cartwright, "An Interview with Wayne Thiebaud," in *Wayne Thiebaud, By Hand: Works on Paper from 1965–2015* (San Diego: University of San Diego, 2015), 12–13, and in this volume, 171, 173.
16. Seth and Art Spiegelman, quoted in Bruce Greenville, et al., *Krazy!: The Delirious World of Anime + Comics + Video Games + Art* (Berkeley and Los Angeles: University of California Press, 2008), 29.
17. Thiebaud once recounted his childhood love of comics and the role it played in his decision to become an artist:

    > "For a long time, I remember I cut out strips and kept them around. Then I would copy them and . . . got more and more interested. By the time I was maybe sixteen [or] fifteen, I started sending in cartoons to magazines. They had these contests . . . In a magazine called *Open Road for Boys* [saying,] 'Draw a cartoon in which you would say how this problem is solved.' And so I did that, and . . . had a couple of things published, and (SUSAN LARSEN: You did?) I was very excited and so on."

    See, Susan C. Larsen, *Oral History Interview with Wayne Thiebaud*, May 17–18, 2001, Smithsonian Archives of American Art: https://www.aaa.si.edu/collections/interviews/oral-history-interview-wayne-thiebaud-12546.
18. Only a few of the Ferbus strips have been published with full references in books devoted to Thiebaud's mature work. See Isabelle Dervaux, "Drawing Keeps You from Cheating," in *Wayne Thiebaud Draftsman* (New York: The Morgan Library and Thames & Hudson, 2018), 17, and Karen Tsujimoto, "Wayne Thiebaud: Formative Years," in *Wayne Thiebaud* (San Francisco: San Francisco Museum of Modern Art, 1985), 20.
19. Adam Gopnik, "An American Painter," in Steven A. Nash, et al., *Wayne Thiebaud: A Paintings Retrospective* (San Francisco: Fine Arts Museums of San Francisco, 2000), 49.
20. See, for instance, my short text, "Freeway Curve, 1995," in *Wayne Thiebaud: Delicious Metropolis* (San Francisco: Chronicle Books, 2019), 104–05.
21. See McGuigan, "Wayne Thiebaud Is Not a Pop Artist," ibid.
22. Kenneth Baker, "A Conversation with Wayne Thiebaud/An American Painter," *SFGate* (January 15, 1995): https://www.sfgate.com/bayarea/article/A-Conversation-With-Wayne-Thiebaud-An-American-3049165.php.
23. Margaretta M. Lovell, "City, River, Mountain: Wayne Thiebaud's California," *Panorama: Journal of the Association of Historians of American Art* 3 (Fall 2017): https://doi.org/10.24926/24716839.1602.
24. Larsen, *Oral History Interview with Wayne Thiebaud*, May 17–18, 2001, op. cit.
25. Some circumstantial evidence for this admittedly speculative interpretation can be found in the way that Thiebaud signed at least one of his pastel drawings on top of a print. That work, *Bow Ties* (1992), bears an otherwise unique signature at lower left, which reads "*? Thiebaud 1992.*" The question about identity is repeated recto upper right: "*? Thiebaud*" as if to call attention to its status as a possible self-portrait. The work in question was sold at auction in 2017: https://www.christies.com/en/lot/lot-6110287.
26. See Julia Friedman, "There ought to be clowns," *The New Criterion*38 (December 2019): 48–150.

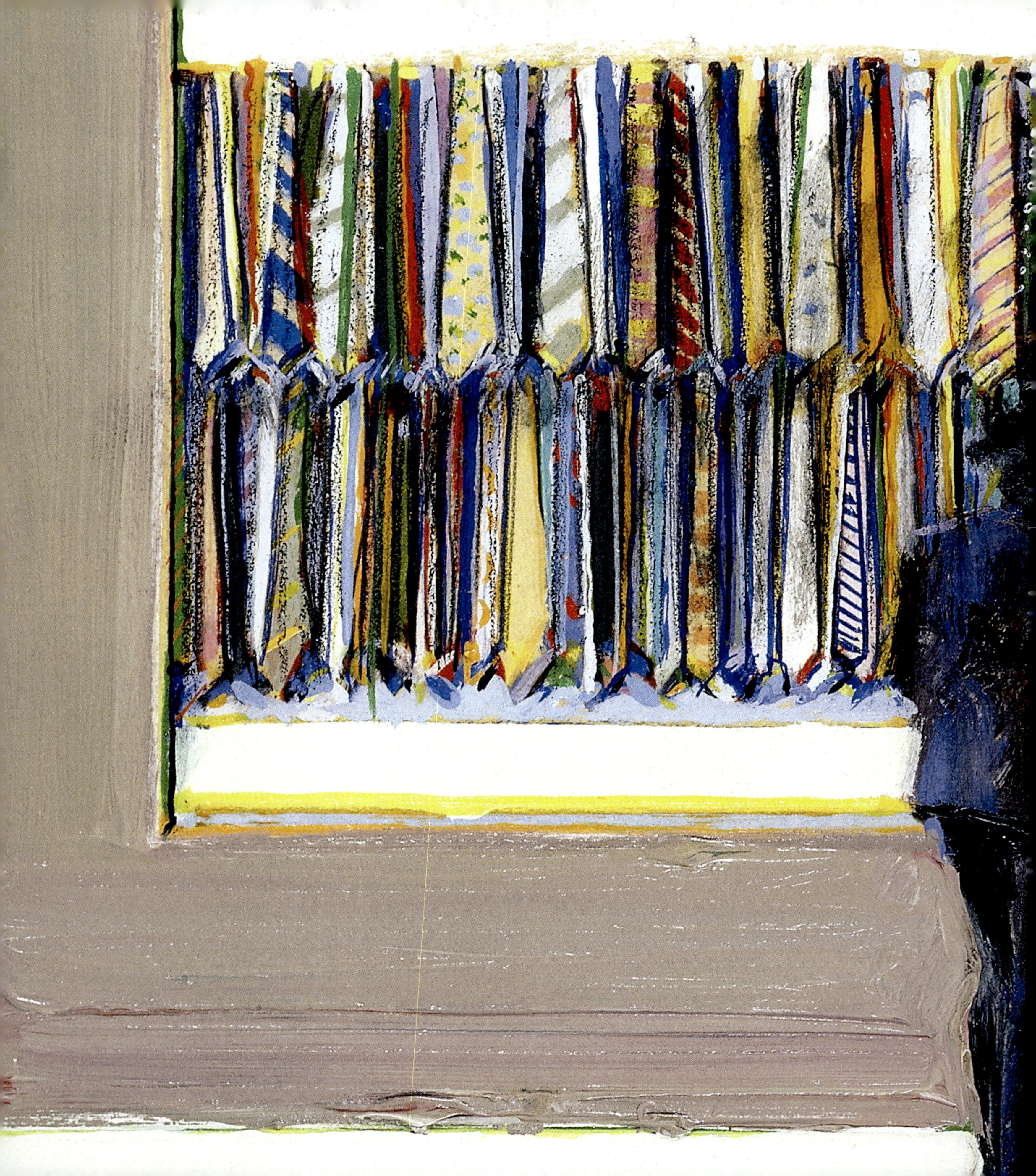

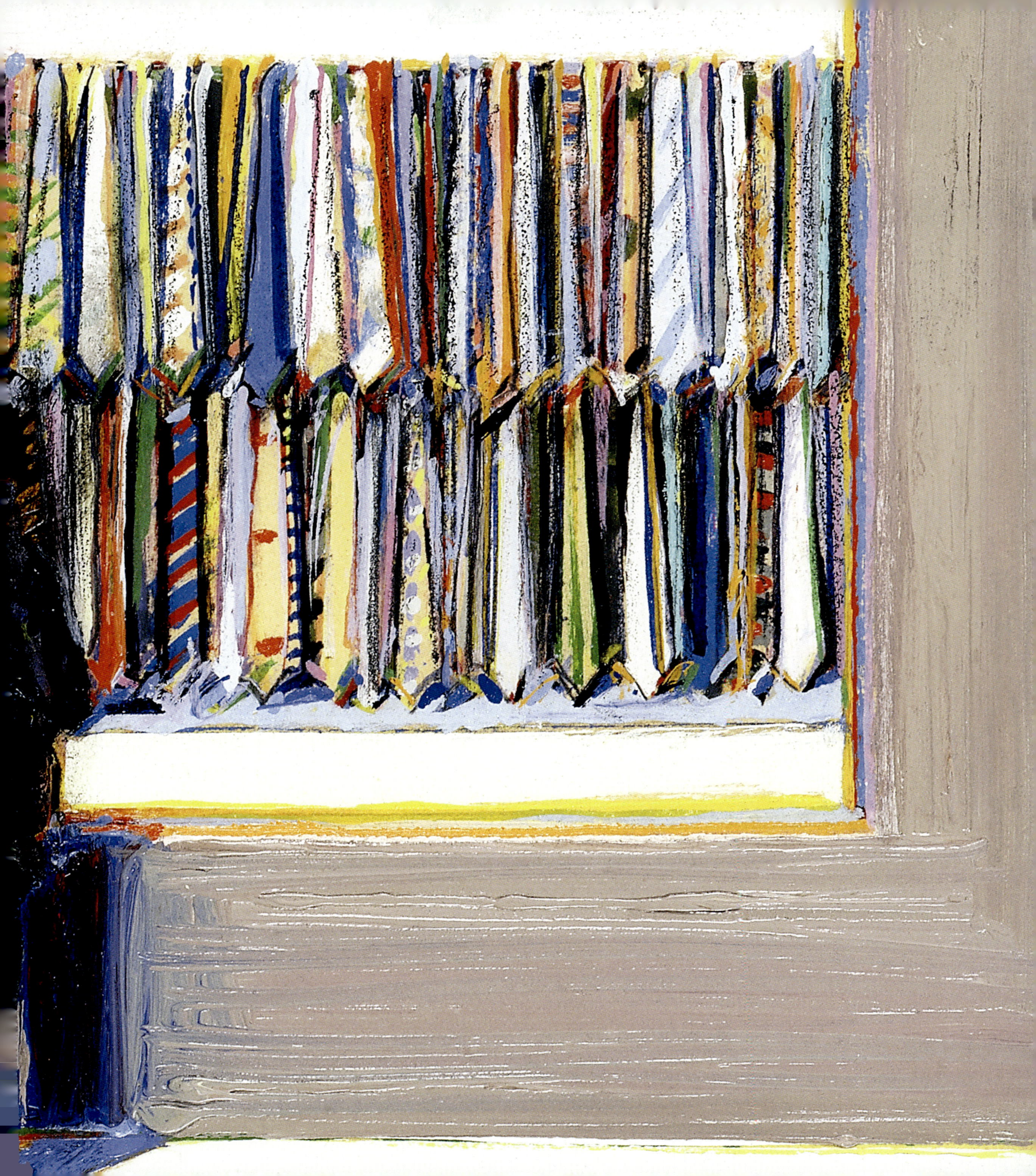

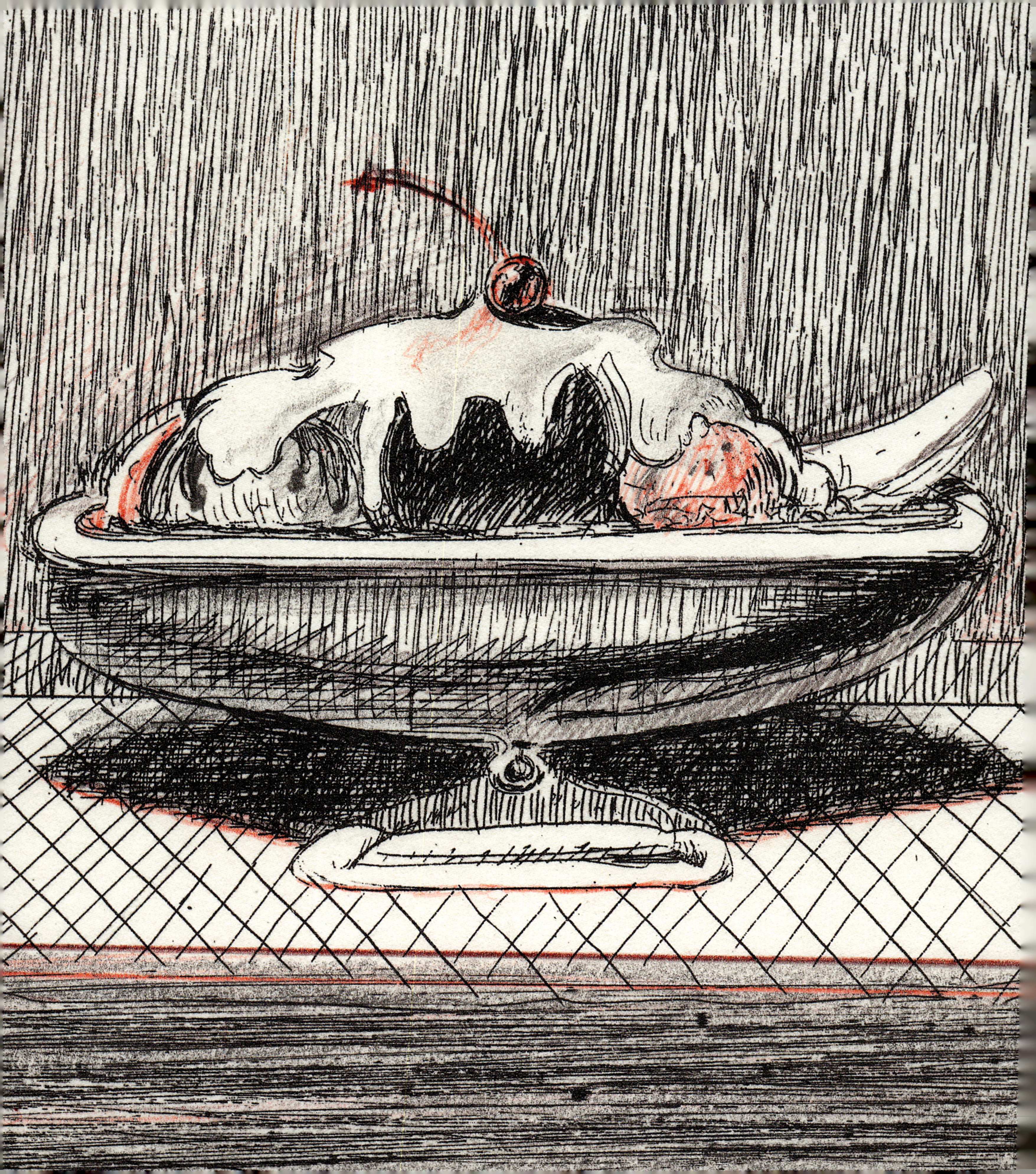

# Interview

## Derrick R. Cartwright
## Wayne Thiebaud

Wayne Thiebaud, **Untitled** (detail), 2016

**DERRICK CARTWRIGHT:** In preparation for this session, I spent some time reading other interviews you've done so I wouldn't bore you by asking the same questions you've heard many times before. One thing I learned quickly is that you've been interviewed quite a bit. You are probably one of the most interviewed people in today's art world. That speaks both to your reputation and to your generosity but, I have to ask, do you even like the interview format?

**WAYNE THIEBAUD:** Well, I guess I do because I don't write about my own work. I have been treated kindly by those who have interviewed me over the years. Also, the other reason for that is because I am interested in teaching and the artist's interview can be a powerful way to communicate ideas to students. So that is a significant part of this format's appeal, I think.

**DC:** You have been teaching for a long time.

**WT:** Yes. I started in 1951 at what is now called Sacramento City College. I had just finished my bachelor's degree at Sacramento State. On the one hand, I thought the last thing I would be was a teacher. On the other, I thought to myself, "if I am going to paint, I had better get into something that I can depend on." It was a desperate move because I had a young family and wrestled with my choices, in the end thinking, "I probably need to do this to keep my family going." That's really why I went into teaching initially—for all of the wrong reasons [laughs]—but it really did entrance me in the end. And it put me on a very humble path of trying to learn something for myself. Teaching was a helpful thing. Then, all of the sudden, among the other things I did at City, I found I was responsible for teaching not just art but for teaching its history, too.

**DC:** Earlier today, while visiting the Crocker Art Museum, I was struck by the opportunity that exists to view your paintings in relation to your students' work, also on display there. For example, there is a big painting by Christopher Brown [*Winter's Blue Cold*, 1990–91] hanging not far from several of your paintings in the contemporary art galleries. When I think about Brown as one of your graduate students at Davis—the purity of formal concerns and the shimmer both of you can achieve in your best work—I tend to appreciate his accomplishments differently. And you can't help but feel an appreciation for how lucky your students have been over the years to have you as a mentor. This recognition of your influence must happen to you all the time as you visit museums throughout the world. Does that experience mean anything to you?

**WT:** It is satisfying and it's a happy thing. I see my former students often and that is certainly a gratifying experience. They are all on a high par when it comes to information and interest, and they've become really good and wonderful people to talk about art with. I do that as regularly as I can. They come here, or I see them in New York, or the Bay Area, and I now give the opportunity to anyone who wants to come and have a critical intervention together to come see me. I am eager to talk with them about their work, and I want them to talk to me about what they see happening with my own work, too. It has worked out to be a very usable and useful idea.

It is important always, at least for me, to recall and remember what a great tradition painting is and, in a way, it is a sort of "secret society." Which for me is a thrilling opportunity to engage in. I wasn't aware of that when I started as a painter, not at all. I wanted to be an artist, but that had to quickly be taken away and [I had to] make sure that I could get down to the business of painting itself. From time to time, I still appreciate the "secret society" aspect.



**DC:** You became a professional artist at a very young age, as a teenager, right?

**WT:** Well, [I became] something, I don't know what. I was really just acting out, being interested in what I was interested in, mostly. Not an artist to start, an illustrator, maybe, and later on a commercial draftsman. I have such respect for all that work of illustration and commercial drawing, believe me, but I didn't start considering myself an artist until much later on.

**DC:** In any case, your work was taken seriously from an early point in your career, something that has only increased with time. For instance, Robert Hughes once called you the "poet of pastry" and Adam Gopnik writes about the nostalgia that pervades your images as a "melancholy little comedy of longing, of exclusion." What do you think when you read those kinds of appreciations of your effort? Do you agree with those interpretations of your art? How do you feel about what art historians say more generally?

**WT:** Well, in the case of the two writers you just mentioned, they both became friends. Adam didn't interview me when he wrote the initial piece about me in *The New Yorker*. It shocked me that he became so interested and that he took the time to write about my work so eloquently. I thanked him and he said, "Well, when you come to New York, let's get acquainted," and so we did and became friends. And that is all extra [pause] extra marvelous. I admire Adam's writings so much, he's so bright. Later he did a series of interviews that resulted in the essay that got published in the catalogue *Wayne Thiebaud: A Paintings Retrospective* (2000).

One of the reasons I have an affinity for well-written art criticism is that, for a long time, I was given the task of teaching a class at UC Davis called "Art Theory and Criticism." It was not your typical art school course. It was, in fact, a big challenge. The head of the department, Richard Allen Nelson, wanted to develop a course in which the painting students had to engage with the problem of actually writing about painting, primarily so that they would not be intimidated by it. The course had to be taught by a painter, too, so that it wasn't your typical survey either. Nelson's approach was modeled after a course taught at UC Berkeley by [Stephen C.] Pepper, who organized it out of the philosophy department. So, to get back to your question, I am more than just pleased by what art historians write. I think art history represents for me the standard for measuring our best accomplishments. It is a measuring device and also, I think, an inspirational tool that we need badly. At its best [art history] has always been taken up by artists, whether [Richard] Diebenkorn or [Willem] de Kooning. They all wanted to talk about art history.

To be a serious artist, you need to be seriously interested in what painters have to say about their art. Right now, I am just finishing reading a book given to me by Rackstraw Downes [*Nature and Art Are Physical: Writings on Art, 1967–2008*]. It is quite a marvelous book about painting. He, unlike me, got his degree in literature from one of the great British universities, and so he was fortunate enough to receive some training to use prose along with historical information in a way that helps him articulate his own views about art, but from a highly personal, yet informed standpoint as well. John Elderfield wrote a foreword to the book and I think you might enjoy reading it, too.

DC: Let's take as an example of your engagement with art history a painting of yours that I just spent some time looking at this morning, *Betty Jean Thiebaud and Book* (1965–69) (P. 172). It is a ravishing picture and put together in that thoughtful way you do so well, Wayne. Betty Jean is wearing a black sweater, with charcoal-gray highlights, and is seated behind a white table, and there is this coral/pink edge to the table that divides the two parts of the picture like an electric charge. I noticed the book that appears on the table. It is open before her and the pages reveal two illustrations. One appears, though it is seen upside down, to be a highly finished sketch for Degas's *Portrait of Diego Martelli* (1879), and the other looks like it is *Seated Boy with a Straw Hat* (1883–84), a study for Georges Seurat's *Bathers at Asnières* (1884). These drawings are facing each other across the open space of the book while Betty Jean looks out at us from within the picture. There's a dialogue about realism going on here, right?

WT: I was pretty much focused on trying to get the best likeness of Betty Jean that I could, to tell you the truth. She was by far my best model. She also was very forgiving. I would tell her, "I am not really making your portrait. I am just trying to make as good a painting as I can." But when I got through, I looked at the painting and there was this great wide "shelf" of white and it bothered me for I don't know how long. I put the book in afterward in a direction, upside down, where only she could easily make out what the illustrations were. I did not expect people to puzzle over them; that is to say, I wasn't thinking too much about the pictures within the picture as you suggest. I admire both Degas and Seurat, of course. And I do a lot of copying of their works, as a type of self-instruction. I ask my students to do this, too, so that they can become, hopefully, more intimately connected to the work of other great artists. For the most part, good painters have always done that over the course of time and continue to do so today.

DC: As a boy, didn't you copy comic strips?

WT: Yes, I suppose I did. I still make copies of cartoons, off and on. As I said, I think it is such great practice to make copies. There is a joy and also an intimacy to committing yourself to the work of another artist. If you try to make a "forgery" of something you always end up learning something new from it. It is a surprise.

I love the whole tradition of cartooning. I love the way it singularizes and it essentializes so many human traits, in all of their ramifications, both positive and negative. That is one of the reasons why I collect original cartoons myself. I have quite a wide selection although they are mostly the ones that are somewhat in touch with the human figure. I don't know if I can put it any other way than that—big noses, big ears, real feet, and real hands.

DC: You like the work of George Herriman, who did *Krazy Kat*.

WT: He is one of my favorites. So many artists were influenced by Herriman in one way

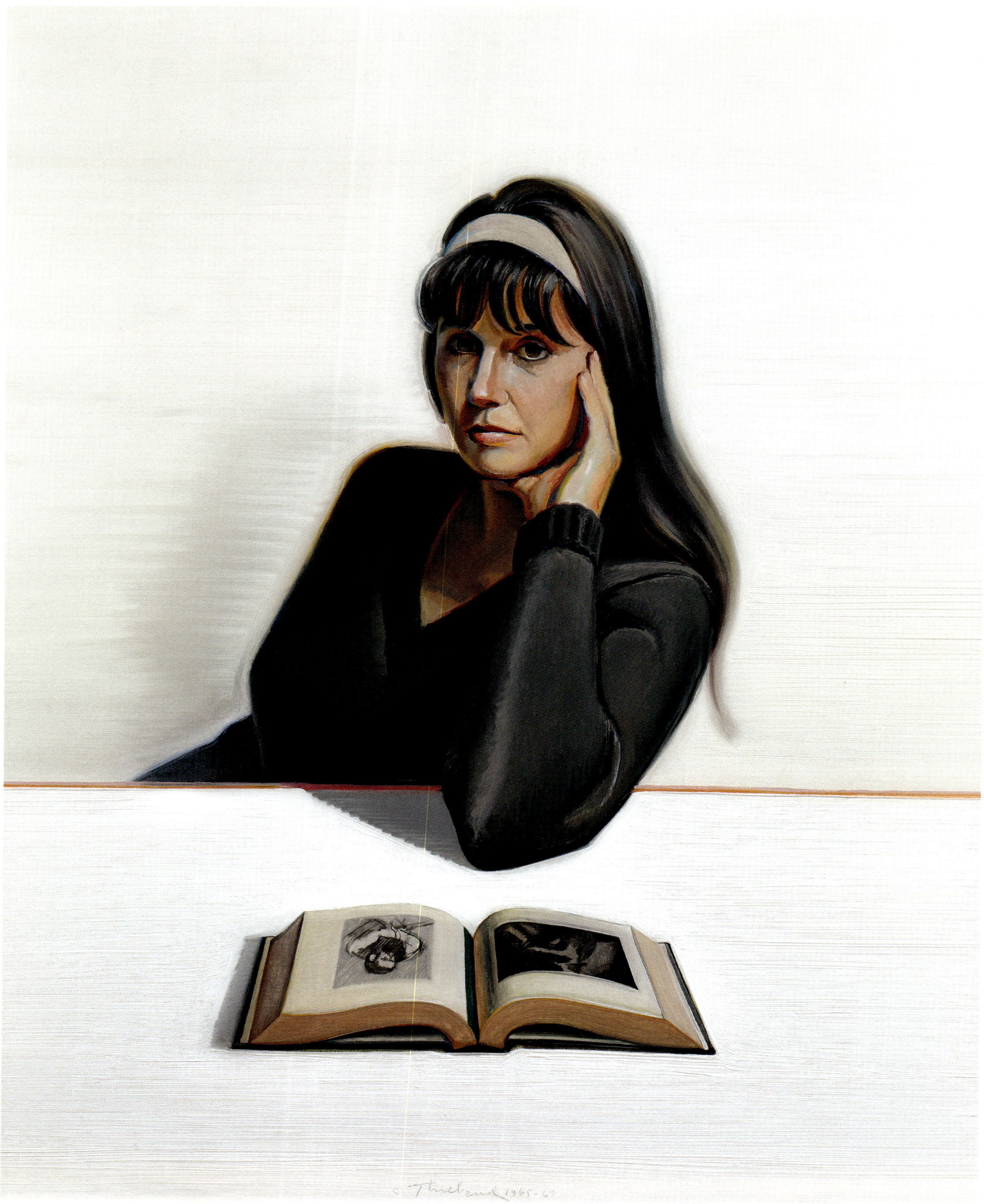

or another—from Picasso to de Kooning, [Elmer] Bischoff and [Philip] Guston, and so on. Although here it is wise to point out that illustrators, cartoonists, and fine artists are all trained in the exact same way, or at least were until very recently. We are all trained in an understanding of the human figure, so whether you choose to be an illustrator or an abstract painter, you need to know the same things. What this means is that really good cartoonists, either explicitly or implicitly, are working within the same human framework as other artists: a framework of empathy.

DC: Humor and empathy seem to be joined in the work of many artists who began as cartoonists. John Sloan, for example. In your work, too, there is this combination of deep caring for human subjects and a certain sly sense of humor. How come?

WT: Well, it is interesting to anyone who cares about cartooning that these two essential aspects of art can happen side by side. Paul [Thiebaud—Wayne's son] once had a show—was it just about *Krazy Kat*?, I can't remember—that was dedicated to cartoons. It was really interesting to me, and, on another occasion, I did the set designs for a ballet staged by the San Francisco Ballet and Ohio Dance Collective that was based on the *Krazy Kat* comic strips. Before that, I did another ballet in Oakland with some of the same people. To tell you the truth, I did not think much of the *Krazy Kat* ballet, and it got bad reviews, which was unfortunate. Transferring comics to the stage was its own challenge, but that particular ballet also tried hard to deal with politics, which detracted some from its success as an autonomous piece of art. Still, it was really fun working on the set designs to transfer Herriman's work to the stage.

Wayne Thiebaud
**Betty Jean Thiebaud and Book**, 1965–69
Oil on canvas
37 ⅝ × 31 ⁷⁄₁₆ in.
Crocker Art Museum
Gift of Mr. and Mrs. Wayne Thiebaud, 1969.21

DC: From time to time, you have referred to your art-making process as "research." Going back into prior work, sometimes years later, you've said, is about investigating problems for yourself. Say more about what you mean by that.

WT: For me, sometimes the most interesting aspect of painting deals with a sort of pure research, as opposed to applied research, where you are trying to find a solution to a problem. Plus, the purity part grows out of not knowing exactly what you are going to learn—a purity of results as well as purity of method. You are risking things and going out to try and find out something without knowing in advance what it is exactly you are looking for. Abstract painting is a lot about that, I think. You can say that a nonobjective painting is nothing more than color and design working into space. Well, yes, but there are also emanations of all kinds of feelings: terror, transcendence, ominousness, the majestic. All of these other things come out of working and, as you work, you must feel something. Is it grandeur? Is it overwhelmed by phenomena? So in terms of talking to students, it is always a question of what you are doing, who the audience is, and how research can help with a pursuit of excellence and those particular qualities of art that will move your work into a realm of being taken seriously.

In the end, it is basically about the nuts and bolts of taking a picture back into the shop and sanding out the rough spots, those places where there are problems. This is not a very helpful thing for the conservators down the line, of course. [laughs] Albert Pinkham Ryder (P. 175) was a like-minded researcher in this mode, I believe. His moon paintings are hugely experimental. He worked on them constantly over long periods. And he ruined many things along the way, but those things he made—at the Met and elsewhere—those are magnificent things. Ryder's work drove Jackson Pollock crazy, in a good way.

**DC:** And you, too?

**WT:** Me, too. What a wonder Ryder's paintings are. But remember, they were also trade pictures for him, which is to say he counted on selling them in order to make a living. I am getting too grandiose, perhaps, but there is that element to this research thing that is critical to making lasting art and keeping yourself in shape as an artist, but it should never become something purely routine.

**DC:** I admire an etching of yours called *Counter Lady* (1991), and it looks like you've been drawn back to that image multiple times, always with different results. It never functions like what you just referred to as "a trade picture," therefore. Sometimes the figure in that work appears to be a phantom-like presence and at other times she looks like a contemporary version of the barmaid in Manet's *A Bar at the Folies-Bergère* (1882)—stoic and bearing the full weight of her confrontation with the viewer.



**WT:** We all know that lady. I always try, as de Kooning cautioned me, to be sure that I am working on something that I know something about and something that I love. Don't manufacture things. The other thing I should say, as a teacher, is that I have occasionally given myself the wrong assignment. Mountains, maybe, are an example of this. I am still working it out [the study of mountains] after many years. It occurs to me that maybe mountains are not something that I truly love, in contrast to the bakeries or San Francisco streets, which keeps me going back to them as subjects. I had full interest in those things. Ties are another example of this. I was once employed as a window dresser and I loved how beautiful a simple display of ties could be (P. 180). Maybe I don't know enough about mountains—or it was too romantic a notion in the end—to be a truly great painter of these subjects. I do know the display counter, however.

**DC:** Because you have been painting mountains in California, it puts you into a lineage with other great landscapists of the state, like Albert Bierstadt. Do you like his pictures?

**WT:** Oh man, what great landscapes those are. Yes, Bierstadt really glorified those mountains, and more. [Pauses, deep in thought] Maybe what I am suggesting is that mountains don't really need to be painted so gloriously any longer since they are already so clearly art. What I mean is: "Why do we go stare at the ocean and the sea?" It is because it is artful and it is a marvel. For an artist to go and try to make these subjects into paintings, is that an ignoble thing? Well, unless you are a Bierstadt, it is going to be really hard to top what nature gives you. My mountains don't compare with that.

**DC:** I am just going to disagree with you.

**WT:** That's all right. We can always disagree and we should always be skeptical. Do you know the writings of Richard Wollheim?

**DC:** He taught at Berkeley when I was a student there.

**WT:** Well, he called me up once and we talked about this idea he had about systematic skepticism, which for him was a continuum, something ongoing. I try to pass this on to my students, equip them with the proper degree of skepticism so that they can get on with their own work and develop their own sense of what it means to be an artist. Wollheim's book [*Painting as an Art*, 1987] is just a terrific thing.

**DC:** Since we are talking about philosophy, Gopnik writes in a philosophical vein about temporality in your work. He uses a term, *tempi*, to describe the rhythmic ways in which you describe forms. Sometimes these result in a kind of halo of brushwork surrounding principal forms in your work. How

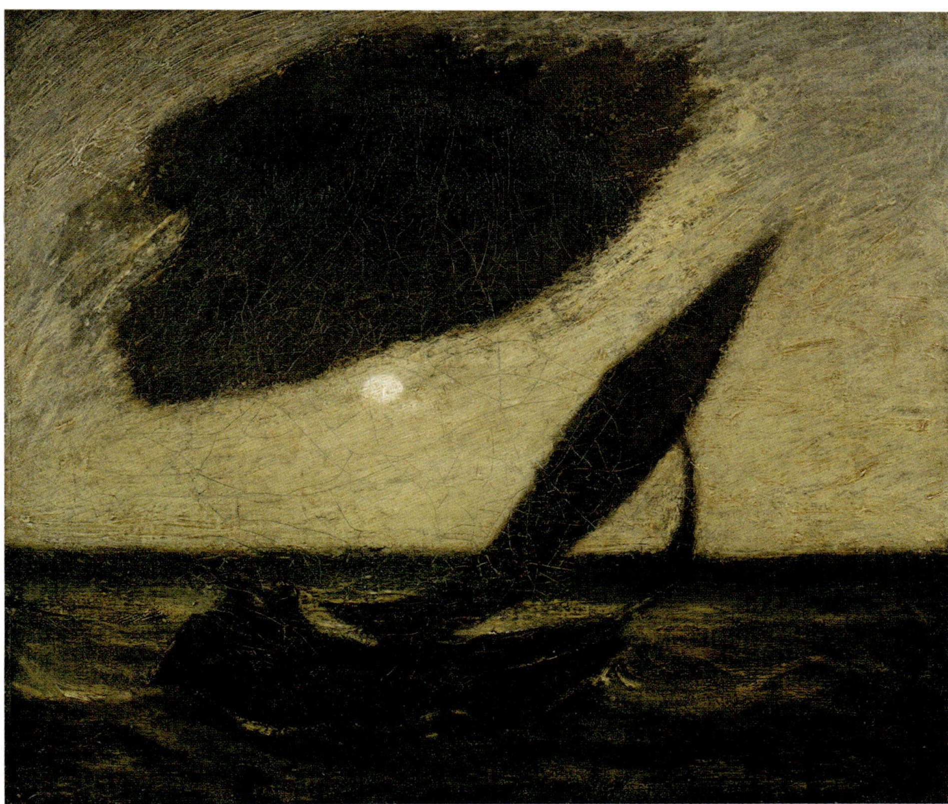

Albert Pinkham Ryder
**Under a Cloud**, ca. 1900
Oil on canvas
20 × 24 in.
Metropolitan Museum of Art, New York
Gift of Alice E. Van Orden, in memory of her husband, Dr. T. Durland Van Orden, 1988

important is time, rhythm, syncopation, and music to an appreciation of your efforts?

**WT:** First, let me say that in addition to the philosophical dimension, there is a physiological phenomenon behind what you have just described, and it is related to the fact that our eyes see two images and that our brain works very hard to merge them, and does so pretty well most of the time. However, if you go out into the sunshine and look at a white egg or something else on a white surface, your eye quickly begins to fatigue and the image itself starts to quiver, and that creates a halation surrounding the objects in your field of vision. I am convinced that is the reason why Vincent van Gogh painted the way he did. He worked in so much sunlight, or else under the unsparing light of an incandescent bulb, and his brilliant, cobalt-blue outlines are the result of this kind of transitional vision. It was just an accident that I found out about this when drawing things against white backgrounds—maybe all it amounted to was a faint yellow vibration at first—but, once I discovered it, I would try to find ways to translate this visual experience into many of my painted surfaces.

**DC:** To some extent, these *tempi* have become a signature of your work.

**WT:** I just have to be careful that I don't overuse them. I don't want them to become a cliché. In regard to Adam's observation about the syncopation that exists in my painting, it has to be considered a compositional base more than anything else. Look at Cézanne's paintings, for instance. If you spend time with them, you notice that an apple is composed of a warm stroke, then alongside he puts a cool stroke, and then another warm stroke, always in the effort to build a sculpted, convincing, three-dimensional form. And those collective brushstrokes are really nothing more than a rhythmic orchestration by the artist's brush. That's what often makes a painting by Paul Cézanne so terrific. Warm and cool is happening simultaneously in Cubism and, if you think about it, it is happening in Diego Velázquez, too. When students ask me "what is the color of flesh," I tell them it is not a color that comes out of a tube labeled "flesh." Velázquez answers their question by showing us [how] a patch of brown, alongside a patch of gray, and yellow and white, set one next to the other, gets read by the eye as a whole and convinces us that it is flesh. That is what a fine sense of rhythm produces in the spectator.

**DC:** Your first drypoint etching was a self-portrait, done in a Cubist-informed, yet also Expressionist manner, reminiscent of Otto Dix or Paul Klee. Shortly after that, you made a linocut that seemed to pay homage to Picasso's *Vollard Suite* (1930–37). Cubism was clearly important to you early on. Is it still?

**WT:** Very much so. We've been having seminars at the graduate level, and I've been talking

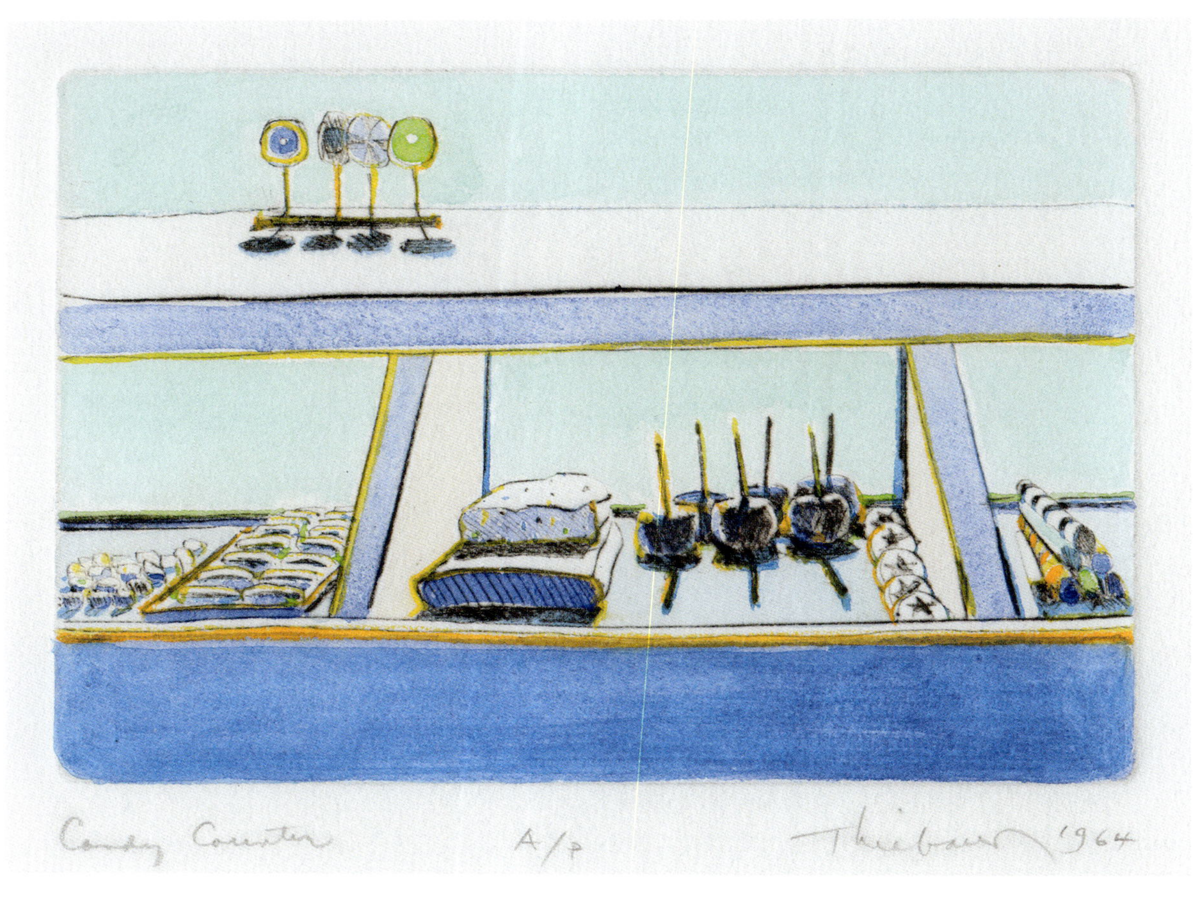




Wayne Thiebaud
**Candy Counter**, 1964
Watercolor over drypoint etching
4 × 6 in.
Private Collection

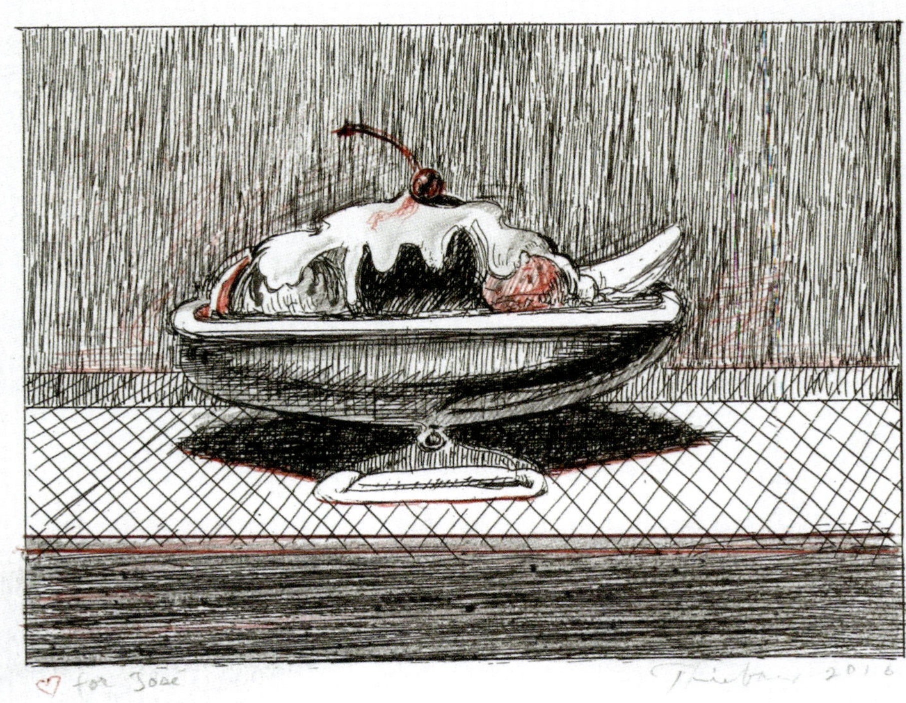




Wayne Thiebaud
**Untitled**, 2016
Handworked lithograph
9 ¾ × 11 ¼ in.
Private Collection

with former students, and as a group we've finally decided that any good painting is essentially Cubist. The importance of the plane is paramount. Take Vermeer. The wonder of his painting is caught up in its use of planes. That is why it is wrong to think of him as merely "photographic." Those maps and walls, the stained glass window and its prismatic planes, the tabletop—he's a marvelous constructor of images in a proto-Cubist manner. When I saw the big exhibition of his works at the Met—and it was the only time I've ever seen something like it—there was total silence in the galleries, although they were very crowded. People were simply awestruck by his painting. That miracle is partly due to the Cubist quality of Vermeer's work.

**DC:** You, too, are fascinated by what could be called "Cubist play" in your landscapes. When spectators confront one of your images of the Sacramento delta, they are struck by aerial perspective and the horizontal views at once. Right?



**WT:** I am so happy you see that. So much good painting uses that technique and it is something that comes right out of the lessons of Cubism. Once when I was on a panel with Thomas Hess [art critic and then editor of *ARTnews*], he said straightaway, "Wayne, you are essentially a Cubist." I was happy he said that, although I was probably a little surprised, like everyone else.

**DC:** What can you do with prints that you can't do with painting?

**WT:** I should start by saying that prints are truly unique. Nothing else can do what prints can do. I can't think of any other artistic method where you can get such resonant, rich, and velvety blacks as you can with an etching, and using the same technique you can also get thin, silvery, spiderweb-like lines, too. Each print medium has its own special qualities and unique terms, whether it is a woodcut, lithograph, serigraph, linocut (PP. 176 AND 177). And I guess I've sinned in all of these areas. Some of my first art courses were printmaking classes, too. I love etching, however.

**DC:** You've made hundreds of prints throughout your career. What's needed is a catalogue raisonné of that part of your oeuvre.

**WT:** Well, those catalogues are such draining things to do.

**DC:** I'd be up for it. One thing I've noticed is that there haven't been that many figurative prints.

**WT:** That's strong, tattletale evidence of my limited ability to use the figure. I like using the figure in paint and think I should face up to it in my prints, but it feels like a big challenge. I sometimes have had to destroy prints where I wasn't satisfied with the way [the figures] looked. Kathan [Brown] tried to help me and, as you know, she is probably the best printer around, and she couldn't get the damn things to look right either. *Clown* (1979) is successful but, you know, it is also a caricature, and I am very comfortable with drawing cartoons, as we've already discussed.

**DC:** Who are some of the other printmakers you admire?

**WT:** I like quite a few. I think about Munch, Whistler, of course, Rembrandt. All of them are endlessly interesting to me. Dick [Diebenkorn], I sure miss him, and I like his prints a whole lot. Jasper Johns—I admire practically every one of his prints.

**DC:** You have something in common with Johns when it comes to the number of progressive proofs that go into making your color etchings. Think of prints you've made, *Steep Street* (1989) or *Sardines* (1982/1990) (P. 148), each of which requires dozens of impressions of separate color, line, and tone to complete the image you had in mind. That reminds me of the kind of thing that Johns has done in a print like *Green Angel 2* (1997), for instance.

**WT:** Yes, that's so. That complexity and labor is always worth it to get the image just right. Another thing, it occurs to me, is that Johns has also not really taken on the figure, except as a photograph or once in a while as a silhouette in certain works like his series *The Seasons* (1987). I am lucky to have become a little bit friendly with Jasper and had breakfast with him once not too long ago. In addition to being a great cook, he's also a real Southern gentleman, and was nice enough to let me know he often uses the Chez Panisse cookbook for which I made illustrations. He and I have had a couple of nice conversations, and I've truly enjoyed knowing him and his work.

**DC:** Let's talk about two prints you made recently at Crown Point Press: *Canyon Bluffs* (2014) and *Reservoir* (2014), both of which we hope to show in San Diego. *Canyon* is an intentionally flat, vertical, and fundamentally linear image and *Reservoir* is all about spatial recession, the curvature of the earth, the spreading volumes of water and land, and a slow, penetrating vista back to a high horizon. Did you mean for these two images to offer contrasting approaches to the problem of representing the land?

**WT:** I did quite a number of paintings of *Reservoir* before turning to making a print of this subject. To tell the truth, I am still not sure if I have gotten it right. There has to be a strong pushback to the planar recession that I have tried to achieve through some tricks—the furrowed verticals to the right, for example. But I don't think you're reading too much by seeing these works in a dialogue with each other. They've always gone together in my mind, and I do think they address some lasting concerns for me when it comes to the basic challenge of making landscapes here in California.

**DC:** Are you comfortable when people refer to you as a California artist?

**WT:** Sure, it is fine. Although I was born in Mesa, Arizona, I came to California when I was, I think, six months old. Almost all of my early years were in Southern California. And now I've spent more than fifty years in Northern California. The only time I ever have a problem with being given the "California" label is when it is used, let's say by New Yorkers, as a limiting device. It was once a way of putting down West Coast artistic practice, and California did suffer that miserably. I don't think it was a deliberate strategy, however. It was fairly unconscious. I remember once asking a New York critic what he thought of artists in California, and he said, something to the effect: "I guess I don't." Now, at first, that statement could be taken as unfair omission. But, unless you think there is such a thing as "California mathematics," there is no such thing as a "California artist" either. You are just an artist and maybe that's what the critic meant.

My work isn't particularly well-known in Europe. Allan [Stone, Thiebaud's New York dealer who passed away in late 2006] never really wanted to show there. He had one bad experience there and never returned. A few of my works are now in Spain and Germany and England, and artists from those countries reach out to me from time to time. I am happy with that and the reputation of being from California. It is nice to be associated with wonderful artists like Diebenkorn, [Elmer] Bischoff, John McLaughlin, [Ed] Ruscha, and Robert Irwin.

**DC:** Occasionally Manny Farber's work has reminded me a little of yours. Do you know those paintings? He was a San Diego artist.

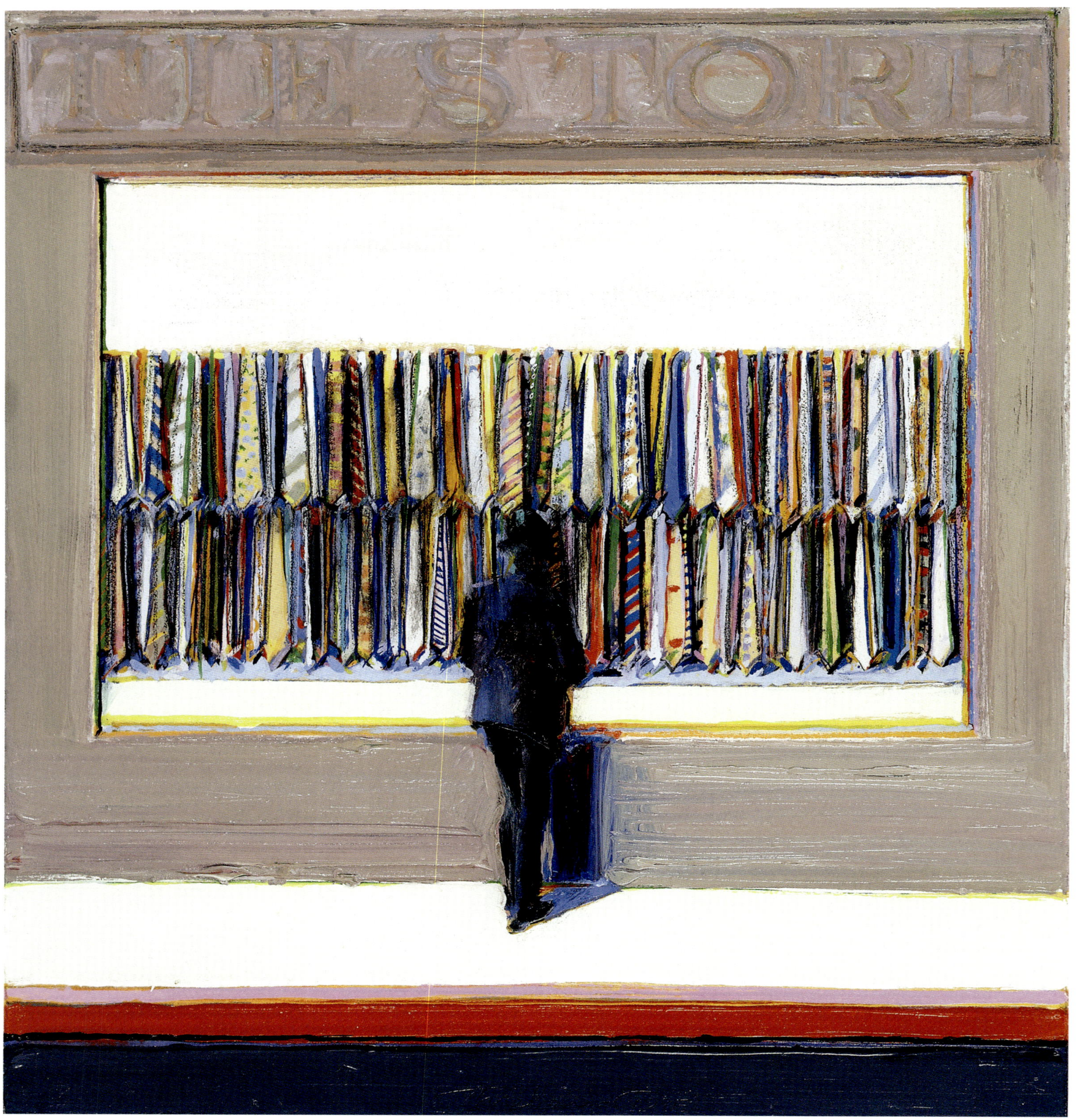


Wayne Thiebaud
**Tie Window**, 1975
Oil on paper on board
15 ⅜ × 14 ¾ in.
Private Collection

**WT:** Yes, I do know Manny Farber's tabletop paintings. He's not well-enough known, but I do enjoy those works. It is hard to see them up here.

**DC:** Your commitment to your own students is legendary. What advice do you have for other young artists, or art historians, for that matter?

**WT:** Let me start with this. I am a fan of academic instruction, the whole rigorous Beaux Arts tradition. At the same time, I am trying to make sense of what happens to those academically trained artists who can't ever seem to move out of it, who are trapped by the singularity of those conventions. The number of academicians who have been able to break away—[Jean-Auguste-Dominique] Ingres is a good example—and accomplish something beyond their training is relatively small. Ingres was an exquisite draftsman and a fine academic painter, but he did something else when he put all those extra vertebrae into his *Grande Odalisque* (1814). Picasso used to copy Ingres, and maybe even developed Cubism by annotating the parts of Ingres's work that could be turned into planes. That practice of transcending your training, of playing with tradition, that moves art forward. It has to go somewhere.

Finding good models for making art is really important. Take Degas. If you have to look at only one artist, he would be a great one to choose. Degas has an academic side, an Impressionist side, an Expressionist side, and all within one extraordinary career. He worked in every medium. He was another fine printmaker, too. Henri Matisse, on the other hand, wasn't really very strong academically. He played with academicism but ultimately escaped it through a kind of Middle Eastern exoticism. He was a great sensualist, designer, and colorist, but you can look for, and won't find, an appreciation of academic grounding in his work.

There seems to be something like a return to academic instruction going on today. This can be dangerous if the work becomes too predictable, too conventional, and people are afraid to interrupt it. Keep in mind that most of what I have done to interrupt academic tradition has been accidental on my part. [Laughter] One other thing I would advise strongly that art students do is to read more, and write more. You can't do enough of that and it often leads to the kind of risk-taking I am talking about.

**DC:** You read poetry, don't you?

**WT:** I do. I loved my English courses when I was a student. Even today, I always read a poem before I give a lecture. Elizabeth Bishop, Emily Dickinson, William Butler Yeats, William Carlos Williams, Philip Levine, and my former colleague at UC Davis, Gary Snyder. Local poets, too. Victoria Dalkey is a very fine poet, married to a painter who was in Paul's gallery, Fred Dalkey.

**DC:** And you either paint or draw pretty much every day?

**WT:** Almost every day.

**DC:** You play tennis, how many times a week?

**WT:** On average, three to four times a week.

**DC:** That's inspiring, Wayne. We started this session by noting that you've been interviewed many times. Is there a question that you've always wished someone would ask you?

**WT:** Well, I have heard so many questions. Let me think. I had a very good question asked of me last year, in Laguna. A woman stood up and wondered, "What do you think [Jean Siméon] Chardin or [Giorgio] Morandi would say if they walked into your studio?" I liked that question a lot. I replied, "Well, you know Chardin was the president of the

French Academy. I think he'd probably tell me to go back and do more drawing. And I think Morandi would question why I use such intense colors in my work." But, you know, those paintings by Morandi really glow from within. I learned so much from studying those two artists, whether it shows or not.

**DC:** Let me return to that question, then, and ask it slightly differently. If you could convene a table of artists, from throughout history, whom would you invite to dinner?

**WT:** And we would talk very seriously about art and eat a really good meal? That is an interesting question. Do you have some time? [Laughs and then pauses to consider] I think we should make it just painters, to test our mettle. Well, I want one of them, even if I am a little afraid of him, to be Degas. You know he wrote quite a lot, wrote sonnets and diaries, and I've read them all. He wrote a beautiful poem to Mary Cassatt when she fell and broke her hip. He was a difficult man, a bit of a monster, and I think he would give me hell, along with everyone else there. Henri de Toulouse-Lautrec admired Degas, but feared him, just as I do. I am sure I'd enjoy listening to Degas. Another one should be Velázquez. And the last should be Van Gogh. That would be a fun dinner for me, one I imagine I would truly enjoy and remember.

**DC:** That sounds like it would be a memorable dinner, just as this conversation has been truly memorable for me, Wayne. Thank you so much.

*This interview with Wayne Thiebaud took place in Sacramento, California, on July 31, 2015. Except for light editing to improve readability, this is a complete transcription of the conversation.*

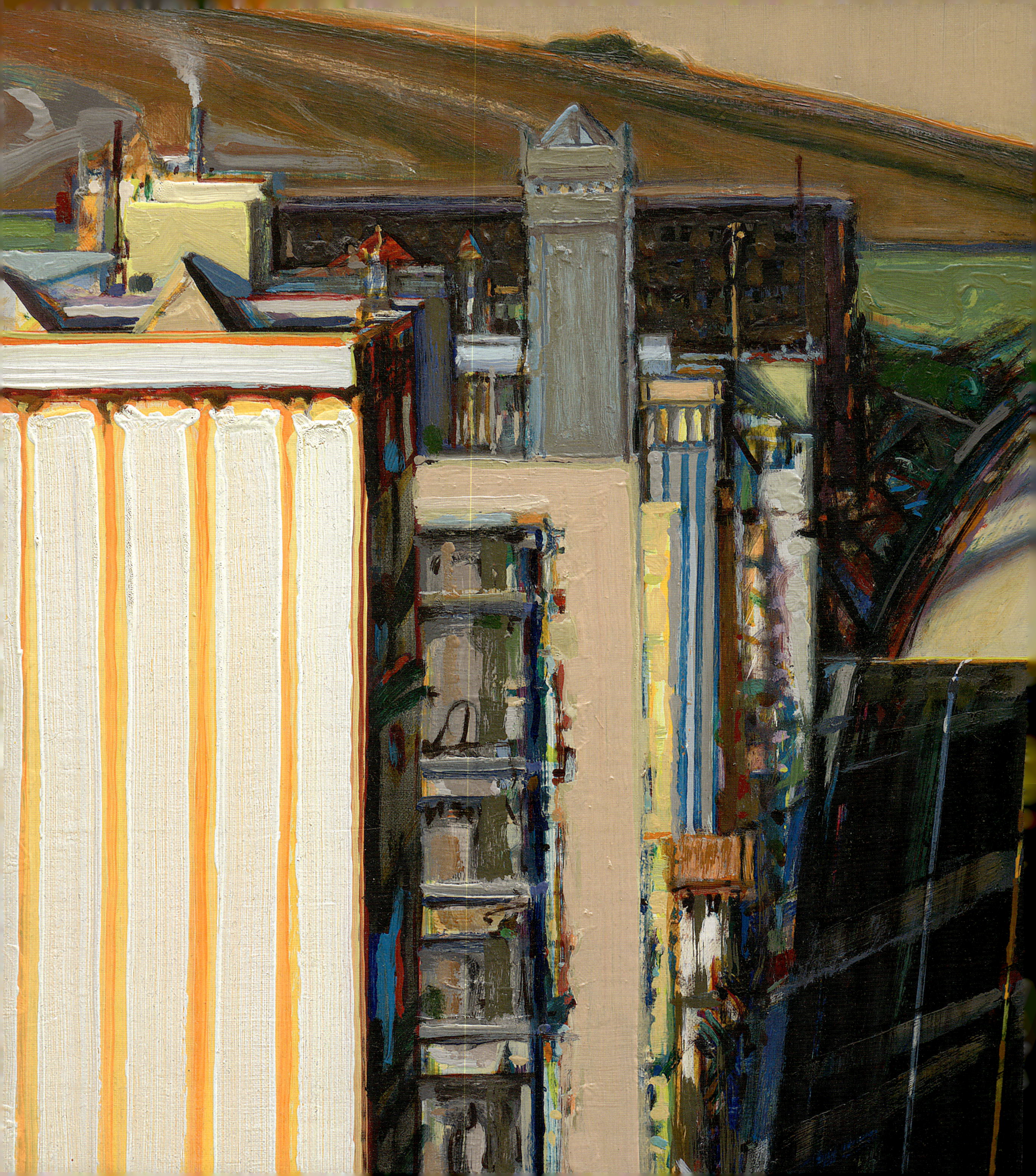

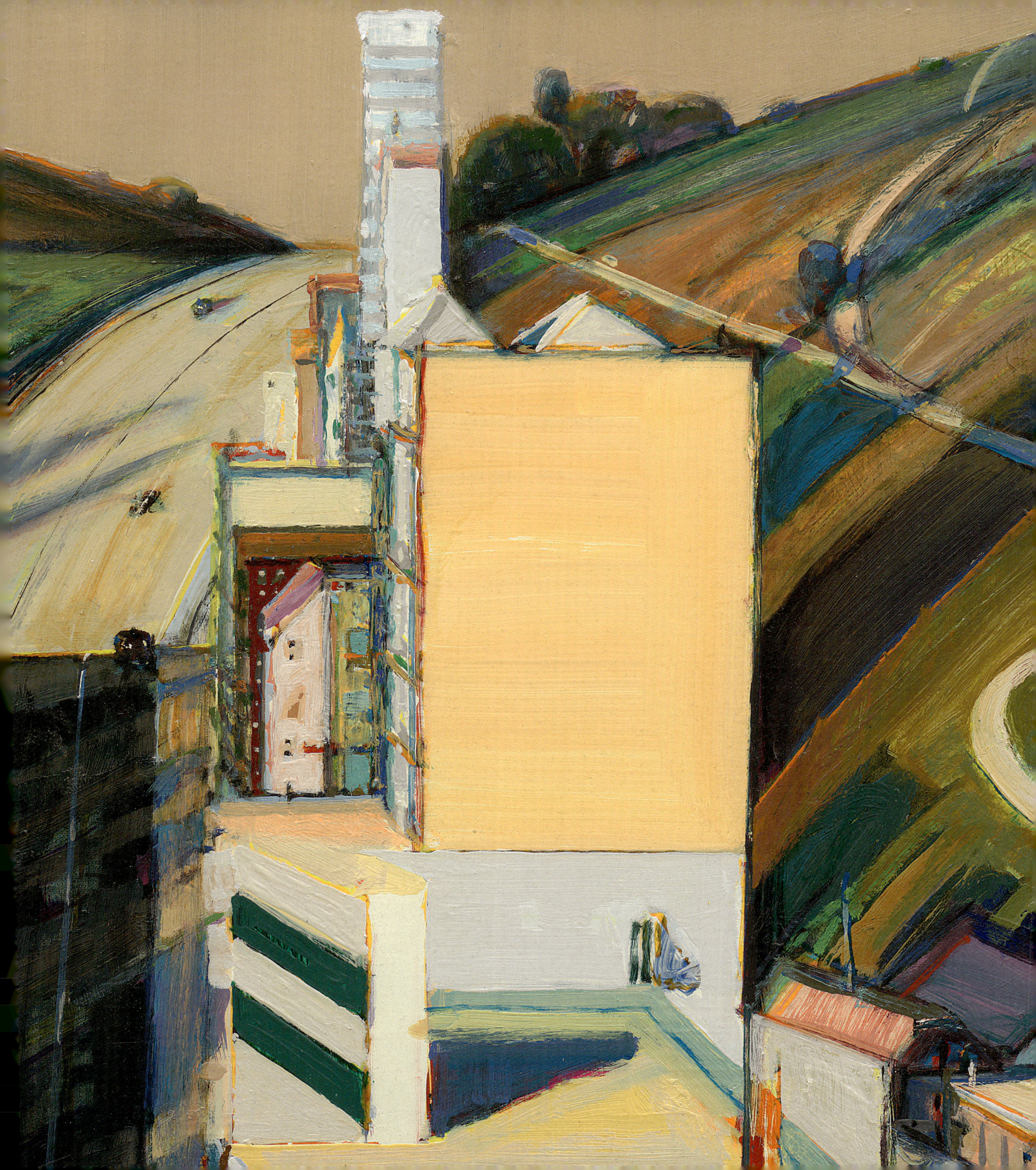

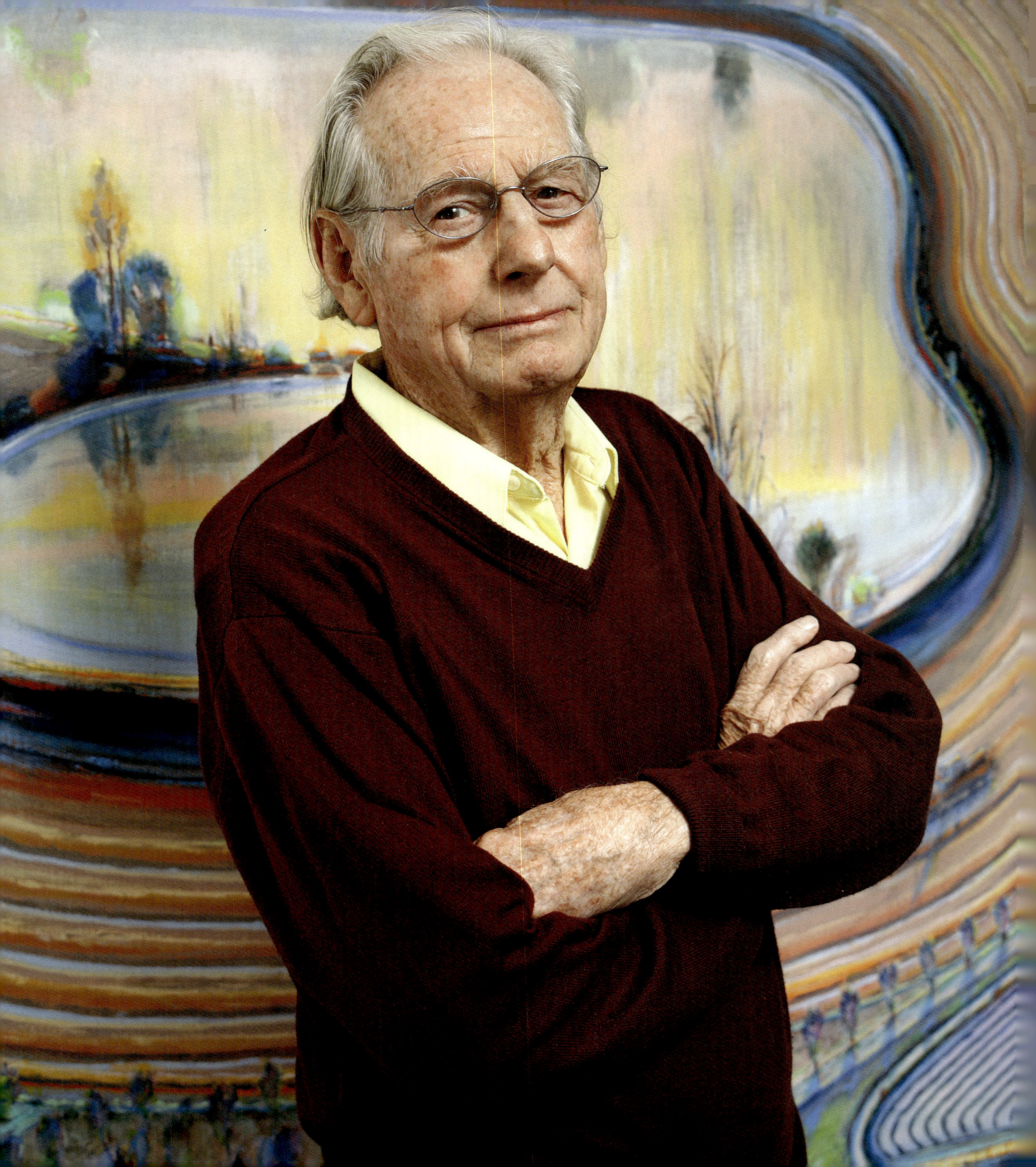

# Wayne Thiebaud: Alive in Art

## Peter Frank

Wayne Thiebaud is considered one of America's most important representational artists from the last half century. He was born in Mesa, Arizona, on November 15, 1920, and lived until December 25, 2021, passing at his longtime home in Sacramento, California. Thiebaud preceded his seven-decade career as a painter and printmaker with jobs in commercial illustration, including animation (with Disney Studios and others) and cartooning, a background that was to have a profound influence on his pictorial sensibility.

Thiebaud grew up in Long Beach, California, outside Los Angeles, but studied, taught, and ultimately came to live and work in the contiguous Sacramento delta and San Francisco Bay Areas. He developed a kind of deadpan realism in his renditions of still life objects and people, but evolved to produce stylized and fanciful renditions of urban and rural spaces based on the San Francisco topography and the patterns of cultivation that mark the delta region.

Thiebaud turned his attention to fine art in the 1950s, and was profoundly influenced by Abstract Expressionism and the parallel practice of gestural figuration, both of which were au courant in the art scene of postwar San Francisco. Thiebaud himself did not come to prominence until the early 1960s, but his rise at that time was meteoric. He became associated with the emergence of Pop Art on both coasts, despite the fact that he did not regard himself a Pop artist. Thiebaud's unusual choices of still life subject matter, including consumer goods, food (especially dessert) display cases, and other items particular to contemporary America, spoke to social and aesthetic issues raised by Pop, but emphasized rather than suppressed the hand of the painter and the elusive effects of light. Thiebaud was less interested in what objects mean than in how we perceive them visually. Still, his cake slices and other edibles presented themselves with such cool élan that they came to be included in early surveys of American Pop.

In great part to escape the Pop label, Thiebaud turned to the figure in the early 1960s. But his uniformed men and women, rendered with the same thick brush and bathed in the same bright, flat light, were Pop images in their own right, blank and isolated, suggestive of the era's middle-class conformity. Nothing about these figures was sensuous except the paint handling; they were more still life than the pie plates. They, too, proved almost more popular than the artist preferred.

From the first, Thiebaud had been interested in the landscape alongside his other motifs. But he held back his involvement with both urban and exurban subjects until the early 1970s (around which time he acquired a pied-à-terre in San Francisco). At that time he increased his plein air activity, painting dramatic views of the Northern California coast, and at the same time turned his attention to the vertiginous net of deeply inclined city streets he now lived among. He would exaggerate the cliffs towering over the beaches and equally the high-rise buildings tottering above tangles of on-ramps to emphasize the role distortion plays in bringing out what is really before our eyes.

Thiebaud went inland with his last major group of paintings, but also moved the farthest he ever had from veristic realism, in his paintings of Sacramento delta views. Such "views" now barely resembled their subjects, showing them as intricate patterns of farming and cultivation, emblazoned with almost tropical colors. Here Thiebaud was done reporting what he could see, and was painting instead what he wanted to see.

But he did not stop painting his other subjects—not the cityscapes, not the figures, not the objects or eats. He liked to circle around constantly to his favored subjects, subjects he had so carefully cultivated over more than half a century. This went hand in hand with his great devotion to teaching, both studio practice and art history. He was answering, again and again, in old ways and new, to the call of art as an evolutionary process. Wayne Thiebaud felt himself part of art history, tasked not only with extending it but with disseminating it through educating, lecturing, and exhibiting, which he did almost to his death at the age of 101.

Wayne Thiebaud, 2007

# Academic and Teaching Career

**1936–37**

At the age of sixteen, works briefly in the Animation Department of Walt Disney Studios, Los Angeles, then attends Frank Wiggins Trade School in Los Angeles to study commercial art.

**1940–41**

Attends Long Beach Community College (now Long Beach City College).

**1949–50**

Attends San Jose State College (now San Jose State University).

**1950–60**

Attends California State College (now California State University) Sacramento. Receives BA in 1951 and MA in 1953, with an art major focused on art history, theory, and education.

Appointed instructor of art at Sacramento City College, 1951, and serves as chairman of the art department 1954–56 and 1958–60. Teaches both art and art history, and introduces new courses in such fields as television production, film, and commercial art.

During the summer months (1951–59), designs exhibits for California State Fair and Exposition in Sacramento. Also active in designing for theatrical productions in the Sacramento area.



In 1954 establishes the Patrician Films Company to produce educational art films. Together with Paul Beckman, initiates national and international art tours for students, teachers, and artists.

Sabbatical leave (1956–57) to live in New York, where he befriends Elaine and Willem de Kooning, Franz Kline, Barnett Newman, Philip Pearlstein, and Milton Resnick, along with critics Harold Rosenberg and Thomas Hess.

Upon returning to Sacramento, in collaboration with Gregory Kondos, Mel Ramos, and Jack Ogden, as well as other Sacramento painters, cofounds the Artists Cooperative Galley.

Guest printmaking instructor at San Francisco Art Institute, 1958.

**1960–2002**

Appointed assistant professor at University of California, Davis. Subsequently appointed associate professor (1963–67) and professor (1967, until retirement at age seventy), and then serves as a professor emeritus until 2002.

Receives appointment as visiting lecturer and artist-in-residence at Cornell University, 1967. Throughout the 1970s and ’80s, accepts similar positions at the University of Victoria in British Columbia, Canada; Rice University, Colorado State University, Stanford University, the University of Utah, the University of Wisconsin, the University of Virginia, Harvard, Yale, Princeton, and the New York School of Drawing, Painting and Sculpture.

Teaches at the New York Studio School in Paris with Elaine de Kooning, summer 1969.

Helps establish a visiting art program at UC Davis, 1970.

Appointed faculty research lecturer, UC Davis, 1972.

Begins weekly drawing sessions in San Francisco with Bay Area artists, including Mark Adams, Theophilus Brown, Gordon Cook, and Beth Van Hoesen, 1976.

# Select Honors

**1956**
Patrician Films (the educational art films company founded by the artist) wins a Chicago Golden Reel Award and first prize at California State Fair's Art Film Festival.

**1972**
Receives the Golden Apple Award for distinguished teaching at UC Davis. Receives an honorary doctorate from California College of Arts and Crafts, Oakland.

**1981**
Receives Award for Distinguished Teaching of Art from the College Art Association.

**1983**
Receives an honorary doctorate from Dickinson College, Carlisle, Pennsylvania.

**1984**
Receives special recognition award from the National Association of Schools of Art and Design.

**1985**
Elected to the American Academy and Institute of Arts and Letters, New York.

**1986**
Elected as Associate of the National Academy of Design, New York.

**1987**
Advances to Academician in the National Academy of Design. Receives the Award of Honor for Distinguished Service in the Arts from the San Francisco Arts Commission. Receives the Cyril Magnin Award for Outstanding Individual Achievement in the Arts. Honored by the American Academy of Achievement.

**1988**
Receives the Prize for Teaching and Scholarly Achievement from UC Davis. Elected as fellow to the American Academy of Arts and Sciences, Boston. Receives an honorary doctorate from the San Francisco Art Institute.

**1990**
Receives the Distinguished Service Award from California State University, Sacramento.

**1991**
Receives the California Arts Council Governor's Award for Lifetime Achievement in the Arts.

**1993**
Receives the Grumbacher Gold Medallion Award for Painting from the American Academy of Design, New York. Awarded an honorary Doctor of Arts degree by the Art Institute of Southern California.

**1994**
Receives a National Medal of Arts awarded by President Bill Clinton.

**1995**
Honored with the Distinguished Artistic Achievement Award by the California Society of Printmakers, Berkeley.

**1996**
Receives the Gold Medal for Lifetime Achievement in the Arts from the National Arts Club, New York.

**1997**
Receives Honorary Doctor of Fine Arts Degree from the Art Institute of Boston.

**1998**
Receives Honorary Doctor of Fine Arts Degree from California State University, Sacramento.

**2000**
Receives Medal for Painting from the Skowhegan School of Painting and Sculpture, Maine.

**2001**
Receives Lifetime Achievement Award for Art from the American Academy of Design, New York.

**2004**
Receives Distinguished Artist Award for Lifetime Achievement from the College Art Association, New York.

**2007**
Receives Bay Area Treasure Award from the San Francisco Museum of Modern Art.

**2010**
Inducted into the California Hall of Fame, California Museum, Sacramento.

**2013**
Receives California Art Award from Laguna Art Museum, Laguna Beach.

**2016**
Receives Lifetime Achievement Award for Innovation from UC Davis.

**2017**
Receives Gold Medal from the American Academy and Institute of Arts and Letters, New York.

# Contributor Biographies

**DERRICK R. CARTWRIGHT** is an art historian who lives in San Diego, California. He is an associate professor in the Department of Art, Architecture + Art History at the University of San Diego. He is also the director of curatorial affairs at the Timken Museum of Art, San Diego. He previously served as director of the University Galleries at the University of San Diego, and at the Seattle Art Museum, San Diego Museum of Art, Hood Museum of Art at Dartmouth College, and Musée d'Art Américain Giverny. Cartwright has lectured internationally and has published on a wide variety of topics, including North American art and architecture, and transatlantic cultural exchange.

**GENE COOPER** is a native Southern Californian. In addition to his bachelor's degree in Japanese art history, he pursued graduate studies in American art history at UCLA, USC, and Yale University. He was a professor of art history at the University of Bridgeport, Connecticut, and California State University, Long Beach, where he is a professor emeritus. Cooper's enduring friendship with Wayne Thiebaud, which began in the early 1970s, afforded both of them insights into art marking and art history. Thiebaud, in his later years, taught Cooper how to paint, which he continues to this day. Cooper carries on his friend's legacy by enthusiastically sharing his knowledge of the celebrated artist with scholars and curators.



**PETER FRANK** is a New York–born, Los Angeles–based art critic, historian, and curator. He has curated for the Solomon R. Guggenheim Museum, El Museo Nacional Centro de Arte Reina Sofía, the Center for Inter-American Relations, the Alternative Museum, Franklin Furnace Archive, the Fort Wayne Museum of Art, and others. He has realized projects for Documenta and the Venice Biennale, and has written and edited for art periodicals worldwide. He served as art critic for *The SoHo Weekly News*, *The Village Voice*, and *LA Weekly*. His essays have been featured in numerous exhibition monographs and catalogues, and he has published several books. He has lectured and taught at universities domestically and abroad. Frank is also a published poet.

**JULIA FRIEDMAN** is an independent art historian and writer based in Los Angeles. She began studying art history at the Hermitage Museum in St. Petersburg, Russia, where she grew up. After receiving her doctorate from Brown University in 2005, she taught and researched in the US, Canada, the UK, and Japan. In 2010, Northwestern University Press published her illustrated monograph *Beyond Symbolism and Surrealism: Alexei Remizov's Synthetic Art*. In the same year, she began reviewing for *Artforum*. In 2015–16, she collaborated on a project with art critic Dave Hickey, editing *Dustbunnies* and *Wasted Words*—two pendant volumes based on his Facebook exchanges. Since 2017, she has been a regular contributor to *The New Criterion* magazine.

**RACHEL TEAGLE** is the founding director of the Jan Shrem and Maria Manetti Shrem Museum of Art at the University of California, Davis, where Wayne Thiebaud taught for more than forty years. Today she continues to define a vision for the museum and its intellectual role in the life of the university. Previously, Teagle was the executive director of The New Children's Museum in San Diego, and curator and department head at the Museum of Contemporary Art San Diego. In San Francisco, she held a curatorial position at the San Francisco Museum of Modern Art and was the first director of the Anderson Collection at Stanford University. Teagle is the author of *Wayne Thiebaud: 1958–1968*, published by University of California Press in 2018.

# In Appreciation

Anderson Collection, Stanford University, CA
Matt and Maria Bult
Corcoran Collection, National Gallery of Art, Washington, DC
The Courtauld Institute of Art, London
Crocker Art Museum, Sacramento
Crown Point Press, San Francisco
Crystal Bridges Museum of American Art, Bentonville, AR
Fine Arts Museums of San Francisco
Hirshhorn Museum and Sculpture Garden, Washington, DC
The Huntington Library, Art Museum, and Botanical Gardens, San Marino
Jan Shrem and Maria Manetti Shrem Museum of Art, UC Davis
Metropolitan Museum of Art, New York
The Morgan Library & Museum, New York
Musée d'Orsay, Paris
Musées royaux des Beaux-Arts de Belgique, Brussels
Museo Morandi/Settore Musei Civici Bologna
Museum of Modern Art, New York
National Gallery of Art, Washington, DC
Nelson-Atkins Museum of Art, Kansas City, MO
Pasadena Art Museum
Ed Ruscha Studio
San Diego Museum of Art
San Francisco Museum of Modern Art
Tasende Gallery, La Jolla
Paul Thiebaud Gallery, San Francisco
Wayne Thiebaud Foundation
University of San Diego Print Collection
Malcolm Warner
Whitney Museum of American Art, New York

First published in the United States of America in 2025 by
Rizzoli Electa, A Division of
Rizzoli International Publications, Inc.
49 West 27th Street
New York, NY 10001
www.rizzoliusa.com


Texts: Derrick R. Cartwright, Gene Cooper, Peter Frank, Julia Friedman, and Rachel Teagle



An earlier version of Julia Friedman's essay, "Anyone Can Be My Protagonist," appeared in the Wayne Thiebaud Foundation publication, *People: Figure Paintings 1936–2021* (2021). The current version is published with permission.

The interview with Wayne Thiebaud by Derrick R. Cartwright, reprinted with permission, originally appeared in the University of San Diego University Galleries publication, *Wayne Thiebaud by Hand: Works on Paper from 1965–2015* (2015).



Publisher: Charles Miers
Associate Publisher: Margaret Rennolds Chace
Senior Editor: Ellen Cohen
Production Manager: Kaija Markoe
Managing Editor: Lynn Scrabis
Copyeditor: Stephanie Cash

Design: Robin Brunelle

Content Development
Director: Mary Beth Petersen
Copyeditor: Julie Dunn
Researchers: Aitor and Betina Tasende

ISBN: 978-0-8478-7574-0
Library of Congress Control Number: 2025934126

Printed in Hong Kong
2025 2026 2027 2028 / 10 9 8 7 6 5 4 3 2 1

The authorized representative in the EU for product safety and compliance is Mondadori Libri S.p.A., via Gian Battista Vico 42, Milan, Italy, 20123, www.mondadori.it

Visit us online:
Instagram.com/RizzoliBooks
Facebook.com/RizzoliNewYork
X: @Rizzoli_Books
Youtube.com/user/RizzoliNY

Front cover: Wayne Thiebaud, *Cloud City* (detail), 1993–94. Photo: Philipp Scholz Rittermann
p. 2: Wayne Thiebaud, *Canyon Mountains* (detail), 2011–12
p. 4: Wayne Thiebaud, *Street and Shadow* (detail), 1982–83/1996
pp. 6–7: Wayne Thiebaud, *Flatland River* (detail), 1997
pp. 12–13: Wayne Thiebaud, *Diagonal Ridge* (detail), 1987
pp. 32–33: Wayne Thiebaud, *Valley Streets* (detail), 2003
pp. 100–101: Wayne Thiebaud, *Napa Valley Ridge* (detail), 1986–97
pp. 118–19: Wayne Thiebaud, *Five Sitting Figures* (detail), 1965
pp. 136–37: Wayne Thiebaud, *Bow Ties* (detail), 1990
pp. 166–67: Wayne Thiebaud, *Tie Window* (detail), 1975
pp. 184–85: Wayne Thiebaud, *Sunset Streets* (detail), 1985
Back cover: Wayne Thiebaud, *Napa Valley Ridge* (detail), 1986–97

Photography:
Philipp Scholz Rittermann, p. 105; Paul Thiebaud Gallery, San Francisco, pp. 17, 23, 24–25, 27, 44, 50–51, 55, 60–61, 65, 67, 68, 76, 81, 82, 92–93, 95, 96, 98, 106–7, 110, 114, 115, 127, 130, 132–33, 134, 151, 186 (photo: Mary Weikert); Wayne Thiebaud Foundation and The Morgan Library, pp. 18, 28 (bottom), 29 (bottom), 157 (bottom); RMN-Grand Palais/Art Resource, NY, p. 28 (top); Museo Morandi/Settore Musei Civici Bologna © 2025 Artists Rights Society (ARS), NY/SAE, Rome, p. 29 (top); Wayne Thiebaud Foundation, p. 30; Bridgeman Images, pp. 40–41, 153 (USA/Bridgeman Images); James Goodwin Gallery, NY/Bridgeman Images, pp. 47, 77; Katherine Du Tiel, pp. 63, 74–75, 90–91; © Christie's Images/Bridgeman Images, p. 64, 88–89, 112–13, 180; John Berggruen Gallery, San Francisco, p. 86; Trask Photography, pp. 99, 117, 141 (right) (photo: Patrick Dullanty); Ben Blackwell, p. 108 (left); Jerry L. Thompson, digital image © Whitney Museum of American Art/Licensed by Scala/Art Resource, NY, p. 109; Cathy Carver, Hirshhorn Museum and Sculpture Garden, Washington, DC, p. 124; © Josse/Bridgeman, p. 129; © The Courtauld/Bridgeman Images, P.1934.SC.234, p. 147 (left); Robert LaPrelle, pp. 154–55.